AGGREGATION, EFFICIENCY, AND MEASUREMENT

Studies in Productivity and Efficiency

Series Editors:

Rolf Färe
Shawna Grosskopf
Oregon State University
R. Robert Russell
University of California, Riverside

Books in the series:

Fox, Kevin J.:
Efficiency in the Public Sector
Ball, V. Eldon and Norton, George W.:
Agricultural Productivity:
Measurement and Sources of Growth
Färe, Rolf and Grosskopf, Shawna:
New Directions:
Efficiency and Productivity
Daraio, C. and Simar, L.:
Advanced Robust and Nonparametric Methods in Efficiency Analysis:
Methods and Applications
Färe, R., Grosskopf, S., and Primont, D.:
Aggregation, Efficiency, and Measurement

AGGREGATION, EFFICIENCY, AND MEASUREMENT

Edited by

Rolf Färe
Oregon State University, Corvallis, OR, USA

Shawna Grosskopf
Oregon State University, Corvallis, OR, USA

Daniel Primont
Southern Illinois University, Carbondale, IL, USA

Springer

e-ISBN 0-387-47677-6
ISBN-13: 978-1-4419-4237-1 e-ISBN-13: 978-0-387-47677-3

Printed on acid-free paper.

9 8 7 6 5 4 3 2 1

springer.com

Contents

Preface

Rolf Färe[1], Shawna Grosskopf[1], and Daniel Primont[2]

[1] Oregon State University
[2] Southern Illinois University

In addition to Daniel Primont's tribute and overview of the contributions of R. Robert Russell to the study of aggregation, efficiency and measurement, this volume consists of nine original papers, which cannot readily be organized into disjoint groups. As Russell pointed out to us when asked how to organize the contributions, defining groups of papers would 'entail serious aggregation error.' We thus chose to include the contribtutions in alphabetical order by first author's surname.

Most of the papers included here were presented and discussed at a symposium held at University of California at Riverside whose title—Conference on Aggregation, Efficiency and Measurement: In Honor of Professor R. Robert Russell—is the basis of the title of this volume. This conference was the brainchild of Taradas Bandyopadhyay, who is a colleague of Russell. Each of the papers in this volume was reviewed by two anonymous referees, to whom we are very grateful. We would also like to thank Lisa Duke and Xiuying Jin for their help in typesetting the manuscript.

What follows is a brief overview of each paper.

Blackorby and Brett study Pareto optima in an overlapping-generations model. In this setting they find that the standard results that obtain in a static general equilibrium model are overturned. In the usual static model Pareto optimality requires the equality of producer and consumer prices; commodity taxes that create a divergence of producer and consumer prices lead to a suboptimal outcome. However, Blackorby and Brett show that in the OLG model in which the government can levy commodity taxes and make generation-specific transfers almost all Pareto optima will involve commodity taxation, subsidies, and taxes on either savings or on capital inputs. Thus, in the OLG setting the government has an important role to play that it does not have in the one-period static case.

Hudgins and Primont show how the usual comparative static results that arise in a model of competitive profit maximization can be derived when using the directional technology distance function as the representation of the firm's technology. They also provide a summary of the derivative restrictions that should be satisfied by a directional technology distance function. Many of these restrictions are the standard ones implied by the assumptions of monotonicity and curvature. However, the restrictions implied by the translation property are unique to directional distance functions and they are the focus of a more detailed scrutiny in the final section of their contribution. These derivative restrictions are useful in formulating econometric models of directional distance functions.

Campbell and Marino distinguish three motivations for mergers, namely 1) market power, 2) technological or efficiency gains from shared fixed inputs and 3) managers' own utility. The first two are included in what the authors call synergistic merger. In contrast to synergy, the authors note that managers' utility can be linked to the 'observability problem' which arises from the principal-agent model. The principal may lose observability of the agents as a consequence of merger. They provide testable predictions of when such mergers are profitable despite the observability problem.

Diewert and Mendoza present a sequence of Data Envelopment Analysis (DEA) models that are used to compute various measures of input efficiency that are in the family of Debreu-Farrell measures that were advocated by R. Robert Russell. They theoretically demonstrate two types of Le-Chatelier results for these measures. In particular, they show that if stronger technological assumptions are imposed on the DEA model then measures of technical input efficiency will decrease and they show that if stronger behavioral assumptions are imposed then overall measures of input efficiency will decrease.

Recent Canadian time-series data are used to illustrate these Le-Chatelier effects. Inspired by Mendoza (1989), their analysis is extended to a comparison of three methods for computing annual rates of productivity change and measures of efficiency loss for each year in the 1961–1980 data set using 1) DEA techniques 2) superlative index numbers and 3) statistical estimation of unit profit functions. The strengths and weaknesses of each approach are highlighted. They conclude that the DEA method can be fruitful, particularly when the other two methods are not practical (or possible.)

In their contribution, Färe, Grosskopf and Zelenyuk try to relate four of the many versions of technical efficiency that have been introduced over the years. They discuss the conditions under which the Farrell measure of technical efficiency and the so-called Russell measure yield the same result. They also study the relationship between the directional distance function and what is referred to as the additive measure in the operations research literature, both of which have an additive structure.

In results that would not surprise Russell, for the two 'multiplicative' measures—Farrell and Russell—to yield the same score the technology must be input homothetic with the input component consistent with equal-weighted Cobb-Douglas form. For the directional distance function to yield the same score as the additive measure, technology must be translation input homothetic with the input aggregator specified as an arithmetic mean.

Grosskopf, Hayes and Taylor provide an empirical interlude by applying the decomposition of labor productivity growth (introduced by Kumar and Russell) to U.S. state manufacturing in the 1990s. They find that the three components: technical change (innovation), efficiency change (diffusion) and capital deepening all played a role, with innovation the primary determinant of manufacturing productivity growth in all states. Capital deepening contributed to labor productivity growth in all but three states, and explains at least half of the labor productivity growth in a dozen states.

In a second stage, these components were related to various policy variables; a growing technology sector is a strong contributor to labor productivity growth, while a growing public sector is largely a drag. Improvements in labor force quality appear to have had little impact on the pace of technical change or the diffusion of technology, but capital deepening was significantly greater in states with a more highly educated population.

Daniel Henderson focuses on technical efficiency and measurement, by providing nonparametric techniques to estimate or measure higher-order moments of technical efficiency. The nonparametric approach allows estimation of these moments without restrictive assumptions on the distribution of inefficiency, which plagued earlier efforts in the stochastic frontier literature. He also provides an empirical example; the estimators are applied to a panel of 17 railway companies over a 14 year time period.

In his contribution, Bill Schworm studies intellectual property rights, efficiency and productivity in a model with endogenous innovation. He uses a stylized version of the Rivera-Batiz and Romer model, which allows him to study equilibria under alternative regimes using standard measures of technical and allocative efficiency. This allows him to compare the efficiency of economies with and without patent rights.

Thijs ten Raa continues the technical efficiency theme, starting with a discussion of the difference between the Farrell (1957) and Debreu (1951) efficiency measures. He chooses the Debreu approach and shows how Debreu's efficiency measure for an economy may be disaggregated into production unit inefficiencies. This contribution gracefully touches on all three issues which unify this volume: aggregation, efficiency and measurement.

Tribute to R. Robert Russell

Daniel Primont

Southern Illinois University, Carbondale, IL.

"The proofs of theorems are pretty. I'd rather look at a nice proof than a work of art."[1]

R. Robert Russell has made intellectual contributions in several areas of economics ranging from microeconomics to macroeconomics, from theoretical economics to empirical economics and to policy analysis. Any attempt to summarize his work in a few pages would be plagued by aggregation errors. Nevertheless, the research that has had the most impact has probably been in microeconomic theory and specifically in the areas of aggregation, efficiency, and measurement. What follows is a selective survey of these three areas.

Russell studied economics as an undergraduate at UC Santa Barbara and as a graduate student at Harvard. He returned to UC Santa Barbara to begin his first academic appointment. His tenure at UC Santa Barbara was interrupted once by an appointment to the professional staff of the Council of Economic Advisers. Several of his early papers were in the field of macroeconomics. However, the direction of his research would soon change.

While at UC Santa Barbara and later at UC San Diego, Russell worked on the theory and applications of duality theory and separability. Russell and his collaborators produced a number of papers on budgeting, decentralized decision making, intertemporal decision making, price and quantity aggregation, partial elasticities of substitution, and testing separability restrictions with flexible functional forms. These results were brought together in a book (aka the yellow book: Blackorby, Primont, and Russell (1978)).

Three of Russell's many separability papers will be highlighted here. In one of these papers, Nissen, Primont and Russell (1973), the problem of intertemporal consistency, first posed by Strotz (1955), is examined in a more general framework. An intertemporal planner (consumer) is said to be inconsistent if he settles on a budget-constrained, utility maximizing intertemporal

[1] Attributed to R.R. Russell by the New York Times, August 12, 1979

plan in the first time period and then, in a later time period, changes the original plan. It is shown that intertemporal consistency is intimately related to "recursive compatibility," a condition that involves separability of the future from the present. In the absence of this separability condition intertemporal inconsistency results.

In a second paper, Blackorby, Primont, and Russell (1977) show that flexible functional forms, interpreted as second-order Taylor series approximations, become inflexible if separability conditions are globally imposed. This negative result has been followed by a great deal of research into finding functional forms with better global properties.

A third paper by Blackorby and Russell (1995) examines the seemingly conflicting practices of proportional budgeting and decentralization. An organization, such as a government or a university, engages in proportional budgeting when it is optimal to increase or decrease its budget by the same proportion across all of its divisions or sectors. Decentralization, on the other hand, requires that each division spends its allocation in a way that is optimal for the overall organization. These two budgeting procedures are simultaneously consistent with overall optimality if and only if the organization's objective function is homothetic and each sector is separable. These strong conditions enable the organization to engage in a simple additive price aggregation scheme but they are unlikely to be met in practice.

Russell took a leave of absence from UC San Diego to become the Deputy Director and, later, the Director of the Council on Wage and Price Stability under the Carter administration. He subsequently accepted a position in the economics department at New York University where he also served as the Director of the C.V. Starr Center for Applied Economics.

Russell's first two papers, Russell (1975) and Blackorby and Russell (1976), on the partial or Allen elasticity of substitution, alluded to above, related certain equality restrictions on the elasticities to separability properties of the cost and input distance functions. Specifically, these papers show that the Allen elasticity of substitution (AES) between inputs i and k is equal to that between inputs j and k if and only if the pair of inputs (i, j) is separable from input k in the cost function (or equivalently, in the input distance function.) These papers were precursors of a third paper, Blackorby and Russell (1981), that found analogous results for the Morishima elasticity of substitution (MES). But there is a fourth paper that is arguably the most important in this series.

In Blackorby and Russell (1989) a rather stark comparison is made between the AES and the MES. The comparison involves asking which measure is a better n-input generalization of the elasticity of substitution first introduced by John Hicks in the two input case.

The answer to this question has several dimensions. First it is shown, using a simple three-input production function, that the AES provides no information about the degree of substitutability between two of the inputs when all three inputs are allowed to adjust to their cost-minimizing values while the MES does provide the correct information. Hence, the MES is the better generalization in this regard.

The original two-good elasticity of substitution had the attractive property that its value could predict how factor shares would change when the factor price ratio changed. It is also shown in this paper that the Allen measure fails miserably on this account and the Morishima measure behaves admirably. Another use of elasticities of substitution is the classification of input pairs as either substitutes or complements. Indeed, many empirical papers that have reported values of the AES have little, or nothing, to say about their interpretation aside from their signs. But, as this paper points out, the sign of the AES for inputs i and j is the same as the sign of the cross-derivative of the input demand for good i with respect to input price j so the AES is unnecessary for this classificatory purpose. This paper has redirected empirical research away from the AES to the MES.

The Debreu-Farrell input measure of technical efficiency is a radial measure, i.e., it is the maximal contraction of an input vector along a ray from the origin holding output constant so that, for example, a measure of 0.8 means that, at most, 80% of the observed input vector is required to produce the observed output. Rolf Färe and Knox Lovell (1978) proposed a set of four properties (or axioms) for a measure of input technical efficiency. Three of these turned out to be of particular interest: indication (I), monotonicity (M), and homogeneity (H).

Färe and Lovell introduced a non-radial measure that they named the Russell measure. This measure is the maximal sum of coordinate-wise proportional contractions of the input vector holding the output vector constant. It was claimed, correctly, that the Debreu-Farrell (DF) measure does not satisfy all four properties and it was claimed, incorrectly, that the Russell measure does.

Russell wrote a series of papers that referred to the Russell measure as the Färe-Lovell measure. This series started while he was at NYU and continued after he accepted an academic appointment at UC Riverside. Henceforth, let us refer to the non-radial measure as the Färe-Lovell (FL) measure since, after all, it was first proposed by Färe and Lovell. Over the course of three papers, Russell (1985, 1988, 1990), four additional properties were introduced. Two of them were variations (weak indication (IW) and weak monotonicity (WM)) and two of them were more substantive (commensurability (C) and continuity.) Russell also introduced the extended Debreu-Farrell (EDF) measure; this is the usual DF measure defined on the disposable hulls of the input requirement sets from the original technology.

It had already been recognized that the FL measure does not satisfy H. Russell showed that it also does not satisfy M. He further showed that M and I are mutually exclusive, that the FL measure satisfies C, I, and WM. and that the EDF measure satisfies C, IW, WM, and H. And finally, he showed that adding continuity rules out I and hence rules out the FL measure. Only the EDF measure remains standing.

In two recent papers, Kumar and Russell (2002) and Henderson and Russell (2005), Russell has turned his attention to the problem of accounting for changes in both productivity and efficiency. Using a cross sectional international data set a production frontier is obtained and changes in labor productivity are decomposed into three components: growth due to 1) technological change (a shift in the frontier) 2) technological catch-up (a change in productive efficiency or the distance from the frontier) and 3) capital accumulation. Traditional growth accounting exercises only incorporated 1) and 3) and hence Russell terms his work as "a growth accounting exercise with a new twist."

Russell has served as an Associate Editor and as an Editor for the *Journal of Productivity Analysis* for the last twenty years. He is also an editor of a book series, Studies in Productivity and Efficiency, for Kluwer Academic Press (Springer Science+Business Media since Spring 2004). Thus, he has not only been an active researcher on the topics of efficiency and productivity but also an intellectual leader in these areas.

Russell's academic research is characterized by a lucid and forceful writing style, intellectual rigor, and proofs of theorems that dazzle like fine art. He enjoys intellectual challenges and working with his students and colleagues to meet those challenges. He excels in the classroom; his lectures are rich in content and delivered in a crisp, engaging style. This volume in his honor is well-deserved.

References

Blackorby, Charles and R. Robert Russell, "Functional Structure and Partial Elasticities of Substitution: An Application of Duality Theory," *Review of Economic Studies* **43** (1976), 285–291.

Blackorby, Charles and R. Robert Russell, "The Morishima Elasticity of Substitution: Symmetry, Constancy, Separability, and Relationship to the Hicks and Allen Elasticities," *Review of Economic Studies* **48** (1981), 147–158.

Blackorby, Charles and R. Robert Russell, "Will the Real Elasticity of Substitution Please Stand Up? A Comparison of the Allen/Uzawa and Morishima Elasticities," *American Economic Review* **79** (1989), 882–888.

Blackorby, Charles and R. Robert Russell, "Proportional Budgeting and Decentralization," *Econometrica* **63** (1995), 431–439.

Blackorby, Charles, David Nissen, Daniel Primont, and R. Robert Russell, "Consistent Intertemporal Decision Making," *Review of Economic Studies* **40** (1973), 239–248.

Blackorby, Charles, Daniel Primont, and R. Robert Russell, "On Testing Separability Restrictions with Flexible Functional Forms," *Journal of Econometrics* **5** (1977), 195–209.

Blackorby, Charles, Daniel Primont, and R. Robert Russell, *Duality, Separability, and Functional Structure: Theory and Economic Applications*, North-Holland, 1978.

Färe, Rolf and C. A. Knox Lovell, "Measuring the Technical Efficiency of Production," *Journal of Economic Theory* **19** (1978), 150–162.

Henderson, Daniel and R. Robert Russell, "Human Capital and Convergence: A Production-Frontier Approach," *International Economic Review.* **46** (2005), 1167–1205.

Kumar, Subodh and R. Robert Russell, "Technological Change, Technological Catch-Up, and Capital Deepening: Relative Contributions to Growth and Convergence," *American Economic Review* **92** (2002), 527–548.

Russell, R. Robert, "Functional Structure and Partial Elasticities of Substitution," *Review of Economic Studies* **42** (1975), 79–85.

Russell, R. Robert, "Measures of Technical Efficiency," *Journal of Economic Theory* **35** (1985), 109–126.

Russell, R. Robert, "On the Axiomatic Approach to the Measurement of Technical Efficiency," in *Measurement in Economics: Theory and Application of Economic Indices* (Wolfgang Eichhorn, ed.), Physica-Verlag, 1988, 207–217.

Russell, R. Robert, "Continuity of Measures of Technical Efficiency," *Journal of Economic Theory* **51** (1990), 255–267.

Strotz, Robert H., "Myopia and Inconsistency in Dynamic Utility Maximization," *Review of Economic Studies* **23** (1955), 165–180.

List of Contributors

Charles Blackorby
Department of Economics
University of Warwick
Gibbet Hill Road
Coventry, CV4 7AL, UK
and
GREQAM
Centre de la Vielle Charité
2 rue de la Charité
13002 Marseille, France
c.blackorby@warwick.ac.uk

Lane Blume Hudgins
Department of Economics
Southern Illinois University
Carbondale, IL 62901
lane@siu.edu

Craig Brett
Canada Research Chair in Canadian Public Policy
Department of Economics
Mount Allison University
Sackville, New Brunswick
Canada E4L 1E6
cbrett@mta.ca

Tim S. Campbell
Department of Finance and Business Economics
Marshall School of Business
University of Southern California
701 Exposition Blvd., Ste. 701
Los Angeles, CA 90089-1427
tcampbell@marshall.usc.edu

W. Erwin Diewert
Department of Economics
University of British Columbia
Vancouver, B.C.
Canada, V6T 1Z1
diewert@econ.ubc.ca

Rolf Färe
Department of Economics
Oregon State University
Corvallis, OR 97331
rolf.fare@orst.edu

Shawna Grosskopf
Department of Economics
Oregon State University
Corvallis, OR 97331
shawna.grosskopf@orst.edu

Kathy Hayes
Department of Economics
Dedman College
Southern Methodist University
Dallas, TX 75275
khayes@smu.edu

Daniel J. Henderson
Department of Economics
State University of New York at Binghamton
Binghamton, NY 13902-6000
djhender@binghamton.edu

Anthony M. Marino
Department of Finance and Business Economics
Marshall School of Business
University of Southern California
701 Exposition Blvd., Ste. 701
Los Angeles, CA 90089-1427
amarino@marshall.usc.edu

M. Nimfa F. Mendoza
School of Economics
University of the Philipines-Diliman
Manila
The Philippines
ma-nimfa.mendoza@up.edu

Daniel Primont
Department of Economics
Southern Illinois University
Carbondale, IL 62901
primo@siu.edu

William Schworm
School of Economics
University of New South Wales
Sydney, NSW 2052
Australia
b.schworm@unsw.edu.au

Lori L. Taylor
George Bush School of Government and Public Service
1098 Allen Building, 4220 TAMU
College Station, TX 77843
ltaylor@bushschool.tamu.edu

Thijs ten Raa
Tilburg University
Box 90153
5000 LE Tilburg
The Netherlands
tenRaa@UvT.nl

Valentin Zelenyuk
Kyiv Economics Institute
Voloska 10
04070 Kiev
Ukraine
and UPEG/EERC
National University
'Kyiv-Mohyla Academy'
vzelenyuk@kei.org.ua

The Pareto-Optima of Finite-Horizon OLG Models

Charles Blackorby[1] and Craig Brett[2*]

[1] Department of Economics, University of Warwick, Gibbet Hill Road, Coventry, CV4 7AL, UK and GREQAM, Centre de la Vieille Charité, 2 rue de la Charité, 13002 Marseille, France c.blackorby@warwick.ac.uk

[2] Department of Mathematics and Computer Science, Mount Allison University, Sackville, New Brunswick, Canada, E4L 1E6. cbrett@mta.ca

Summary. In a simple overlapping-generations model where the government has the power to levy commodity taxes and to implement generation-specific transfers, we show that the second-best optima are not first-best, that is, commodity taxes and subsidies are almost always part of the efficient solution. Provided that savings is positive, we also show that taxes on saving and on capital inputs are required for efficiency at almost all optima.

Key words: overlapping generations, commodity taxes, tax-reform.

1 Introduction

The way in which economists think about the merits of government intervention is profoundly influenced by the first and second theorems of welfare economics. According to these theorems, competition insures that the economy is at a Pareto-optimum and, moreover, that any such optimum can be implemented by a competitive market, as long as initial endowments of resources can be altered via lump-sum transfers. Even when the economy cannot obtain such a first-best outcome,[3] our understanding of the structure of the set of Pareto-optimal allocations in competitive economies lies behind much of our reasoning. In overlapping-generations models of the economy we also

* This research has been generously supported by the Social Science Research Council of Canada. Blackorby is grateful for the many conversations with Paul Beaudry and Francisco Gonzalez and a very productive lunch with Ivar Ekeland. We are particularly grateful to Sushama Murty.

[3] This may be for any of a myriad of reasons, e.g., inability to effectuate individual lump-sum transfers, informational asymmetries, or imperfect competition.

need to evaluate alternative economic policies. Are capital taxes inefficient, are taxes on savings less efficient because of the so-called double taxation, should investment in human capital be taxed in the same fashion as investment in physical capital? In order to answer such questions we need first to have some idea of the nature of the set of Pareto-optimal allocations in a model with overlapping generations. That is, we need to have a clear idea of what constitutes an efficient outcome before undertaking an analysis of the policies that would best correct some distortion. To the best of our knowledge no such characterization exists.

In this paper we characterize the set of Pareto-optima in a finite-horizon overlapping-generations model where the government has the power to levy commodity taxes and to implement generation-specific transfers. That is, in an overlapping-generations model, we give the government the instruments and knowledge that would bring about a first-best allocation in a Walrasian economy and study the resulting set of Pareto-optimal allocations. We show that almost none of the Pareto optima in this economy are first-best; that is, commodity taxes and subsidies are part of almost all efficient solutions. Taxes on savings and or on capital inputs (but not both) are also required at almost all Pareto-optima. This implies that government intervention in the market place is essential if the economy is to achieve its true potential. In particular, the usual practice of assuming that consumer prices are equal to producer prices in a finite-horizon overlapping-generations model with saving leads to an equilibrium that is Pareto-inferior to one with commodity and services taxes and generation-specific transfers.

Our results are in stark contrast to the well-known results in a static general equilibrium model with the same instruments, in which a first-best outcome would result. There are several reasons for this. Here the government can do no better than the consumers in transferring wealth from one period to another. That is, the government must engage in capital market transactions in order to transfer income. In addition, each generation, except for generation zero, must satisfy two budget constraints which are connected only through the capital market. Hence, in period t the budget constraints of generations $t-1$ and t depend only on period t prices and capital market considerations. Thus all information about past and future prices are transmitted by capital transactions. Our results rest on the observation that the taxation authority does not have sufficient control of prices to offset this second-best constraint. It is true that with positive savings each generation faces a single lifetime budget constraint. However, attempts to decentralize these intertemporal budget constraints must also account for the fact that each lifetime budget constraint must decompose into two budget constraints that are intertemporally consistent. These distinctions place additional constraints on the model that do not exist in a standard general equilibrium model and account for the second-best nature of the outcome.

We use the tax reform methodology.[4] Starting with an economy at an arbitrary tight equilibrium, we ask what changes in taxes, transfers, and producer prices are strictly Pareto-improving and equilibrium preserving. If there are no such changes then the economy is at a Pareto optimum. We show that these optima usually require government intervention in the market place.

The next section of the paper presents a simple finite horizon overlapping generations model with three generations. Unlike many such models in the literature, we allow for many consumption goods, in order to give some content to the issue of within period relative price changes. In Section 3 we describe the tax reform methodology and characterize strictly Pareto improving directions of policy reform. This also furnishes a description of the Pareto optima of the economy. This is followed by a section detailing the somewhat delicate issue of price normalizations. We show that producer prices and the price of capital can be normalized period by period, but that only one consumer price normalization is admitted. The overlapping generations structure links relative prices across generations, so that independent normalization is impossible. Section 5 contains a description of the geometric structure of the tax equilibria. We show that, locally, the Pareto manifold is of dimension two (one less than the number of consumers). Zero tax rates are optimal only at an isolated set of equilibria—those in which the rate of interest is zero. Section 6 has concluding remarks and Section 7 contains the many calculations needed in the text.

2 The Model

We consider the simplest possible overlapping generations model.[5] The economy lasts for three periods: a start-up phase, a single period of the type usually examined in overlapping generations models, and a shut-down period.

2.1 Goods and Consumers

There is a single consumer in each generation, so consumer and generation are used interchangeably. Consumers have preferences over a vector $\alpha \in \mathcal{R}^n$ of non-storable goods and services; there is a storable good, κ that is the basis for the capital stock.

An initial generation, denoted by 0, is born old. It enters at date 1 in possession of the initial capital stock, κ_0. It consumes goods and services, α_1^0, receives a generation-specific lump-sum transfer, m_1, and sells its capital stock. If any of the elements of α_1^0 are negative these are services supplied to

[4] See Guesnerie (1977,1995), Diewert (1978), Weymark (1979); a good textbook treatment is in Myles (1995).

[5] This is a simple version of the model introduced by Allais (1947), Samuelson (1958), and analyzed by Diamond (1965).

the market. Also alive at time 1 is a generation born young. This generation lives for two periods. During period 1, it consumes α_1^1 and may also purchase an amount of the storable good, κ_1^1, to carry forward with it into the second period. Again, if any elements of α_1^1 are negative, then these are services supplied to the market. In period 2 it spends its accumulated wealth and its lump-sum transfer, m_2, on the consumption of α_2^1. Also alive in period 2 is a young generation which works, consumes, and saves. In period 3, the final period of our model, this generation sells its capital stock, κ_2^2, receives its lump-sum transfer, m_3, and consumes α_3^3.

The production sector is composed of an aggregate profit–maximizing firm whose technology is not assumed to be the same in every period. During periods 1 and 2, this firm can produce both a and b using a and k as inputs. In period 3 it does not produce any b.[6]

2.2 Prices

A complete specification of a price system requires a separate price for each good, at each date in time. In addition, to allow for taxes, a set consumer prices and a set of producer prices must be specified. We express all prices in present value form. Let p_t be the producer price vector for a_t. π_t denotes the corresponding consumer price vector. r_t is the producer price of the storable good at time t, while ρ_t is its consumer price. In addition the firm buys at time t the capital stock from generation $t-1$ at a price s_{t-1} while generation $t-1$ receives σ_{t-1}. For the moment we make no price normalizations but show subsequently that the question of what can be normalized is a delicate issue.

2.3 The Flows of Resources

Besides levying specific commodity taxes, the government is assumed to tax away all pure profit[7] and it has the power to transfer income in a lump-sum to each generation. The transfer at date t, denoted by m_t, is paid to the old generation at that time. The planner may purchase the storable good in amounts κ_1^g in period 1 and κ_2^g in period 2 to finance part of these lump sums. It has no means, however, of producing manna to bestow upon generation 0. This makes the redistributive powers of the government less than pure lump–sum because it can engage in only those transfers implementable through capital market transactions.

Generation 0 enters the economy in possession of the capital stock, κ_0. It sells this capital to the firm receiving σ_0 per unit. It carries out its purchases

[6] We use roman letters to indicate quantities produced and Greek letters to indicate quantities consumed. The symbols α and a refer to goods of identical characteristics. The same correspondence applies to κ and k. An inconsistency in notation arises in that the supply of κ is denoted b.

[7] Alternatively, one could assume constant returns-to-scale, implying zero profits.

with the proceeds of this sale and its lump–sum income. Given the lump-sum transfer, the budget constraint of generation 0 is[8]

$$\pi_1^T \alpha_1^0 \leq \sigma_0 \kappa_0 + m_1. \tag{1}$$

The indirect utility function of generation 0 and its related expenditure function are given by

$$u_0 = V^0(\sigma_0, \pi_1, m_1) \longleftrightarrow m_1 = E^0(u_0, \sigma_0, \pi_1). \tag{2}$$

Generation 1 uses its wage income to purchase consumption goods and services in period 1 and to buy an amount of the storable good to hold until the second period. At the beginning of the second period, it sells its capital to the firm, receiving σ_1 per unit. At this time, it also receives its lump-sum payment from the government. Thus, its behavior is consistent with the joint budget constraints:

$$\begin{aligned} \pi_1^T \alpha_1^1 + \rho_1 \kappa_1^1 &\leq 0; \\ \pi_2^T \alpha_2^1 &\leq \sigma_1 \kappa_1^1 + m_2. \end{aligned} \tag{3}$$

Combining these budget constraints yields

$$\frac{\sigma_1}{\rho_1} \pi_1^T \alpha_1^1 + \pi_2^T \alpha_2^1 \leq m_2. \tag{4}$$

Letting

$$\tilde{\pi}_1 := \frac{\sigma_1}{\rho_1} \pi_1 \tag{5}$$

the indirect utility function and expenditure function—conditional on positive savings—are given by

$$u_1 = V^1(\tilde{\pi}_1, \pi_2, m_2) \longleftrightarrow m_2 = E^1(u_1, \tilde{\pi}_1, \pi_2). \tag{6}$$

Similarly, the value functions of generation 2—conditional on positive savings—are given by

$$u_2 = V^2(\tilde{\pi}_2, \pi_3, m_3) \longleftrightarrow m_3 = E^2(u_2, \tilde{\pi}_2, \pi_3). \tag{7}$$

Each consumer maximizes lifetime utility, given the prices it faces and the lump–sum income it receives from the government. Generation 0 has a static problem. Generation 1 decides on a consumption plan for its two periods of life. Similarly for generation 2. We assume that the preferences are such that the indirect utility functions are differentially strongly quasi-convex.[9]

[8] We use subscripts to denote the date at which a commodity is produced or consumed. When ambiguity is possible, we use superscripts to denote the birth date of the consuming agent.

[9] See Blackorby and Diewert (1979).

It is worth noting that the above problem imposes substantial structure on the optimal purchases of the capital stock. For example, from (3), κ_1^1 is homogeneous of degree zero in (π_1, ρ_1) and (π_2, σ_1, m_2). From (4), it is homogeneous of degree zero in $(\tilde{\pi}_1, \pi_2, m_2)$. Note that the latter implies that κ_1^1 is also homogeneous of degree zero in (σ_1, ρ_1). A similar argument holds for the purchases of κ_2^2.

Subsequently we need to know the directions of change in consumer prices and lump-sum transfers that improve the well-being of the three generations. Using Roy's theorem and the envelope conditions these can be written as

$$du_0 > 0 \longleftrightarrow \kappa_0 d\sigma_0 - \alpha_1^{0T} d\pi_1 + dm_1 > 0, \tag{8}$$

$$du_1 > 0 \longleftrightarrow -\frac{\sigma_1}{\rho_1}\alpha_1^{1T} d\pi_1 + \frac{\sigma_1}{\rho_1^2}\pi_1^T \alpha_1^1 d\rho_1 - \frac{1}{\rho_1}\pi_1^T \alpha_1^1 d\sigma_1 - \alpha_2^{1T} d\pi_2 + dm_2 > 0 \tag{9}$$

and

$$du_2 > 0 \longleftrightarrow -\frac{\sigma_2}{\rho_2}\alpha_2^{2T} d\pi_2 + \frac{\sigma_2}{\rho_2^2}\pi_2^T \alpha_2^2 d\rho_2 - \frac{1}{\rho_2}\pi_2^T \alpha_2^2 d\sigma_2 - \alpha_3^{2T} d\pi_3 + dm_3 > 0. \tag{10}$$

In period 1, the firm uses the capital it purchases from generation 0 in combination with the services supplied by generations 0 and 1 to produce a vector of (net) outputs. The profit-maximizing behavior of the firm yields net supply functions:

$$a_1 = A^1(s_0, p_1, r_1), \quad b_1 = B^1(s_0, p_1, r_1), \quad \text{and} \quad k_1 = K^1(s_0, p_1, r_1). \tag{11}$$

In periods 2 and 3, the firm faces essentially identical problems to the one it faced in period 1 yielding

$$a_2 = A^2(s_1, p_2, r_2), \quad b_2 = B^2(s_1, p_2, r_2), \quad \text{and} \quad k_2 = K^2(s_1, p_2, r_2) \tag{12}$$

and

$$a_3 = A^3(s_2, p_3), \quad \text{and} \quad k_3 = K^3(s_2, p_3). \tag{13}$$

Because the technology is not assumed to be the same in each period, this formulation is consistent with any rate of capital depreciation. We assume that the profit functions of the firm are twice continuously differentiable and strongly convex in each period.[10]

2.4 Equilibrium

Depending upon which region of the Pareto-frontier is under consideration, in periods one and two, the planner may or may not be purchasing the capital good in order to transfer resources from period t to period $t+1$ for $t = 1, 2$.

---

[10] See Diewert, Avriel, and Zang (1981).

These quantities are denoted, κ_1^g and κ_2^g respectively. A collection of consumer and producer prices give rise to an equilibrium if all markets clear. The market clearing conditions are:

$$
\begin{aligned}
&\kappa_0 - k_1 \geq 0, \\
&-\alpha_1^0 - \alpha_1^1 + a_1 \geq 0, \\
&-\kappa_1^1 - \kappa_1^g + b_1 \geq 0, \\
&\kappa_1^1 + \kappa_1^g - k_2 \geq 0, \\
&-\alpha_2^1 - \alpha_2^2 + a_2 \geq 0, \\
&-\kappa_2^2 - \kappa_2^g + b_2 \geq 0, \\
&\kappa_2^2 + \kappa_2^g - k_3 \geq 0, \\
&-\alpha_3^2 + a_3 \geq 0, \\
&\kappa_1^g \geq 0, \quad \text{and} \\
&\kappa_2^g \geq 0.
\end{aligned}
\tag{14}
$$

It is straightforward to show that the government budget is balanced in every period.[11] One is free, however, to interpret purchases of the storable good as a form of government saving.

3 Tax Reforms

We assume that the economy is initially in a tight equilibrium;[12] that is, the initial vector of consumer prices, producer prices and transfer incomes is such that (14) all hold with equality with the possible exception of the last two. Depending upon the region of the Pareto-frontier being considered, either, both, or neither of these relations may hold with equality. This implies that there are four potentially different regimes that must be considered. For example, if both κ_1^g and κ_2^g are positive, then neither of the last two equations in (2.4) is relevant. This takes place in that region of the Pareto-frontier where the planner is moving resources away from generation zero in order to increase the demogrants to generations one and two. At the other extreme, both of these constraints are binding, the government would like to move resources from generation two to generations zero and one but is limited in its ability to do so by the non-negativity constraints on capital.

The planner may effect marginal changes in prices and generation-specific transfers. In general, the second-best outcomes that are feasible depend upon the instruments available to the government. Formally, the government has

[11] See Chapter 2 in Guesnerie (1995) for a general discussion of this issue; a proof is provided in the section entitled *Tedious Calculations*.

[12] See Guesnerie (1995) for a discussion of the non-tight case.

control over lump-sum transfers (using, when feasible, capital purchases) and commodity taxes while producer prices are adjusting so as to maintain equilibrium. If there are no restrictions on the use of taxes then the government can equivalently use consumer prices and the lump-sum transfers as instruments. If, however, there are restrictions on which taxes can be used these two procedures are no longer equivalent.[13] Because we investigate the conditions under which some taxes may, without loss of generality, be set at zero we use producer prices, taxes and the lump-sum transfers as instruments throughout. The taxes are already defined implicitly and are given by

$$\pi_t = p_t + \tau_t^a, \quad \sigma_t = s_t + \tau_t^k, \quad \text{and} \quad \rho_t = r_t + \tau_t^b. \tag{15}$$

The directions of change are given by

$$\gamma^T := [\gamma_p^T, \gamma_\tau^T, \gamma_m^T, \gamma_\kappa^T] \tag{16}$$

where

$$\begin{aligned} \gamma_p^T &:= [ds_0, dp_1^T, dr_1, ds_1, dp_2^T, dr_2, ds_2, dp_3^T]; \\ \gamma_\tau^T &:= [d\tau_0^k, d\tau_1^{aT}, d\tau_1^b, d\tau_1^k, d\tau_2^{aT}, d\tau_2^b, d\tau_2^k, d\tau_3^{aT}]; \\ \gamma_m^T &:= [dm_1, dm_2, dm_3]; \\ \gamma_\kappa^T &:= [d\kappa_1^g, d\kappa_2^g]. \end{aligned} \tag{17}$$

These vectors correspond (respectively) to changes in producer prices, taxes, lump-sum transfers, and government capital purchases.

3.1 Directions of Change

In order to proceed we need to find those directions of change that are strictly Pareto-improving and feasible. We first collect information on those changes in consumer prices and incomes that increase utility and then those that preserve equilibrium. The relevant changes in prices and incomes in the consumer sector are given by

$$P_\pi := \begin{bmatrix} \kappa_0 & -\alpha_1^{0T} & 0 & 0 & 0_n^T & 0 & 0 & 0_n^T \\ 0 & -\frac{\sigma_1}{\rho_1}\alpha_1^{1T} & \frac{\sigma_1}{\rho_1^2}\pi_1^T\alpha_1^1 & -\frac{1}{\rho_1}\pi_1^T\alpha_1^1 & -\alpha_2^{1T} & 0 & 0 & 0_n^T \\ 0 & 0_n^T & 0 & 0 & -\frac{\sigma_2}{\rho_2}\alpha_2^{2T} & \frac{\sigma_2}{\rho_2^2}\pi_2^T\alpha_2^2 & -\frac{1}{\rho_2}\pi_2^T\alpha_2^2 & -\alpha_3^{2T} \end{bmatrix} \tag{18}$$

and

$$P_m := \begin{bmatrix} 1 & 0 & 0 \\ 0 & 1 & 0 \\ 0 & 0 & 1 \end{bmatrix}. \tag{19}$$

[13] See Blackorby and Brett (1998).

The feasibility conditions can be described in matrix form. Let α_t denote the total amount of the consumer goods demanded by all consumers alive at date t.[14]

$$E_\pi := \begin{bmatrix} 0 & 0_n^T & 0 & 0 & 0_n^T & 0 & 0 & 0_n^T \\ -\nabla_{\sigma_0}\alpha_1^0 & -\nabla_{\pi_1}\alpha_1 & -\nabla_{\rho_1}\alpha_1^1 & -\nabla_{\sigma_1}\alpha_1^1 & -\nabla_{\pi_2}\alpha_1^1 & 0_n & 0_n & 0_{n\times n} \\ 0 & -\nabla_{\pi_1}\kappa_1^1 & -\nabla_{\rho_1}\kappa_1^1 & -\nabla_{\sigma_1}\kappa_1^1 & -\nabla_{\pi_2}\kappa_1^1 & 0 & 0 & 0_n^T \\ 0 & +\nabla_{\pi_1}\kappa_1^1 & +\nabla_{\rho_1}\kappa_1^1 & +\nabla_{\sigma_1}\kappa_1^1 & +\nabla_{\pi_2}\kappa_1^1 & 0 & 0 & 0_n^T \\ 0 & -\nabla_{\pi_1}\alpha_2^1 & -\nabla_{\rho_1}\alpha_2^1 & -\nabla_{\sigma_1}\alpha_2^1 & -\nabla_{\pi_2}\alpha_2 & -\nabla_{\rho_2}\alpha_2^2 & -\nabla_{\sigma_2}\alpha_2^2 & -\nabla_{\pi_3}\alpha_2^2 \\ 0 & 0_n^T & 0 & 0 & -\nabla_{\pi_2}\kappa_2^2 & -\nabla_{\rho_2}\kappa_2^2 & -\nabla_{\sigma_2}\kappa_2^2 & -\nabla_{\pi_3}\kappa_2^2 \\ 0 & 0_n^T & 0 & 0 & +\nabla_{\pi_2}\kappa_2^2 & +\nabla_{\rho_2}\kappa_2^2 & +\nabla_{\sigma_2}\kappa_2^2 & +\nabla_{\pi_3}\kappa_2^2 \\ 0_n & 0_{n\times n} & 0_n & 0_n & -\nabla_{\pi_2}\alpha_3^2 & -\nabla_{\rho_2}\alpha_3^2 & -\nabla_{\sigma_2}\alpha_3^2 & -\nabla_{\pi_3}\alpha_3^2 \end{bmatrix}; \tag{20}$$

$$E_m := \begin{bmatrix} 0 & 0 & 0 \\ -\nabla_{m_1}\alpha_1^0 & -\nabla_{m_2}\alpha_1^1 & 0 \\ 0 & -\nabla_{m_2}\kappa_1^1 & 0 \\ 0 & \nabla_{m_2}\kappa_1^1 & 0 \\ 0 & -\nabla_{m_2}\alpha_2^1 & -\nabla_{m_3}\alpha_2^2 \\ 0 & 0 & -\nabla_{m_3}\kappa_2^2 \\ 0 & 0 & \nabla_{m_3}\kappa_2^2 \\ 0 & 0 & -\nabla_{m_3}\alpha_3^2 \end{bmatrix}; \tag{21}$$

$$E_p := \begin{bmatrix} -\nabla_{s_0}k_1 & -\nabla_{p_1}k_1 & -\nabla_{r_1}k_1 & 0 & 0_n^T & 0 & 0 & 0_n^T \\ \nabla_{s_0}a_1 & \nabla_{p_1}a_1 & \nabla_{r_1}a_1 & 0_n & 0_{n\times n} & 0_n & 0_n & 0_{n\times n} \\ \nabla_{s_0}b_1 & \nabla_{p_1}b_1 & \nabla_{r_1}b_1 & 0 & 0_n^T & 0 & 0 & 0_n^T \\ 0 & 0_n^T & 0 & -\nabla_{s_1}k_2 & -\nabla_{p_2}k_2 & -\nabla_{r_2}k_2 & 0 & 0_n^T \\ 0_n & 0_{n\times n} & 0_n & \nabla_{s_1}a_2 & \nabla_{p_2}a_2 & \nabla_{r_2}a_2 & 0 & 0_n^T \\ 0 & 0_n^T & 0 & \nabla_{s_1}b_2 & \nabla_{p_2}b_2 & \nabla_{r_2}b_2 & 0 & 0_n^T \\ 0 & 0_n^T & 0 & 0 & 0_n^T & 0 & -\nabla_{s_2}k_3 & -\nabla_{p_3}k_3 \\ 0_n & 0_{n\times n} & 0_n & 0_n & 0_{n\times n} & 0_n & \nabla_{s_2}a_3 & \nabla_{p_3}a_3 \end{bmatrix}; \tag{22}$$

and

$$E_\kappa := \begin{bmatrix} 0 & 0 \\ 0_n & 0_n \\ -1 & 0 \\ 1 & 0 \\ 0_n & 0_n \\ 0 & -1 \\ 0 & 1 \\ 0_n & 0_n \end{bmatrix}. \tag{23}$$

[14] We introduce a second use of the capital E at this point. Whenever a capital E appears without a superscript, it refers to a matrix representation of equilibrium-preserving directions of change. A capital E with a superscript refers to the expenditure function of the consumer named by the superscript.

In addition to the above we have the non-negativity constraint on the government's purchases of capital,

$$d\kappa_1^g + \kappa_1^g \geq 0 \quad \text{and} \quad d\kappa_2^g + \kappa_2^g \geq 0. \tag{24}$$

3.2 Strictly Pareto-Improving Equilibrium Preserving Directions of Change

A set of changes is strictly Pareto-improving if and only if

$$P_\pi \gamma_p + P_\pi \gamma_\tau + P_m \gamma_m + \mathbf{0}\gamma_\kappa \gg 0 \tag{25}$$

where $\mathbf{0}$ is an appropriately dimensioned matrix of zeros. A direction is equilibrium-preserving if and only if

$$[E_\pi + E_p]\gamma_p + E_\pi \gamma_\tau + E_m \gamma_m + E_\kappa \gamma_\kappa \geq 0. \tag{26}$$

In addition the capital constraints on government must be satisfied, see (24). There are strictly Pareto-improving changes that are simultaneously equilibrium-preserving if and only (25), (26), and (24) have a solution. Together these constitute a non homogeneous system which we convert to the following homogeneous system.[15]

$$\begin{bmatrix} P_\pi & P_\pi & P_m & 0_{n\times 2} & 0_n \\ 0_n^T & 0_n^T & 0_3^T & 0_2^T & 1 \end{bmatrix} \begin{bmatrix} \gamma \\ \gamma_\eta \end{bmatrix} \gg 0 \tag{27}$$

and

$$\begin{bmatrix} E_\pi + E_p & E_\pi & E_m & E_\kappa & 0_n \\ 0_n^T & 0_n^T & 0_3^T & I_{2\times 2} & \kappa^g \end{bmatrix} \begin{bmatrix} \gamma \\ \gamma_\eta \end{bmatrix} \geq 0 \tag{28}$$

where $\kappa^g = [\kappa_1^g, \kappa_2^g]$ and γ_η is the dummy variable used to convert the non homogeneous system to a homogeneous one. If there is no solution we are at a second-best optimum. Using Motzkin's Theorem[16] the economy is at a second-best optimum if and only if

$$\begin{bmatrix} \xi^T & \theta \end{bmatrix} \begin{bmatrix} [P_\pi & P_\pi & P_m & 0 & 0 \\ 0_n^T & 0_n^T & 0_3^T & 0_2^T & 1 \end{bmatrix} + \begin{bmatrix} v^T & \eta^T \end{bmatrix} \begin{bmatrix} E_\pi + E_p & E_\pi & E_m & E_\kappa & 0 \\ 0_n^T & 0_n^T & 0_3^T & I_{2\times 2} & \kappa^g \end{bmatrix} \tag{29}$$

$= 0,$

where $0 \neq [\xi^T, \theta] \geq 0$ and $[v^T, \eta^T] \geq 0$.

Before analyzing the structure of the Pareto-optimal set and the implied taxes and subsidies, we examine the question of price-normalizations. That is, how many producer and consumer prices are actually redundant.

[15] See the second subsection of *Tedious Calculations* for this argument.

[16] See Mangasarian (1969, pp. 28–29) for a statement and proof of this result.

4 Normalizations

In this section we investigate the legitimacy of normalizing prices. We do this formally by adding constraints to the original system of equations preventing some prices from changing. If the multiplier on this constraint can be shown to be zero, then this normalization places no restrictions on the optimal solution and is permissible. If however, this multiplier cannot be shown to be zero, then such a normalization is inconsistent with an efficient equilibrium. The results of this exercise are summarized at the end of this section. It is important to note that if one normalizes more prices than are admitted by the above procedure, then the resulting set of equilibria are not Pareto-optimal.

4.1 Producer Price Normalizations

First we show that at most one producer price can be normalized in each period. To set

$$s_0 = 1, \quad s_1 = 1, \quad \text{and} \quad s_2 = 1 \tag{30}$$

and to look for the Pareto-improving directions that are equilibrium-preserving and satisfy (30) define

$$\mathcal{I} = \begin{bmatrix} 1 & 0_n^T & 0 & 0 & 0_n^T & 0 & 0 & 0_n^T \\ 0 & 0_n^T & 0 & 1 & 0_n^T & 0 & 0 & 0_n^T \\ 0 & 0_n^T & 0 & 0 & 0_n^T & 0 & 1 & 0_n^T \end{bmatrix}. \tag{31}$$

(30) is satisfied if and only if

$$\mathcal{I}\gamma_p + \mathbf{0}\gamma_\tau + \mathbf{0}\gamma_m + \mathbf{0}\gamma_\kappa + 0_n\gamma_\eta = 0, \tag{32}$$

where $\mathbf{0}$ is an appropriately dimensioned block of zeroes.

There exist strictly Pareto-improving changes that are simultaneously equilibrium-preserving with three producer price normalizations if and only if (27), (28), and (32) have a solution. If there is no such solution we are at a second-best optimum. Using Motzkin's Theorem the economy is at a second-best optimum if and only if

$$[\xi^T \quad \theta]\begin{bmatrix} P_\pi & P_\pi & P_m & \mathbf{0} & 0 \\ 0_n^T & 0_n^T & 0_3^T & 0_2^T & 1 \end{bmatrix} + [v^T \quad \eta^T]\begin{bmatrix} E_\pi + E_p & E_\pi & E_m & E_\kappa & 0 \\ 0_n^T & 0_n^T & 0_3^T & I_{2\times 2} & \kappa^g \end{bmatrix}$$

$$+ w^T[\mathcal{I} \quad \mathbf{0} \quad \mathbf{0} \quad \mathbf{0} \quad 0_n] = 0, \tag{33}$$

or, expanding

$$\xi^T P_\pi + v^T[E_\pi + E_p] + w^T\mathcal{I} = 0, \tag{34}$$

$$\xi^T P_\pi + v^T E_\pi = 0, \tag{35}$$

$$\xi^T P_m + v^T E_m = 0. \tag{36}$$

$$v^T E_\kappa + \eta^T = 0, \tag{37}$$

and

$$\theta + \eta^T \kappa^g = 0. \tag{38}$$

Subtracting (35) from (34) yields

$$v^T E_p + w^T \mathcal{I} = 0 \tag{39}$$

or, using (22),

$$v^{1T} \begin{bmatrix} -\nabla_{s_0} k_1 & -\nabla_{p_1} k_1 & -\nabla_{r_1} k_1 \\ \nabla_{s_0} a_1 & \nabla_{p_1} a_1 & \nabla_{r_1} a_1 \\ \nabla_{s_0} b_1 & \nabla_{p_1} b_1 & \nabla_{r_1} b_1 \end{bmatrix} + (w_1, 0_n^T, 0) = 0,$$

$$v^{2T} \begin{bmatrix} -\nabla_{s_1} k_2 & -\nabla_{p_2} k_2 & -\nabla_{r_2} k_2 \\ \nabla_{s_1} a_2 & \nabla_{p_2} a_2 & \nabla_{r_2} a_2 \\ \nabla_{s_1} b_2 & \nabla_{p_2} b_2 & \nabla_{r_2} b_2 \end{bmatrix} + (w_2, 0_n^T, 0) = 0, \tag{40}$$

and

$$v^{3T} \begin{bmatrix} -\nabla_{s_2} k_3 & -\nabla_{p_3} k_3 \\ \nabla_{s_2} a_3 & \nabla_{p_3} a_3 \end{bmatrix} + (w_3, 0_n^T) = 0$$

where $v^T = (v^{1T}, v^{2T}, v^{3T})$ is defined implicitly by the above; v^{1T} and v^{2T} are $n+2$ tuples, and v^{3T} is a $n+1$ tuple. Post-multiply (40) by the producer price vector to obtain

$$w_1 s_0 = 0, \quad w_2 s_1 = 0 \quad \text{and} \quad w_3 s_2 = 0. \tag{41}$$

Because prices are positive, this implies that $w = 0$ and hence that the constraints embodying the normalizations do not bind at the second-best optimum; that is, (30) places no restrictions on the optimum. It is easy to see that if another producer price were normalized then some of these constraints would be strictly binding.

4.2 Producer and Capital Input (or Savings) Price Normalizations

Before proceeding to a formal analysis first note that intuition suggests that several prices can be normalized without loss of generality. The budget constraint of generation zero is given by

$$\pi_1 \alpha_1^0 \leq (s_0 + \tau_0^k)\kappa_0 + m_1. \tag{42}$$

Clearly the tax on the fixed amount of the capital stock, τ_0^k, is a perfect substitute for the lump-sum transfer, m_1, and is redundant in a Pareto-optimum. The budget constraint of generation one is given by

$$\left[\frac{s_1 + \tau_1^k}{r_1 + \tau_1^b}\right] \pi_1 \alpha_1^1 + \pi_2 \alpha_2^1 \leq m_2. \tag{43}$$

From this it is clear that either τ_1^k or τ_1^b is redundant. The budget constraint of generation two is given by

$$\left[\frac{s_2 + \tau_2^k}{r_2 + \tau_2^b}\right] \pi_2 \alpha_2^2 + \pi_3 \alpha_3^2 \leq m_3. \tag{44}$$

From this it is clear that either τ_2^k or τ_2^b is redundant. We show formally that these suggestions are correct.

Suppose now, that in addition to (30) we constrain the taxes on the inputs purchases to be zero, that is,

$$\tau_0^k = 0, \quad \tau_1^k = 0, \quad \text{and} \quad \tau_2^k = 0. \tag{45}$$

A direction is strictly Pareto-improving and equilibrium-preserving when the price normalizations (30) and (45) are satisfied if and only if (27), (28), and

$$\begin{bmatrix} \mathcal{I} \\ \mathbf{0} \end{bmatrix} \gamma_p + \begin{bmatrix} \mathbf{0} \\ \mathcal{I} \end{bmatrix} \gamma_\tau + \begin{bmatrix} \mathbf{0} \\ \mathbf{0} \end{bmatrix} \gamma_m \begin{bmatrix} \mathbf{0} \\ \mathbf{0} \end{bmatrix} \gamma_\kappa + \begin{bmatrix} 0_n \\ 0_n \end{bmatrix} \gamma_\eta = 0 \tag{46}$$

are satisfied. If there is no such solution we are at a second-best optimum. Using Motzkin's Theorem the economy is at a second-best optimum if and only if

$$\begin{bmatrix} \xi^T & \theta \end{bmatrix} \begin{bmatrix} [P_\pi & P_\pi & P_m & \mathbf{0} & 0 \\ 0_n^T & 0_n^T & 0_3^T & 0_2^T & 1 \end{bmatrix} + \begin{bmatrix} v^T & \eta^T \end{bmatrix} \begin{bmatrix} E_\pi + E_p & E_\pi & E_m & E_\kappa & 0 \\ 0_n^T & 0_n^T & 0_3^T & I_{2\times 2}\kappa^g & \end{bmatrix}$$

$$+(w^T, z^T) \begin{bmatrix} \mathcal{I} & \mathbf{0} & \mathbf{0} & \mathbf{0} & 0_n \\ \mathbf{0} & \mathcal{I} & \mathbf{0} & \mathbf{0} & 0_n \end{bmatrix} = 0, \tag{47}$$

or, expanding

$$\xi^T P_\pi + v^T [E_\pi + E_p] + w^T \mathcal{I} = 0, \tag{48}$$

$$\xi^T P_\pi + v^T E_\pi + z^T \mathcal{I} = 0, \tag{49}$$

$$\xi^T P_m + v^T E_m = 0, \tag{50}$$

$$v^T E_\kappa + \eta^T = 0, \tag{51}$$

and

$$\theta + \eta^T \kappa^g = 0. \tag{52}$$

This means that we cannot simply proceed as above, subtracting (49) from (48). If we are to show that some consumer prices can be normalized without loss of generality then this now has to come from (49). Only when the shadow value of the constraints on consumer prices are shown to be identically zero can we proceed as above. Let

$$v^T = \left(v_1, v_2^T, v_3, v_4, v_5^T, v_6, v_7, v_8^T\right). \tag{53}$$

For this to be consistent with the above,

$$v^{1T} = (v_1, v_2^T, v_3), v^{2T} = (v_4, v_5^T, v_6), \text{and } v^{3T} = (v_7, v_8^T). \tag{54}$$

Expanding (50) yields

$$\xi_1 = v_2^T \nabla_{m_1} \alpha_1^0, \tag{55}$$

$$\xi_2 = v_2^T \nabla_{m_2} \alpha_1^1 + (v_3 - v_4) \nabla_{m_2} \kappa_1^1 + v_5^T \nabla_{m_2} \alpha_2^1, \tag{56}$$

and

$$\xi_3 = v_5^T \nabla_{m_3} \alpha_2^2 + (v_6 - v_7) \nabla_{m_3} \kappa_2^2 + v_8^T \nabla_{m_3} \alpha_3^2. \tag{57}$$

Expanding (49), using (55) -57), and the Slutsky equation repeatedly yields[17]

$$-\xi_1 \kappa_0 = -v_2^T \nabla_{\sigma_0} \alpha_1^0 + z_1, \tag{58}$$

$$\begin{bmatrix} v_2^T & v_5^T & v_8^T \end{bmatrix} \begin{bmatrix} E^0_{\pi_1\pi_1} + \frac{\sigma_1}{\rho_1} E^1_{\tilde{\pi}_1\tilde{\pi}_1} & E^1_{\tilde{\pi}_1\pi_2} & 0 \\ \frac{\sigma_1}{\rho_1} E^1_{\pi_2\tilde{\pi}_1} & E^1_{\pi_2\pi_2} + \frac{\sigma_2}{\rho_2} E^2_{\tilde{\pi}_2\tilde{\pi}_2} & E^2_{\tilde{\pi}_2\pi_3} \\ 0 & \frac{\sigma_2}{\rho_2} E^2_{\pi_3\tilde{\pi}_2} & E^2_{\pi_3\pi_3} \end{bmatrix}$$

$$= \begin{bmatrix} (v_4 - v_3)(\nabla_{\pi_1}\kappa_1^1 + \nabla_{m_2}\kappa_1^1 \frac{\sigma_1}{\rho_1} \alpha_1^{1T}) \\ (v_4 - v_3)(\nabla_{\pi_2}\kappa_1^1 + \nabla_{m_2}\kappa_1^1 \alpha_2^{1T}) + (v_7 - v_6)(\nabla_{\pi_2}\kappa_2^2 + \nabla_{m_3}\kappa_2^2 \frac{\sigma_2}{\rho_2} \alpha_2^{2T}) \\ (v_7 - v_6)(\nabla_{\pi_3}\kappa_2^2 + \nabla_{m_3}\kappa_2^2 \alpha_3^{2T}) \end{bmatrix}^T \tag{59}$$

$$v_2^T \frac{\sigma_1}{\rho_1^2} E^1_{\tilde{\pi}_1\tilde{\pi}_1} \pi_1 + v_5^T \frac{\sigma_1}{\rho_1^2} E^1_{\pi_2\tilde{\pi}_1} \pi_1 = (v_4 - v_3)(\nabla_{m_2}\kappa_1^1 \frac{\sigma_1}{\rho_1^2} \pi_1^T \alpha_1^1 - \nabla_{\rho_1}\kappa_1^1), \tag{60}$$

$$v_2^T \frac{1}{\rho_1} E^1_{\tilde{\pi}_1\tilde{\pi}_1} \pi_1 + v_5^T \frac{1}{\rho_1} E^1_{\pi_2\tilde{\pi}_1} \pi_1 = (v_4 - v_3)(\nabla_{\sigma_1}\kappa_1^1 + \nabla_{m_2}\kappa_1^1 \frac{1}{\rho_1} \pi_1^T \alpha_1^1) + z_2, \tag{61}$$

$$v_5^T \frac{\sigma_2}{\rho_2^2} E^2_{\tilde{\pi}_2\tilde{\pi}_2} \pi_2 + v_8^T \frac{\sigma_2}{\rho_2^2} E^2_{\pi_3\tilde{\pi}_2} \pi_2 = (v_7 - v_6)(\nabla_{m_3}\kappa_2^2 \frac{\sigma_2}{\rho_2^2} \alpha_2^{2T} \pi_2 - \nabla_{\rho_2}\kappa_2^2), \tag{62}$$

and

$$v_5^T \frac{1}{\rho_2} E_{\tilde{\pi}_2\tilde{\pi}_2} \pi_2 + v_8^T \frac{1}{\rho_2} E^2_{\pi_3\tilde{\pi}_2} \pi_2 = (v_7 - v_6)(\nabla_{\sigma_2}\kappa_2^2 + \nabla_{m_3}\kappa_2^2 \frac{1}{\rho_2} \alpha_2^{2T} \pi_2) + z_3, \tag{63}$$

First note that τ_0^k can be set equal to zero without any loss of generality. Multiply (55) by κ_0 and add it to (58) to obtain

$$z_1 = 0. \tag{64}$$

This means that the input taxes on capital in period one can be set equal to zero without loss of generality. This is a consequence of the start-up features of the model. The income of generation zero is given by $\kappa_0(s_0 + t_0^k) + m_1$ so that taxing the fixed capital stock is the same as reducing the lump-sum transfer. This tax is therefore redundant and confirms the above intuition.

---

[17] See the normalization subsection in *Tedious Calculations*.

Multiply (60) by ρ_1, (61) by σ_1 and subtract to obtain

$$(v_4 - v_3)(\rho_1 \nabla_{\rho_1} \kappa_1^1 + \sigma_1 \nabla_{\sigma_1} \kappa_1^1) + z_2\sigma_1 = 0; \tag{65}$$

similarly from (60) and (61) obtain

$$(v_7 - v_6)(\rho_2 \nabla_{\rho_2} \kappa_2^2 + \sigma_2 \nabla_{\sigma_2} \kappa_2^2) + z_3\sigma_2 = 0. \tag{66}$$

Because κ_t is homogeneous of degree zero in (ρ_t, σ_t), (65) and (66) imply that

$$z_2\sigma_1 = 0 \quad \text{and} \quad z_3\sigma_2 = 0 \tag{67}$$

which in turn implies that $z_2 = 0$ and $z_3 = 0$, the normalizations of the input prices are not binding. It is clear from the above argument that instead of setting $\tau_1^k = 0$, we could have set $\tau_1^b = 0$, but not both. Similarly we could have chosen to normalize at $\tau_2^b = 0$ instead of setting $\tau_2^k = 0$, but again, not both. This too confirms our above stated intuition. Now subtract (49) from (48) and as in the previous subsection and we find still that one producer price can be normalized in each period.

4.3 Consumer Prices Too

Finally we address the question of how many consumer prices can be normalized. In order to make the argument clear we normalize one consumer price in period one and one consumer price in period two and show that, in conjunction with what has been assumed already, this in not consistent with the achievement of a Pareto-optimum; hence only one consumer price can be normalized.

Suppose that in addition to (30) and (45) we set the first component of τ_1^a equal to zero and the first component of τ_2^a equal to zero. Let

$$\tilde{\mathcal{I}} = \begin{bmatrix} 1 & 0_n^T & 0 & 0 & 0_n^T & 0 & 0 & 0_n^T \\ 0 & 1, 0_{n-1}^T & 0 & 0 & 0_n^T & 0 & 0 & 0_n^T \\ 0 & 0_n^T & 0 & 1 & 0_n^T & 0 & 0 & 0_n^T \\ 0 & 0_n^T & 0 & 0 & 1, 0_{n-1}^T & 0 & 0 & 0_n^T \\ 0 & 0_n^T & 0 & 0 & 0_n^T & 0 & 1 & 0_n^T \end{bmatrix}. \tag{68}$$

These normalizations are imposed by

$$\begin{bmatrix} \mathcal{I} \\ \mathbf{0} \end{bmatrix} \gamma_p + \begin{bmatrix} \mathbf{0} \\ \tilde{\mathcal{I}} \end{bmatrix} \gamma_\tau + \begin{bmatrix} \mathbf{0} \\ \mathbf{0} \end{bmatrix} \gamma_m + \begin{bmatrix} \mathbf{0} \\ \mathbf{0} \end{bmatrix} \gamma_\kappa + \begin{bmatrix} 0_n \\ 0_n \end{bmatrix} \gamma_\eta = 0. \tag{69}$$

There are strict Pareto-improving changes that are simultaneously equilibrium-preserving with three producer price normalizations and three capital inputs price (27), (28) solution. If there is no such solution we are at a second-best optimum. Using Motzkin's Theorem the economy is at a second-best optimum if and only if

$$
\begin{bmatrix} \xi^T & \theta \end{bmatrix} \begin{bmatrix} [P_\pi & P_\pi & P_m & \mathbf{0} & 0 \\ 0_n^T & 0_n^T & 0_3^T & 0_2^T & 1 \end{bmatrix} + \begin{bmatrix} v^T & \eta^T \end{bmatrix} \begin{bmatrix} E_\pi + E_p & E_\pi & E_m & E_\kappa & 0 \\ 0_n^T & 0_n^T & 0_3^T & I_{2\times 2} & \kappa^g \end{bmatrix}
$$

$$
+(w^T, z^T) \begin{bmatrix} \mathcal{I} & \mathbf{0} & \mathbf{0} & \mathbf{0} & 0_n \\ \mathbf{0} & \tilde{\mathcal{I}} & \mathbf{0} & \mathbf{0} & 0_n \end{bmatrix} = 0, \tag{70}
$$

Expanding (70) in the same manner as (50) was expanded previously yields

$$
\xi_1 = v_2^T \nabla_{m_1} \alpha_1^0, \tag{71}
$$

$$
\xi_2 = v_2^T \nabla_{m_2} \alpha_1^1 + (v_3 - v_4) \nabla_{m_2} \kappa_1^1 + v_5^T \nabla_{m_2} \alpha_2^1, \tag{72}
$$

and

$$
\xi_3 = v_5^T \nabla_{m_3} \alpha_2^2 + (v_6 - v_7) \nabla_{m_3} \kappa_2^2 + v_8^T \nabla_{m_3} \alpha_3^2 \tag{73}
$$

Expanding (70), using (71)-(73), and the Slutsky equation repeatedly yields[18]

$$
-\xi_1 \kappa_0 = -v_2^T \nabla_{\sigma_0} \alpha_1^0 + \tilde{z}_1, \tag{74}
$$

$$
\begin{bmatrix} v_2^T & v_5^T & v_8^T \end{bmatrix} \begin{bmatrix} E^0_{\pi_1\pi_1} + \frac{\sigma_1}{\rho_1} E^1_{\tilde{\pi}_1\tilde{\pi}_1} & E^1_{\tilde{\pi}_1\pi_2} & 0 \\ \frac{\sigma_1}{\rho_1} E^1_{\pi_2\tilde{\pi}_1} & E^1_{\pi_2\pi_2} + \frac{\sigma_2}{\rho_2} E^2_{\tilde{\pi}_2\tilde{\pi}_2} & E^2_{\tilde{\pi}_2\pi_3} \\ 0 & \frac{\sigma_2}{\rho_2} E^2_{\pi_3\tilde{\pi}_2} & E^2_{\pi_3\pi_3} \end{bmatrix} =
$$

$$
\begin{bmatrix} (v_4 - v_3)(\nabla_{\pi_1} \kappa_1^1 + \nabla_{m_2} \kappa_1^1 \frac{\sigma_1}{\rho_1} \alpha_1^{1T}) + (\tilde{z}_2, 0_{n-1}^T) \\ (v_4 - v_3)(\nabla_{\pi_2} \kappa_1^1 + \nabla_{m_2} \kappa_1^1 \alpha_2^{1T}) + (v_7 - v_6)(\nabla_{\pi_2} \kappa_2^2 + \nabla_{m_3} \kappa_2^2 \frac{\sigma_2}{\rho_2} \alpha_2^{2T}) + (\tilde{z}_4, 0_{n-1}^T) \\ (v_7 - v_6)(\nabla_{\pi_3} \kappa_2^2 + \nabla_{m_3} \kappa_2^2 \alpha_3^{2T}) \end{bmatrix}^T, \tag{75}
$$

$$
v_2^T \frac{\sigma_1}{\rho_1^2} E^1_{\tilde{\pi}_1\tilde{\pi}_1} \pi_1 + v_5^T \frac{\sigma_1}{\rho_1^2} E^1_{\pi_2\tilde{\pi}_1} \pi_1 = (v_4 - v_3)(\nabla_{m_2} \kappa_1^1 \frac{\sigma_1}{\rho_1^2} \pi_1^T \alpha_1^1 - \nabla_{\rho_1} \kappa_1^1), \tag{76}
$$

$$
v_2^T \frac{1}{\rho_1} E^1_{\tilde{\pi}_1\tilde{\pi}_1} \pi_1 + v_5^T \frac{1}{\rho_1} E^1_{\pi_2\tilde{\pi}_1} \pi_1 = (v_4 - v_3)(\nabla_{\sigma_1} \kappa_1^1 + \nabla_{m_2} \kappa_1^1 \frac{1}{\rho_1} \pi_1^T \alpha_1^1) + \tilde{z}_3, \tag{77}
$$

$$
v_5^T \frac{\sigma_2}{\rho_2^2} E^2_{\tilde{\pi}_2\tilde{\pi}_2} \pi_2 + v_8^T \frac{\sigma_2}{\rho_2^2} E^2_{\pi_3\tilde{\pi}_2} \pi_2 = (v_7 - v_6)(\nabla_{m_3} \kappa_2^2 \frac{\sigma_2}{\rho_2^2} \alpha_2^{2T} \pi_2 - \nabla_{\rho_2} \kappa_2^2), \tag{78}
$$

and

$$
v_5^T \frac{1}{\rho_2} E_{\tilde{\pi}_2\tilde{\pi}_2} \pi_2 + v_8^T \frac{1}{\rho_2} E^2_{\pi_3\tilde{\pi}_2} \pi_2 = (v_7 - v_6)(\nabla_{\sigma_2} \kappa_2^2 + \nabla_{m_3} \kappa_2^2 \frac{1}{\rho_2} \alpha_2^{2T} \pi_2) + \tilde{z}_5, \tag{79}
$$

Post-multiplying (75) by the consumer price vector, $(\pi^{1T}, \pi^{2T}, \pi^{3T})$ yields

$$
(\tilde{z}_2, 0_{n-1}^T)\pi_1 + (\tilde{z}_4, 0_{n-1}^T)\pi_2 = 0, \tag{80}
$$

implying that the two multipliers on the consumer prices are not zero and hence that two such normalizations are binding constraints and not consistent with Pareto-optimality. Repeating the above exercise with only one consumer price normalization shows immediately that one price can be normalized.

[18] See the normalization subsection in *Tedious Calculations*.

Continuing now as above simply repeats the previous normalization argument.

4.4 Other Regimes

Next we consider the other possible regimes. Suppose that initially the government is buying positive amounts of the capital stock in both periods. Then we drop the last two equations in (14), and drop the last two rows from E_p, E_m, and E_κ and repeat the above argument. The vector of shadow prices is now given by $v^T = (v^{1T}, v^{2T}, v^{3T})$; that is, v^{4T} has been expunged. However, none of the calculations above depended upon E_κ or upon v^{4T}. Hence the entire argument can be repeated without loss of generality. Similar arguments result in the same set of normalizations in the other two regimes.

We summarize this section with the following result.

Theorem 1 At an efficient optimum with positive savings, one producer price can be normalized in each period, the tax on the initial consumer capital stock can be set equal to zero, either the capital input taxes or the taxes on savings can be set equal to zero in each period (but not both), and at most one consumer tax can be set equal to zero.

This means that, as far as simple normalizations are concerned, almost all efficient outcomes require taxes either on capital inputs or on savings. If these taxes are to be zero at the optimum, it must result from the structure of the Pareto-set and not merely from some normalization argument.

5 The Structure of the Set of Pareto-Optima

In this section we formally explore the structure of the set of Pareto-optima. More specifically, we show that this set has dimension two. We first examine in detail the region where the purchases by the government of capital stocks is zero in the initial equilibrium; that is, where there is no government saving.

The set of second-best optima are characterized by (29); expanding these yields

$$\xi^T P_\pi + v^T [E_\pi + E_p] = 0, \tag{81}$$

$$\xi^T P_\pi + v^T E_\pi = 0, \tag{82}$$

$$\xi^T P_m + v^T E_m = 0, \tag{83}$$

$$v^T E_\kappa + \eta^T = 0, \tag{84}$$

and

$$\theta + \eta^T \kappa^g = 0. \tag{85}$$

Subtracting (82) from (81) yields

$$v^T E_p = 0 \tag{86}$$

or, using, (22),

$$v^{1T}\begin{bmatrix} -\nabla_{s_0} k_1 & -\nabla_{p_1} k_1 & -\nabla_{r_1} k_1 \\ \nabla_{s_0} a_1 & \nabla_{p_1} a_1 & \nabla_{r_1} a_1 \\ \nabla_{s_0} b_1 & \nabla_{p_1} b_1 & \nabla_{r_1} b_1 \end{bmatrix} = 0,$$

$$v^{2T}\begin{bmatrix} -\nabla_{s_1} k_2 & -\nabla_{p_2} k_2 & -\nabla_{r_2} k_2 \\ \nabla_{s_1} a_2 & \nabla_{p_2} a_2 & \nabla_{r_2} a_2 \\ \nabla_{s_1} b_2 & \nabla_{p_2} b_2 & \nabla_{r_2} b_2 \end{bmatrix} = 0, \tag{87}$$

and

$$v^{3T}\begin{bmatrix} -\nabla_{s_2} k_3 & -\nabla_{p_3} k_3 \\ \nabla_{s_2} a_3 & \nabla_{p_3} a_3 \end{bmatrix} = 0$$

The vector v represents the shadow price of commodity and services to the economy; these are the prices that should be used to evaluate any public project. Given the strong convexity of the profit functions, the eigenvector associated with the zero eigenvalue of each Hessian in (87) is equal to the producer price vector up to a positive multiple. Given the regularity conditions on production (87) implies that the social shadow prices are proportional to producer prices so that

$$(v^{1T}, v^{2T}, v^{3T}) = \Big(\mu_1[s_0, p_1^T, r_1], \mu_2[s_1, p_2^T, r_2], \mu_3[s_2, p_3^T]\Big) \tag{88}$$

where $\mu_t > 0$ for $t = 1, 2, 3$. Because of the temporal decomposition of production, μ_t is a function only of the prices in period t.

Rewrite (81) through (86) in conjunction with repeated use of the Slutsky equation to obtain[19]

$$[\,\mu_1 p_1^T \quad \mu_2 p_2^T \quad \mu_3 p_3^T\,]\begin{bmatrix} E^0_{\pi_1\pi_1} + \frac{\sigma_1}{\rho_1}E^1_{\tilde{\pi}_1\tilde{\pi}_1} & E^1_{\tilde{\pi}_1\pi_2} & 0 \\ \frac{\sigma_1}{\rho_1}E^1_{\pi_2\tilde{\pi}_1} & E^1_{\pi_2\pi_2} + \frac{\sigma_2}{\rho_2}E^2_{\tilde{\pi}_2\tilde{\pi}_2} & E^2_{\tilde{\pi}_2\pi_3} \\ 0 & \frac{\sigma_2}{\rho_2}E^2_{\pi_3\tilde{\pi}_2} & E^2_{\pi_3\pi_3} \end{bmatrix}$$

$$= \begin{bmatrix} (\mu_2 s_1 - \mu_1 r_1)(\nabla_{\pi_1}\kappa_1^1 + \nabla_{m_2}\kappa_1^1 \frac{\sigma_1}{\rho_1}\alpha_1^{1T}) \\ (\mu_2 s_1 - \mu_1 r_1)(\nabla_{\pi_2}\kappa_1^1 + \nabla_{m_2}\kappa_1^1 \alpha_2^{1T}) + (\mu_3 s_2 - \mu_2 r_2)(\nabla_{\pi_2}\kappa_2^2 + \nabla_{m_3}\kappa_2^2 \frac{\sigma_2}{\rho_2}\alpha_2^{2T}) \\ (\mu_3 s_2 - \mu_2 r_2)(\nabla_{\pi_3}\kappa_2^2 + \nabla_{m_3}\kappa_2^2 \alpha_3^{2T}) \end{bmatrix}^T, \tag{89}$$

$$-\mu_1 r_1 + \mu_2 s_1 + \eta_1 = 0 \quad \text{and} \quad -\mu_2 r_2 + \mu_3 s_2 + \eta_2 = 0 \tag{90}$$

and the complementary slackness conditions

$$\eta_1 \kappa_1^g = 0 \quad \text{and} \quad \eta_2 \kappa_2^g = 0. \tag{91}$$

In conjunction with (14) and (88), (89)–(91) determine the set of Pareto-optima in the economy. First note that there is one more normalization; dividing (89)–(91) by μ_1 does not change the set of optima. Hence there are

[19] See the section entitled *Tedious Calculations* for details.

eight normalizations possible, the seven we established in the previous section plus this one. Next, notice that this set of equations is not linearly independent. Post-multiplying (89) by consumer prices, $(\pi_1^T, \pi_2^T, \pi_3^T)^T$, shows that of the $3n$ equations in (89), only $3n - 1$ are linearly independent. Eliminating one of these equations let the mapping determined by (14 and (89)–(90) be called ϕ; it is a mapping from the space of consumer prices (dimension $3n+5$), producer prices (dimension $3n+5$), incomes (dimension 3), and multipliers (dimension 5 $(\mu_1, \mu_2, \mu_3, \eta_1, \eta_2)$))[20] into an $6n+10$-dimensional space determined by the $3n+5$ equilibrium conditions and the additional $3n+3$ conditions for a Pareto-optimum. Remembering that there are eight normalizations feasible, $\phi : \mathbf{R}^{6n+10} \mapsto \mathbf{R}^{6n+8}$. Supposing that ϕ is smooth, zero is a regular value of the mapping by construction, thus $\phi^{-1}(0)$ is a smooth manifold of dimension two.[21] This means that the entire set of Pareto-optima can be parameterized in terms of two variables, say, m_1 and m_2 or τ_1^b and τ_2^b.

Also of interest to us is the structure of the tax system in the set of Pareto-optima. That is, for example, are there regions of the Pareto-frontier that entail commodity taxes and taxes on savings and other regions that entail either no taxes or no taxes on savings?

Consider first the case where η_1 and η_2 are equal to zero, that is, neither government capital constraint is strictly binding. This implies that the right side of (89)–(91) are equal to zero and that

$$\mu_1 r_1 = \mu_2 s_1 \quad \text{and} \quad \mu_2 r_2 = \mu_3 s_2. \tag{92}$$

Rewriting (89) now yields

$$[p_1^T \quad r_1 p_2^T \quad r_2 p_3^T] \begin{bmatrix} E^0_{\pi_1\pi_1} + \frac{\sigma_1}{\rho_1} E^1_{\tilde{\pi}_1\tilde{\pi}_1} & E^1_{\tilde{\pi}_1\pi_2} & 0 \\ \frac{\sigma_1}{\rho_1} E^1_{\pi_2\tilde{\pi}_1} & E^1_{\pi_2\pi_2} + \frac{\sigma_2}{\rho_2} E^2_{\tilde{\pi}_2\tilde{\pi}_2} & E^2_{\tilde{\pi}_2\pi_3} \\ 0 & \frac{\sigma_2}{\rho_2} E^2_{\pi_3\tilde{\pi}_2} & E^2_{\pi_3\pi_3} \end{bmatrix} = 0. \tag{93}$$

First note that in general a set of zero taxes solves this system of equations. Remembering that our normalizations require that $s_1 = 1 = s_2$, the first element of (93) can be written as

$$p_1^T E^0_{\pi_1\pi_1}(u_0, p_1) + \frac{p_1}{r_1} E^1_{\tilde{\pi}_1\tilde{\pi}_1}(u_1, \frac{p_1}{r_1}, p_2) + p_2^T E^1_{\pi_2\tilde{\pi}_1}(u_1, \frac{p_1}{r_1}, p_2) \tag{94}$$

which by the homogeneity and symmetry properties of the expenditure function is identically zero. Factoring r_1 out of the second element of (93) and $r_1 r_2$ out of the third element shows that they too are identically zero by homogeneity. Thus, with government saving and private savings, zero taxes are Pareto-optimal.

[20] The total is $6n + 18$.

[21] This follows from the Pre-image Theorem; see Guillemin and Pollack (1974). In general equilibrium models this is a standard result; see Guesnerie (1979, 1995), and Fuchs and Guesnerie (1983). If there were H generations instead of three, the Pareto manifold would have dimension $H - 1$.

Now consider the case where either η_1 or η_2 is not equal to zero; it follows trivially from the above argument that zero taxes cannot be part of the set of Pareto-optima. This is that part of the Pareto-frontier in which the government is trying to redistribute from later generations to earlier ones. Here that non negativity constraints on government capital purchases are binding and the redistribution program must work through the indirect tax system. Indeed, a parameterization of the equilibrium manifold in terms of η_1 and η_2 would provide a straightforward way to classify the regions of the Pareto frontier according to their need for indirect taxes.

Theorem 2 The second-best optimum of the overlapping generations model with generation-specific lump-sum taxes is characterized by shadow prices that are proportional to producer prices which, in turn, are proportional to consumer prices only when desired government saving is nonnegative. The set of Pareto-optima has a region of zero taxes and a region of non zero taxes. Both regions have dimension two.

6 Conclusion

In this paper we have shown, in a finite-horizon overlapping-generations model, that government intervention in the markets in terms of taxes on commodities and on either savings or capital inputs (but not both) is required for a non negligible set of Pareto-optima. This follows basically because the government cannot use the capital market to effect intertemporal transfers of income from later to earlier generations. This imposes a second-best constraint on the model that does not exist in a standard general equilibrium framework.

Our results are of interest not only in their own right, but also in the context of optimal taxes. It is sometimes claimed that expenditure taxes are preferable to income taxes because the latter entail some version of double taxation.[22] At the very least, it is sometimes maintained that taxes on savings are not optimal. Our results give no support to this claim. At the very least, it is hoped that our results demonstrate that extending the analysis of overlapping generations models to include many consumption goods is both feasible and rewarding.

7 Tedious Calculations

This section contains the many tedious calculations necessary for the main results in the previous sections. We first show that the government's budget must be balanced in each period, and then do a complete expansion of the

[22] See Meade (1975), Ordover and Phelps (1975, 1979), Ordover (1976), and Park (1991).

second-best optima before using those calculations to do the expansions for the normalizations.

7.1 Budget Balance

It is sufficient to examine period one where government expenditure is given by

$$m_1 + r_1 \kappa_1^g. \tag{95}$$

Adopting the innocuous normalization $\tau_0 = 0$, governments revenue, taxes plus profits, is given by

$$t_1^{aT}(\alpha_1^0 + \alpha_1^1) + t_1^b \kappa_1^1 + [p_1^T a_1 + r_1 b_1 - s_0 \kappa_0]. \tag{96}$$

Equilibrium requires that

$$\alpha_1^0 + \alpha_1^1 - a_1 = 0 \tag{97}$$

and

$$\kappa_1^1 + \kappa_1^g - b_1 = 0. \tag{98}$$

Assuming local nonsatitation in preferences, consumers are on their respective budget constraints so that

$$\pi_1^T \alpha_1^0 = s_0 \kappa_0 + m_1 \tag{99}$$

and

$$\pi_1^T \alpha_1^1 + \rho_1 \kappa_1^1 = 0. \tag{100}$$

Summing the budget constraints and using the definition of consumer prices yields

$$(p_1^T + \tau_1^{aT})(\alpha_1^0 + \alpha_1^1) + r_1 \kappa_1^1 + \tau_1^b \kappa_1^1 = s_0 \kappa_0 + m_1. \tag{101}$$

Adding $r_1 \kappa_1^g$ to both sides and rearranging yields

$$(p_1^T + \tau_1^{aT})(\alpha_1^0 + \alpha_1^1) + r_1(\kappa_1^1 + \kappa_1^g) + \tau_1^b \kappa_1^1 - s_0 \kappa_0 = m_1 + r_1 \kappa_1^g. \tag{102}$$

Using the equilibrium conditions yields

$$p_1^T a_1 + r_1 b_1 - s_0 \kappa_0 + \tau_1^{aT}(\alpha_1^0 + \alpha_1^1) + \tau_1^b \kappa_1^1 = m_1 + r_1 \kappa_1^g, \tag{103}$$

which shows that the government budget is balanced.

7.2 Motzkin's Theorem

We want to show that the non homogeneous version of Motzkin's Theorem,

$$Ax \gg 0, \quad Bx \geq 0, \quad Dx \geq \xi, \quad \text{and} \quad Cx = 0, \tag{104}$$

is equivalent to the homogeneous version of Motzkin's Theorem,

$$\begin{bmatrix} A & 0_a \\ 0_n^T & 1 \end{bmatrix} \begin{bmatrix} x \\ z \end{bmatrix} \gg 0, \quad \begin{bmatrix} B & 0_b \\ D & \xi \end{bmatrix} \begin{bmatrix} x \\ z \end{bmatrix} \geq 0, \quad \text{and} \quad \begin{bmatrix} C & 0_c \\ 0_n^T & 0 \end{bmatrix} \begin{bmatrix} x \\ z \end{bmatrix} = 0 \tag{105}$$

where $x \in \mathcal{R}^n$ and 0_a has the same number of rows as A.

If (104) has a solution, then (105) has a solution with $z = 1$. If (105) has a solution, then, dividing by through by z shows that (104)has a solution.

7.3 Second-Best Calculations

We obtain from (83)

$$\xi^T + v^T E_m = 0 \tag{106}$$

which becomes

$$\xi_1 = \mu_1 p_1^T \nabla_{m_1} \alpha_1^0, \tag{107}$$

$$\xi_2 = \mu_1 p_1^T \nabla_{m_2} \alpha_1^1 + (\mu_1 r_1 - \mu_2 s_1) \nabla_{m_2} \kappa_1^1 + \mu_2 p_2^T \nabla_{m_2} \alpha_2^1, \tag{108}$$

and

$$\xi_3 = \mu_2 p_2^T \nabla_{m_3} \alpha_2^2 + (\mu_2 r_2 - \mu_3 s_2) \nabla_{m_3} \kappa_2^2 + \mu_3 p_3^T \nabla_{m_3} \alpha_3^2. \tag{109}$$

Finally we have from (82)

$$\xi^T P_\pi + v^T E_\pi = 0. \tag{110}$$

Expanding (110) yields

$$-\xi_1 \kappa_0 = -\mu_1 p_1^T \nabla_{\sigma_0} \alpha_1^0, \tag{111}$$

$$\xi_1 \alpha_1^{0T} + \xi_2 \frac{\sigma_1}{\rho_1} \alpha_1^{1T} = -\mu_1 p_1^T \nabla_{\pi_1} \alpha_1 - (\mu_1 r_1 - \mu_2 s_1) \nabla_{\pi_1} \kappa_1^1 - \mu_2 p_2^T \nabla_{\pi_1} \alpha_2^1, \tag{112}$$

$$-\xi_2 \frac{\sigma_1}{\rho_1^2} \pi_1^T \alpha_1^1 = -\mu_1 p_1^T \nabla_{\rho_1} \alpha_1^1 - (\mu_1 r_1 - \mu_2 s_1) \nabla_{\rho_1} \kappa_1^1 - \mu_2 p_2^T \nabla_{\rho_1} \alpha_2^1, \tag{113}$$

$$\xi_2 \frac{1}{\rho_1} \pi_1^T \alpha_1^1 = -\mu_1 p_1^T \nabla_{\sigma_1} \alpha_1^1 - (\mu_1 r_1 - \mu_2 s_1) \nabla_{\sigma_1} \kappa_1^1 - \mu_2 p_2^T \nabla_{\sigma_1} \alpha_2^1, \tag{114}$$

$$\begin{aligned} \xi_2 \alpha_2^{1T} + \xi_3 \frac{\sigma_2}{\rho_2} \alpha_2^{2T} &= -\mu_1 p_1^T \nabla_{\pi_2} \alpha_1^1 - (\mu_1 r_1 - \mu_2 s_1) \nabla_{\pi_2} \kappa_1^1 \\ &-\mu_2 p_2^T \nabla_{\pi_2} \alpha_2 - (\mu_2 r_2 - \mu_3 s_2) \nabla_{\pi_2} \kappa_2^2 - \mu_3 p_3^T \nabla_{\pi_2} \alpha_3^2, \end{aligned} \tag{115}$$

$$-\xi_3 \frac{\sigma_2}{\rho_2^2} \pi_2^T \alpha_2^2 = -\mu_2 p_2^T \nabla_{\rho_2} \alpha_2^2 - (\mu_2 r_2 - \mu_3 s_2) \nabla_{\rho_2} \kappa_2^2 - \mu_3 p_3^T \nabla_{\rho_2} \alpha_3^2, \tag{116}$$

$$\xi_3 \frac{1}{\rho_2} \pi_2^T \alpha_2^2 = -\mu_2 p_2^T \nabla_{\sigma_2} \alpha_2^2 - (\mu_2 r_2 - \mu_3 s_2) \nabla_{\sigma_2} \kappa_2^2 - \mu_3 p_3^T \nabla_{\sigma_2} \alpha_3^2, \tag{117}$$

$$\xi_3 \alpha_3^{2T} = -\mu_2 p_2^T \nabla_{\pi_3} \alpha_2^2 - (\mu_2 r_2 - \mu_3 s_2) \nabla_{\pi_3} \kappa_2^2 - \mu_3 p_3^T \nabla_{\pi_3} \alpha_3^2. \tag{118}$$

First note that, by (1), (111) is just (107) in disguise. Expanding (112)–(118), using the values of ξ_i from (107)–(109) and the Slutsky equation repeatedly yields[23]

$$\mu_1 p_1^T E^0_{\pi_1\pi_1} + \mu_1 p_1^T \frac{\sigma_1}{\rho_1} E^1_{\tilde{\pi}_1\tilde{\pi}_1} + \mu_2 p_2^T \frac{\sigma_1}{\rho_1} E^1_{\pi_2\tilde{\pi}_1}$$
$$= (\mu_2 s_1 - \mu_1 r_1)(\nabla_{\pi_1}\kappa_1^1 + \nabla_{m_2}\kappa_1^1 \frac{\sigma_1}{\rho_1}\alpha_1^{1T}), \tag{119}$$

$$\mu_1 p_1^T \frac{\sigma_1}{\rho_1^2} E^1_{\tilde{\pi}_1\tilde{\pi}_1}\pi_1 + \mu_2 p_2^T \frac{\sigma_1}{\rho_1^2} E^1_{\pi_2\tilde{\pi}_1}\pi_1 = (\mu_2 s_1 - \mu_1 r_1)(\nabla_{m_2}\kappa_1^1 \frac{\sigma_1}{\rho_1^2}\pi_1^T\alpha_1^1 - \nabla_{\rho_1}\kappa_1^1), \tag{120}$$

$$\mu_1 p_1^T \frac{1}{\rho_1} E^1_{\tilde{\pi}_1\tilde{\pi}_1}\pi_1 + \mu_2 p_2^T \frac{1}{\rho_1} E^1_{\pi_2\tilde{\pi}_1}\pi_1 = (\mu_2 s_1 - \mu_1 r_1)(\nabla_{\sigma_1}\kappa_1^1 + \nabla_{m_2}\kappa_1^1 \frac{1}{\rho_1}\pi_1^T\alpha_1^1), \tag{121}$$

$$\mu_1 p_1^T E^1_{\tilde{\pi}_1\pi_2} + \mu_2 p_2^T E^1_{\pi_2\pi_2} + \mu_2 p_2^T \frac{\sigma_2}{\rho_2} E^2_{\tilde{\pi}_2\tilde{\pi}_2} + \mu_3 p_3^T \frac{\sigma_2}{\rho_2} E^2_{\pi_3\tilde{\pi}_2}$$
$$= (\mu_2 s_1 - \mu_1 r_1)(\nabla_{\pi_2}\kappa_1^1 + \nabla_{m_2}\kappa_1^1\alpha_2^{1T}) + (\mu_3 s_2 - \mu_2 r_2)(\nabla_{\pi_2}\kappa_2^2 + \nabla_{m_3}\kappa_2^2 \frac{\sigma_2}{\rho_2}\alpha_2^{2T}), \tag{122}$$

$$\mu_2 p_2^T \frac{\sigma_2}{\rho_2^2} E^2_{\tilde{\pi}_2\tilde{\pi}_2}\pi_2 + \mu_3 p_3^T \frac{\sigma_2}{\rho_2^2} E^2_{\pi_3\tilde{\pi}_2}\pi_2 = (\mu_3 s_2 - \mu_2 r_2)(\nabla_{m_3}\kappa_2^2 \frac{\sigma_2}{\rho_2^2}\alpha_2^{2T}\pi_2 - \nabla_{\rho_2}\kappa_2^2), \tag{123}$$

$$\mu_2 p_2^T \frac{1}{\rho_2} E_{\tilde{\pi}_2\tilde{\pi}_2}\pi_2 + \mu_3 p_3^T \frac{1}{\rho_2} E^2_{\pi_3\tilde{\pi}_2}\pi_2 = (\mu_3 s_2 - \mu_2 r_2)(\nabla_{\sigma_2}\kappa_2^2 + \nabla_{m_3}\kappa_2^2 \frac{1}{\rho_2}\alpha_2^{2T}\pi_2), \tag{124}$$

$$\mu_2 p_2^T E^2_{\tilde{\pi}_2\pi_3} + \mu_3 p_3^T E^2_{\pi_3\pi_3} = (\mu_3 s_2 - \mu_2 r_2)(\nabla_{\pi_3}\kappa_2^2 + \nabla_{m_3}\kappa_2^2\alpha_3^{2T}). \tag{125}$$

Finally, note that writing (119), (122), and (125) in matrix form yields

$$[\,\mu_1 p_1^T \quad \mu_2 p_2^T \quad \mu_3 p_3^T\,] \begin{bmatrix} E^0_{\pi_1\pi_1} + \frac{\sigma_1}{\rho_1}E^1_{\tilde{\pi}_1\tilde{\pi}_1} & E^1_{\tilde{\pi}_1\pi_2} & 0 \\ \frac{\sigma_1}{\rho_1}E^1_{\pi_2\tilde{\pi}_1} & E^1_{\pi_2\pi_2} + \frac{\sigma_2}{\rho_2}E^2_{\tilde{\pi}_2\tilde{\pi}_2} & E^2_{\tilde{\pi}_2\pi_3} \\ 0 & \frac{\sigma_2}{\rho_2}E^2_{\pi_3\tilde{\pi}_2} & E^2_{\pi_3\pi_3} \end{bmatrix}$$
$$= \begin{bmatrix} (\mu_2 s_1 - \mu_1 r_1)(\nabla_{\pi_1}\kappa_1^1 + \nabla_{m_2}\kappa_1^1\frac{\sigma_1}{\rho_1}\alpha_1^{1T}) \\ (\mu_2 s_1 - \mu_1 r_1)(\nabla_{\pi_2}\kappa_1^1 + \nabla_{m_2}\kappa_1^1\alpha_2^{1T}) + (\mu_3 s_2 - \mu_2 r_2)(\nabla_{\pi_2}\kappa_2^2 + \nabla_{m_3}\kappa_2^2\frac{\sigma_2}{\rho_2}\alpha_2^{2T}) \\ (\mu_3 s_2 - \mu_2 r_2)(\nabla_{\pi_3}\kappa_2^2 + \nabla_{m_3}\kappa_2^2\alpha_3^{2T}) \end{bmatrix} T. \tag{126}$$

In addition, the fact that κ_1 is homogeneous of degree zero in ρ_1 and σ_1 implies that (120) and (121) are not independent. Similarly, (123) and (124) are not independent, yielding

$$\mu_1 p_1^T \frac{\sigma_1}{\rho_1} E^1_{\tilde{\pi}_1\tilde{\pi}_1}\pi_1 + \mu_2 p_2^T \frac{\sigma_1}{\rho_1} E^1_{\pi_2\tilde{\pi}_1}\pi_1 = (\mu_2 s_1 - \mu_1 r_1)(\nabla_{m_2}\kappa_1^1 \frac{\sigma_1}{\rho_1}\pi_1^T\alpha_1^1 - \rho_1\nabla_{\rho_1}\kappa_1^1), \tag{127}$$

---

[23] See the following subsections for the details.

and

$$\mu_2 p_2^T \frac{\sigma_2}{\rho_2} E^2_{\tilde{\pi}_2\tilde{\pi}_2}\pi_2 + \mu_3 p_3^T \frac{\sigma_2}{\rho_2} E^2_{\pi_3\tilde{\pi}_2}\pi_2 = (\mu_3 s_2 - \mu_2 r_2)(\nabla_{m_3}\kappa_2^2 \frac{\sigma_2}{\rho_2}\alpha_2^{2T}\pi_2 - \rho_2 \nabla_{\rho_2}\kappa_2^2). \tag{128}$$

Note that multiplying the first element of (126) by π_1 and using the homogeneity of κ_1^1 yields (127); then multiplying the second element of (126) by π_2, adding (127) to it and using homogeneity yields (128).

Finally, from (84) and (85) we have

$$-\mu_1 r_1 + \mu_2 s_1 + \eta_1 = 0 \quad \text{and} \quad -\mu_2 r_2 + \mu_3 s_2 + \eta_2 = 0 \tag{129}$$

and

$$\theta + \eta_1 \kappa_1^g + \eta_2 \kappa_2^g = 0. \tag{130}$$

Because each element of this is non negative this yields $\theta = 0$ and the complementary slackness conditions

$$\eta_1 \kappa_1^g = 0 \quad \text{and} \quad \eta_2 \kappa_2^g = 0. \tag{131}$$

7.4 (112) → (119)

First note that the Slutsky equations can be written as

$$\nabla_{\pi_1}\alpha_1^0 = E^0_{\pi_1\pi_1} - \nabla_{m_1}\alpha_1^0\alpha_1^{0T}, \tag{132}$$

$$\nabla_{\pi_1}\alpha_1^1 = \frac{\sigma_1}{\rho_1}\nabla_{\tilde{\pi}_1}\alpha_1^1 = \frac{\sigma_1}{\rho_1}\Big[E^1_{\tilde{\pi}_1\tilde{\pi}_1} - \nabla_{m_2}\alpha_1^1\alpha_1^{1T}\Big], \tag{133}$$

$$\nabla_{\pi_1}\alpha_2^1 = \frac{\sigma_1}{\rho_1}\nabla_{\tilde{\pi}_1}\alpha_2^1 = \frac{\sigma_1}{\rho_1}\Big[E^1_{\pi_2\tilde{\pi}_1} - \nabla_{m_2}\alpha_2^1\alpha_1^{1T}\Big]. \tag{134}$$

Substituting these into (112) and rearranging yields

$$\begin{aligned}
&\xi_1\alpha_1^{0T} + \xi_2\tfrac{\sigma_1}{\rho_1}\alpha_1^{1T}\\
&= -\mu_1 p_1^T E^0_{\pi_1\pi_1} + \mu_1 p_1^T \nabla_{m_1}\alpha_1^0\alpha_1^{0T} - \mu_1 p_1^T \tfrac{\sigma_1}{\rho_1} E^1_{\tilde{\pi}_1\tilde{\pi}_1} + \mu_1 p_1^T \nabla_{m_2}\alpha_1^1\alpha_1^{1T}\\
&\quad -\mu_2 p_2^T \tfrac{\sigma_1}{\rho_1} E^1_{\pi_2\tilde{\pi}_1} + \mu_2 p_2^T \tfrac{\sigma_1}{\rho_1}\nabla_{m_2}\alpha_2^1\alpha_1^{1T} - (\mu_1 r_1 - \mu_2 s_1)\nabla_{\pi_1}\kappa_1^1\\
&= -\mu_1 p_1^T E^0_{\pi_1\pi_1} - \mu_1 p_1^T \tfrac{\sigma_1}{\rho_1} E^1_{\tilde{\pi}_1\tilde{\pi}_1} - \mu_1 p_1^T \tfrac{\sigma_1}{\rho_1} E^1_{\pi_2\tilde{\pi}_1} + \mu_1 p_1^T \nabla_{m_1}\alpha_1^0\alpha_1^{0T}\\
&\quad +\tfrac{\sigma_1}{\rho_1}\Big[\mu_1 p_1^T \nabla_{m_2}\alpha_1^1 + \mu_2 p_2^T \nabla_{m_2}\alpha_2^1\Big]\alpha_1^{1T} - (\mu_1 r_1 - \mu_2 s_1)\nabla_{\pi_1}\kappa_1^1\\
&= -\mu_1 p_1^T E^0_{\pi_1\pi_1} - \mu_1 p_1^T \tfrac{\sigma_1}{\rho_1} E^1_{\tilde{\pi}_1\tilde{\pi}_1} - \mu_1 p_1^T \tfrac{\sigma_1}{\rho_1} E^1_{\pi_2\tilde{\pi}_1} + \xi_1\alpha_1^{0T}\\
&\quad +\tfrac{\sigma_1}{\rho_1}\Big[\xi_2 - (\mu_1 r_1 - \mu_2 s_1)\nabla_{m_2}\kappa_1^1\Big]\alpha_1^{1T} - (\mu_1 r_1 - \mu_2 s_1)\nabla_{\pi_1}\kappa_1^1.
\end{aligned} \tag{135}$$

The final line in this derivation follows from (108).

Rearranging yields

$$\mu_1 p_1^T E^0_{\pi_1\pi_1} + \mu_1 p_1^T \frac{\sigma_1}{\rho_1} E^1_{\tilde{\pi}_1\tilde{\pi}_1} + \mu_1 p_1^T \frac{\sigma_1}{\rho_1} E^1_{\pi_2\tilde{\pi}_1} = (\mu_2 s_1 - \mu_1 r_1)\Big[\nabla_{\pi_1}\kappa_1^1 + \nabla_{m_2}\kappa_1^1\Big]\alpha_1^{1T} \tag{136}$$

which is in fact (119).

7.5 (113) → (120)

Using the Slutsky equations yields

$$\nabla_{\rho_1}\alpha_1^1 = -\frac{\sigma_1}{\rho_1^2}\nabla_{\tilde{\pi}_1}\alpha_1^1\pi_1 = -\frac{\sigma_1}{\rho_1^2}\left[E^1_{\tilde{\pi}_1\tilde{\pi}_1} - \nabla_{m_2}\alpha_1^1\alpha_1^{1T}\right]\pi_1 \tag{137}$$

and

$$\nabla_{\rho_1}\alpha_2^1 = -\frac{\sigma_1}{\rho_1^2}\nabla_{\tilde{\pi}_1}\alpha_2^1\pi_1 = -\frac{\sigma_1}{\rho_1^2}\left[E^1_{\pi_2\tilde{\pi}_1} - \nabla_{m_2}\alpha_2^1\alpha_1^{1T}\right]\pi_1. \tag{138}$$

Substituting these into (113) and using (108) yields

$$\begin{aligned}
&-\xi_2\tfrac{\sigma_1}{\rho_1^2}\pi_1^T\alpha_1^1\\
&= \mu_1 p_1^T\tfrac{\sigma_1}{\rho_1^2}E^1_{\tilde{\pi}_1\tilde{\pi}_1}\pi_1 + \mu_2 p_2^T\tfrac{\sigma_1}{\rho_1^2}E^1_{\pi_2\tilde{\pi}_1}\pi_1 - \tfrac{\sigma_1}{\rho_1^2}\left[\mu_1 p_1^T\nabla_{m_2}\alpha_1^1 + \mu_2 p_2^T\nabla_{m_2}\alpha_2^1\right]\alpha_1^{1T}\pi_1\\
&\quad -(\mu_1 r_1 - \mu_2 s_1)\nabla_{\rho_1}\kappa_1^1\\
&= \mu_1 p_1^T\tfrac{\sigma_1}{\rho_1^2}E^1_{\tilde{\pi}_1\tilde{\pi}_1}\pi_1 + \mu_2 p_2^T\tfrac{\sigma_1}{\rho_1^2}E^1_{\pi_2\tilde{\pi}_1}\pi_1 - \tfrac{\sigma_1}{\rho_1^2}\left[\xi_2 - (\mu_1 r_1 - \mu_2 s_1)\nabla_{m_2}\kappa_1^1\right]\alpha_1^{1T}\pi_1\\
&\quad -(\mu_1 r_1 - \mu_2 s_1)\nabla_{\rho_1}\kappa_1^1.
\end{aligned} \tag{139}$$

Rearranging (139) yields

$$\mu_1 p_1^T\frac{\sigma_1}{\rho_1^2}E^1_{\tilde{\pi}_1\tilde{\pi}_1}\pi_1 + \mu_2 p_2^T\frac{\sigma_1}{\rho_1^2}E^1_{\pi_2\tilde{\pi}_1}\pi_1 = (\mu_1 r_1 - \mu_2 s_1)\left[\nabla_{\rho_1}\kappa_1^1 - \nabla_{m_2}\kappa_1^1\frac{\sigma_1}{\rho_1^2}\alpha_1^{1T}\pi_1\right] \tag{140}$$

which is (120).

7.6 (114) → (121)

Using the Slutsky equations yields

$$\nabla_{\sigma_1}\alpha_1^1 = \frac{1}{\rho_1}\nabla_{\tilde{\pi}_1}\alpha_1^1\pi_1 = \frac{1}{\rho_1}\left[E^1_{\tilde{\pi}_1\tilde{\pi}_1} - \nabla_{m_2}\alpha_1^1\alpha_1^{1T}\right]\pi_1 \tag{141}$$

and

$$\nabla_{\sigma_1}\alpha_2^1 = \frac{1}{\rho_1}\nabla_{\tilde{\pi}_1}\alpha_2^1\pi_1 = \frac{1}{\rho_1}\left[E^1_{\pi_2\tilde{\pi}_1} - \nabla_{m_2}\alpha_2^1\alpha_1^{1T}\right]\pi_1. \tag{142}$$

Substituting these into (113) and using (108) yields

$$\begin{aligned}
&\xi_2\tfrac{1}{\rho_1}\alpha_1^{1T}\pi_1\\
&= -\tfrac{1}{\rho_1}\left[\mu_1 p_1^T E^1_{\tilde{\pi}_1\tilde{\pi}_1} + \mu_2 p_2^T E^1_{\pi_2\tilde{\pi}_1}\right]\pi_1\\
&\quad +\tfrac{1}{\rho_1}\left[\mu_1 p_1^T\nabla_{m_2}\alpha_1^1 + \mu_2 p_2^T\nabla_{m_2}\alpha_2^1\right]\alpha_1^{1T}\pi_1 - (\mu_1 r_1 - \mu_2 s_1)\nabla_{\sigma_1}\kappa_1^1 \qquad (143)\\
&= -\tfrac{1}{\rho_1}\left[\mu_1 p_1^T E^1_{\tilde{\pi}_1\tilde{\pi}_1} + \mu_2 p_2^T E^1_{\pi_2\tilde{\pi}_1}\right]\pi_1\tfrac{1}{\rho_1}\Big[\xi_2\\
&\quad -(\mu_1 r_1 - \mu_2 s_1)\nabla_{m_2}\kappa_1^1\Big]\alpha_1^{1T}\pi_1 - (\mu_1 r_1 - \mu_2 s_1)\nabla_{\sigma_1}\kappa_1^1.
\end{aligned}$$

Rearranging yields

$$\frac{1}{\rho_1}\Big[\mu_1 p_1^T E^1_{\tilde{\pi}_1\tilde{\pi}_1} + \mu_2 p_2^T E^1_{\pi_2\tilde{\pi}_1}\Big]\pi_1 = (\mu_2 s_1 - \mu_1 r_1)\Big[\nabla_{\sigma_1}\kappa_1^1 + \frac{1}{\rho_1}\nabla_{m_2}\kappa_1^1\alpha_1^{1T}\pi_1\Big] \tag{144}$$

which is (121).

7.7 (115) → (122)

Using the Slutsky equations yields

$$\nabla_{\pi_2}\alpha_1^1 = E^1_{\pi_2\pi_2} - \nabla_{m_2}\alpha_1^1\alpha_2^{1T}, \tag{145}$$

$$\nabla_{\pi_2}\alpha_2^1 = E^1_{\tilde{\pi}_1\pi_2} - \nabla_{m_2}\alpha_1^1\alpha_2^{1T}, \tag{146}$$

$$\nabla_{\pi_2}\alpha_2^2 = \frac{\sigma_2}{\rho_2}\nabla_{\tilde{\pi}_2}\alpha_2^2 = \frac{\sigma_2}{\rho_2}\Big[E^2_{\tilde{\pi}_2\tilde{\pi}_2} - \nabla_{m_3}\alpha_2^2\alpha_2^{2T}\Big], \tag{147}$$

and

$$\nabla_{\pi_2}\alpha_3^2 = \frac{\sigma_2}{\rho_2}\Big[E^2_{\pi_3\tilde{\pi}_2} - \nabla_{m_3}\alpha_3^2\alpha_2^{2T}\Big]. \tag{148}$$

Substituting these into (115), using (108) and (109), yields

$$\begin{aligned}
&\xi_2\alpha_2^{1T} + \xi_3\tfrac{\sigma_2}{\rho_2}\alpha_2^{2T}\\
&= -\mu_1 p_1^T E^1_{\tilde{\pi}_1\pi_2} - \mu_2 p_2^T E^1_{\pi_2\pi_2} - \mu_2 p_2^T\tfrac{\sigma_2}{\rho_2}E^2_{\tilde{\pi}_2\tilde{\pi}_2} - \mu_3 p_3^T\tfrac{\sigma_2}{\rho_2}E^2_{\pi_3\tilde{\pi}_2}\\
&\quad+\Big[\mu_1 p_1^T\nabla_{m_2}\alpha_1^1 + \mu_2 p_2^T\nabla_{m_2}\alpha_2^1\Big] + \tfrac{\sigma_2}{\rho_2}\Big[\mu_2 p_2^T\nabla_{m_3}\alpha_2^2 + \mu_3 p_3^T\nabla_{m_3}\alpha_3^2\Big]\\
&\quad-(\mu_1 r_1 - \mu_2 s_1)\nabla_{\pi_2}\kappa_1^1 - (\mu_2 r_2 - \mu_3 s_2)\nabla_{\pi_2}\kappa_2^2\\
&= -\mu_1 p_1^T E^1_{\tilde{\pi}_1\pi_2} - \mu_2 p_2^T E^1_{\pi_2\pi_2} - \mu_2 p_2^T\tfrac{\sigma_2}{\rho_2}E^2_{\tilde{\pi}_2\tilde{\pi}_2} - \mu_3 p_3^T\tfrac{\sigma_2}{\rho_2}E^2_{\pi_3\tilde{\pi}_2}\\
&\quad+\Big[\xi_2 - (\mu_1 r_1 - \mu_2 s_1)\nabla_{m_2}\kappa_1^1\Big]\alpha_2^{1T} + \tfrac{\sigma_2}{\rho_2}\Big[\xi_3 - (\mu_2 r_2 - \mu_3 s_2)\nabla_{m_3}\kappa_2^2\Big]\alpha_2^{2T}\\
&\quad-(\mu_1 r_1 - \mu_2 s_1)\nabla_{\pi_2}\kappa_1^1 - (\mu_2 r_2 - \mu_3 s_2)\nabla_{\pi_2}\kappa_2^2.
\end{aligned} \tag{149}$$

Rearranging (149) yields

$$\begin{aligned}
&\mu_1 p_1^T E^1_{\tilde{\pi}_1\pi_2} + \mu_2 p_2^T E^1_{\pi_2\pi_2} + \mu_2 p_2^T\tfrac{\sigma_2}{\rho_2}E^2_{\tilde{\pi}_2\tilde{\pi}_2} + \mu_3 p_3^T\tfrac{\sigma_2}{\rho_2}E^2_{\pi_3\tilde{\pi}_2}\\
&= (\mu_2 s_1 - \mu_1 r_1)\Big[\nabla_{\pi_2}\kappa_1^1 + \nabla_{m_2}\kappa_1^1\alpha_2^{1T}\Big]\\
&\quad+(\mu_3 s_2 - \mu_2 r_2)\Big[\nabla_{\pi_2}\kappa_2^2 + \tfrac{\sigma_2}{\rho_2}\nabla_{m_3}\kappa_2^2\alpha_2^{2T}\Big]
\end{aligned} \tag{150}$$

which is (122).

7.8 (116) → (123)

The Slutsky equations yield

$$\nabla_{\rho_2}\alpha_2^2 = \frac{\sigma_2}{\rho_2^2}\nabla_{\tilde{\pi}_2}\alpha_2^2\pi_2^T = -\frac{\sigma_2}{\rho_2^2}\left[E^2_{\tilde{\pi}_2\tilde{\pi}_2} - \nabla_{m_3}\alpha_2^2\alpha_2^{2T}\right]\pi_2 \tag{151}$$

and

$$\nabla_{\rho_2}\alpha_3^2 = -\frac{\sigma_2}{\rho_2^2}\left[E^2_{\pi_3\tilde{\pi}_2} - \nabla_{m_3}\alpha_3^2\alpha_2^{2T}\right]\pi_2. \tag{152}$$

Substituting these into (116) yields

$$\begin{aligned}
&-\xi_3\tfrac{\sigma_2}{\rho_2^2}\alpha_2^{2T}\pi_2\\
&= \mu_2 p_2^T\tfrac{\sigma_2}{\rho_2^2}E^2_{\tilde{\pi}_2\tilde{\pi}_2}\pi_2 + \mu_3 p_3^T\tfrac{\sigma_2}{\rho_2^2}E^2_{\pi_3\tilde{\pi}_2}\pi_2\\
&\quad -\tfrac{\sigma_2}{\rho_2^2}\left[\mu_2 p_2^T\nabla_{m_3}\alpha_2^2 + \mu_3 p_3^T\nabla_{m_3}\alpha_3^2\right]\alpha_2^{2T}\pi_2 - (\mu_2 r_2 - \mu_3 s_2)\nabla_{\rho_2}\kappa_2^2 \qquad (153)\\
&= \mu_2 p_2^T\tfrac{\sigma_2}{\rho_2^2}E^2_{\tilde{\pi}_2\tilde{\pi}_2}\pi_2 + \mu_3 p_3^T\tfrac{\sigma_2}{\rho_2^2}E^2_{\pi_3\tilde{\pi}_2}\pi_2\\
&\quad -\tfrac{\sigma_2}{\rho_2^2}\left[\xi_3 - (\mu_2 r_2 - \mu_3 s_2)\nabla_{m_3}\kappa_2^2\right]\alpha_2^{2T}\pi_2 - (\mu_2 r_2 - \mu_3 s_2)\nabla_{\rho_2}\kappa_2^2.
\end{aligned}$$

Rearranging (55) yields

$$\mu_2 p_2^T\frac{\sigma_2}{\rho_2^2}E^2_{\tilde{\pi}_2\tilde{\pi}_2}\pi_2 + \mu_3 p_3^T\frac{\sigma_2}{\rho_2^2}E^2_{\pi_3\tilde{\pi}_2}\pi_2 = (\mu_3 s_2 - \mu_2 r_2)\left[\frac{\sigma_2}{\rho_2^2}\nabla_{m_3}\kappa_2^2\alpha_2^{2T}\pi_2 - \nabla_{\rho_2}\kappa_2^2\right] \tag{154}$$

which is (123).

7.9 Normalization Calculations

Collecting (58)–(63) of the text and using the Slutsky equation yields

$$-\xi_1\kappa_0 = -v_2^T\nabla_{\sigma_0}\alpha_1^0 + z_1, \tag{155}$$

$$\xi_1\alpha_1^{0T} + \xi_2\frac{\sigma_1}{\rho_1}\alpha_1^{1T} = -v_2^T\nabla_{\pi_1}\alpha_1 - (v_3 - v_4)\nabla_{\pi_1}\kappa_1^1 - v_5^T\nabla_{\pi_1}\alpha_2^1, \tag{156}$$

$$-\xi_2\frac{\sigma_1}{\rho_1^2}\pi_1^T\alpha_1^1 = -v_2^T\nabla_{\rho_1}\alpha_1^1 - (v_3 - v_4)\nabla_{\rho_1}\kappa_1^1 - v_5^T\nabla_{\rho_1}\alpha_2^1, \tag{157}$$

$$\xi_2\frac{1}{\rho_1}\pi_1^T\alpha_1^1 = -v_2^T\nabla_{\sigma_1}\alpha_1^1 - (v_3 - v_4)\nabla_{\sigma_1}\kappa_1^1 - v_5^T\nabla_{\sigma_1}\alpha_2^1 + z_2, \tag{158}$$

$$\begin{aligned}\xi_2\alpha_2^{1T} + \xi_3\tfrac{\sigma_2}{\rho_2}\alpha_2^{2T} &= -v_2^T\nabla_{\pi_2}\alpha_1^1 - (v_3 - v_4)\nabla_{\pi_2}\kappa_1^1 - v_5^T\nabla_{\pi_2}\alpha_2\\ &\quad -(v_6 - v_7)\nabla_{\pi_2}\kappa_2^2 - v_8^T\nabla_{\pi_2}\alpha_3^2,\end{aligned} \tag{159}$$

$$-\xi_3\frac{\sigma_2}{\rho_2^2}\pi_2^T\alpha_2^2 = -v_5^T\nabla_{\rho_2}\alpha_2^2 - (v_6 - v_7)\nabla_{\rho_2}\kappa_2^2 - v_8^T\nabla_{\rho_2}\alpha_3^2, \tag{160}$$

$$\xi_3 \frac{1}{\rho_2} \pi_2^T \alpha_2^2 = -v_5^T \nabla_{\sigma_2} \alpha_2^2 - (v_6 - v_7) \nabla_{\sigma_2} \kappa_2^2 - v_8^T \nabla_{\sigma_2} \alpha_3^2 + z_3, \tag{161}$$

$$\xi_3 \alpha_3^{2T} = -v_5^T \nabla_{\pi_3} \alpha_2^2 - (v_6 - v_7) \nabla_{\pi_3} \kappa_2^2 - v_8^T \nabla_{\pi_3} \alpha_3^2. \tag{162}$$

Expanding (156)-(162), using the values of ξ_i from (55)–(57) and the Slutsky equation repeatedly yields

$$v_2^T E^0_{\pi_1\pi_1} + v_2^T \frac{\sigma_1}{\rho_1} E^1_{\tilde{\pi}_1\tilde{\pi}_1} + v_5^T \frac{\sigma_1}{\rho_1} E^1_{\pi_2\tilde{\pi}_1} = (v_4 - v_3)(\nabla_{\pi_1}\kappa_1^1 + \nabla_{m_2}\kappa_1^1 \frac{\sigma_1}{\rho_1}\alpha_1^{1T}), \tag{163}$$

$$v_2^T \frac{\sigma_1}{\rho_1^2} E^1_{\tilde{\pi}_1\tilde{\pi}_1}\pi_1 + v_5^T \frac{\sigma_1}{\rho_1^2} E^1_{\pi_2\tilde{\pi}_1}\pi_1 = (v_4 - v_3)(\nabla_{m_2}\kappa_1^1 \frac{\sigma_1}{\rho_1^2}\pi_1^T \alpha_1^1 - \nabla_{\rho_1}\kappa_1^1), \tag{164}$$

$$v_2^T \tfrac{1}{\rho_1} E^1_{\tilde{\pi}_1\tilde{\pi}_1}\pi_1 + v_5^T \tfrac{1}{\rho_1} E^1_{\pi_2\tilde{\pi}_1}\pi_1 = (v_4 - v_3)(\nabla_{\sigma_1}\kappa_1^1 + \nabla_{m_2}\kappa_1^1 \tfrac{1}{\rho_1}\pi_1^T \alpha_1^1) + z_2, \tag{165}$$

$$\begin{aligned} &v_2^T E^1_{\tilde{\pi}_1\pi_2} + v_5^T E^1_{\pi_2\pi_2} + v_5^T \tfrac{\sigma_2}{\rho_2} E^2_{\tilde{\pi}_2\tilde{\pi}_2} + v_8^T \tfrac{\sigma_2}{\rho_2} E^2_{\pi_3\tilde{\pi}_2} \\ &= (v_4 - v_3)(\nabla_{\pi_2}\kappa_1^1 + \nabla_{m_2}\kappa_1^1 \alpha_2^{1T}) + (v_7 - v_6)(\nabla_{\pi_2}\kappa_2^2 + \nabla_{m_3}\kappa_2^2 \tfrac{\sigma_2}{\rho_2}\alpha_2^{2T}), \end{aligned} \tag{166}$$

$$v_5^T \frac{\sigma_2}{\rho_2^2} E^2_{\tilde{\pi}_2\tilde{\pi}_2}\pi_2 + v_8^T \frac{\sigma_2}{\rho_2^2} E^2_{\pi_3\tilde{\pi}_2}\pi_2 = (v_7 - v_6)(\nabla_{m_3}\kappa_2^2 \frac{\sigma_2}{\rho_2^2}\alpha_2^{2T}\pi_2 - \nabla_{\rho_2}\kappa_2^2), \tag{167}$$

$$v_5^T \frac{1}{\rho_2} E_{\tilde{\pi}_2\tilde{\pi}_2}\pi_2 + v_8^T \frac{1}{\rho_2} E^2_{\pi_3\tilde{\pi}_2}\pi_2 = (v_7 - v_6)(\nabla_{\sigma_2}\kappa_2^2 + \nabla_{m_3}\kappa_2^2 \frac{1}{\rho_2}\alpha_2^{2T}\pi_2) + z_3, \tag{168}$$

$$v_5^T E^2_{\tilde{\pi}_2\pi_3} + v_8^T E^2_{\pi_3\pi_3} = (v_7 - v_6)(\nabla_{\pi_3}\kappa_2^2 + \nabla_{m_3}\kappa_2^2 \alpha_3^{2T}). \tag{169}$$

Rewrite (163), (166), and (169) in matrix form to obtain

$$\begin{aligned} &[\, v_2^T \quad v_5^T \quad v_8^T \,] \begin{bmatrix} E^0_{\pi_1\pi_1} + \frac{\sigma_1}{\rho_1} E^1_{\tilde{\pi}_1\tilde{\pi}_1} & E^1_{\tilde{\pi}_1\pi_2} & 0 \\ \frac{\sigma_1}{\rho_1} E^1_{\pi_2\tilde{\pi}_1} & E^1_{\pi_2\pi_2} + \frac{\sigma_2}{\rho_2} E^2_{\tilde{\pi}_2\tilde{\pi}_2} & E^2_{\tilde{\pi}_2\pi_3} \\ 0 & \frac{\sigma_2}{\rho_2} E^2_{\pi_3\tilde{\pi}_2} & E^2_{\pi_3\pi_3} \end{bmatrix} \\ &= \begin{bmatrix} (v_4 - v_3)(\nabla_{\pi_1}\kappa_1^1 + \nabla_{m_2}\kappa_1^1 \frac{\sigma_1}{\rho_1}\alpha_1^{1T}) \\ (v_4 - v_3)(\nabla_{\pi_2}\kappa_1^1 + \nabla_{m_2}\kappa_1^1 \alpha_2^{1T}) + (v_7 - v_6)(\nabla_{\pi_2}\kappa_2^2 + \nabla_{m_3}\kappa_2^2 \frac{\sigma_2}{\rho_2}\alpha_2^{2T}) \\ (v_7 - v_6)(\nabla_{\pi_3}\kappa_2^2 + \nabla_{m_3}\kappa_2^2 \alpha_3^{2T}) \end{bmatrix}^T . \end{aligned} \tag{170}$$

References

Allais, M., *Economie et Intérêt*, Imprimerie Nationale, Paris, 1947.

Blackorby, C. and C. Brett, "Fiscal Federalism Revisited", UBC Discussion Paper 98-09, 1998 (http://web.arts.ubc.ca/econ/).

Blackorby, C. and W. Diewert, "Expenditure Functions, Local Duality, and Second Order Approximations", *Econometrica* **47** (1979), 579–601.

Diamond, P., "National Debt in a Neoclassical Growth Model", *American Economic Review* **55** (1965), 1125–1150.

Diewert, W., "Optimal Tax Perturbations", *Journal of Public Economics* **10** (1978), 139–177.

Diewert, W., M. Avriel, and I. Zang, "Nine Kinds of Quasi-Concavity and Concavity", *Journal of Economic Theory* **25** (1981), 397–420.

Fuchs, G. and R. Guesnerie, "Structure of Tax Equilibria", *Econometrica* **51** (1983), 403–434.

Guillemin, V. and A. Pollack, *Differential Topology*, Prentice-Hall, 1974.

Guesnerie, R., "On The Direction of Tax Reform", *Journal of Public Economics* **7** (1977), 179–202.

Guesnerie, R., "Financing Public Goods with Taxes: The Tax Reform View Point", *Econometrica* **47** (1979), 393–421.

Guesnerie, R., *A Contribution to the Pure Theory of Taxation*, Cambridge University Press, 1995.

Mangasarian, O., *Nonlinear Programming*, McGraw-Hill, 1969.

Meade, J., *The Intelligent Radical's Guide to Economic Policy*, Allen and Unwin, 1975.

Myles, G., *Public Economics*, Cambridge University Press, 1995.

Ordover, J. "Distributive Justice and Optimal Taxation of Wages and Interest in a Growing Economy", *Journal of Public Economics* **5** (1976), 139–160.

Ordover, J. and E. Phelps, "Linear Taxation of Wealth and Wages for Intragenerational Lifetime Justice: Some Steady-State Cases", *American Economic Review* **65** (1975), 660–673.

Ordover, J. and E. Phelps, "The Concept of of Optimal Taxation in the Overlapping-Generations Model of Capital and Wealth", *Journal of Public Economics* **12** (1979), 1–26.

Park, N. "Steady-State Solutions of Optimal Tax Mixes in and Overlapping-Generations Model", *Journal of Public Economics* **46** (1991), 227–246.

Samuelson, P., "An Exact Consumption-Loan Model of Interest With or Without the Social Contrivance of Money, *Journal of Political Economy* **46** (1958), 467–482.

Weymark, J., "A Reconciliation of Recent Results in Optimal Taxation", *Journal of Public Economics* **12** (1979),171–189.

Derivative Properties of Directional Technology Distance Functions

Lane Blume Hudgins[1] and Daniel Primont[2]

[1] Department of Economics Southern Illinois University Carbondale Carbondale, Illinois 62901, lane@siu.edu
[2] Department of Economics Southern Illinois University Carbondale Carbondale, Illinois 62901, primo@siu.edu

1 Introduction

Properties of the directional technology distance function have been given in a paper by Chambers, Chung, and Färe (1998). This function, $\vec{\mathbf{D}}\ (x, y; g_x, g_y)$, is an implicit representation of an M-output, N-input production technology. An input-output vector, (x, y), is feasible if and only if $\vec{\mathbf{D}}\ (x, y; g_x, g_y) \geqq 0$, where (g_x, g_y) is a "direction" vector to be described later. An important antecedent of the directional technology distance function is the shortage function, introduced by Luenberger (1992, 1995).

In this paper the theory of the directional technology distance function is extended by deriving a set of restrictions on the first and second derivatives of the directional technology distance functions. These restrictions would be useful in building an econometric model based on the directional technology distance function. It is then shown that the usual comparative static results for a competitive firm are easily established. In the final section we present flexible functional forms for estimating directional technology distance functions and some of the required parametric restrictions.

Let $x \in R_+^N$ be the input vector and let $y \in R_+^M$ be the output vector. The technology T is given by

$$T = \{(x, y) : x \text{ can produce } y\}\,.$$

Assume (see Chambers, Chung, Färe (1998))

- T1. T is closed
- T2. Free disposability: if $(x, y) \in T, x' \geq x$, and $y' \leq y$ then $(x', y') \in T$.
- T3. No free lunch: if $(x, y) \in T$ and $x = 0$ then $y = 0$.
- T4. Possibility of inaction: $(0, 0) \in T$.
- T5. T is convex.

The directional technology distance function is a particular representation of a multi-output, multi-input production technology. Following Chambers, Chung, and Färe (1998),

$$\vec{\mathbf{D}}\,(x,y;g_x,g_y) = \begin{cases} \max\{\beta : (x,y)+\beta(-g_x,g_y)\in T\} \\ \qquad \text{if } (x,y)+\beta(-g_x,g_y)\in T \text{ for some } \beta \\ -\infty \quad \text{otherwise.} \end{cases} \tag{1}$$

The calculation of the directional technology distance function is depicted in Figure 1.

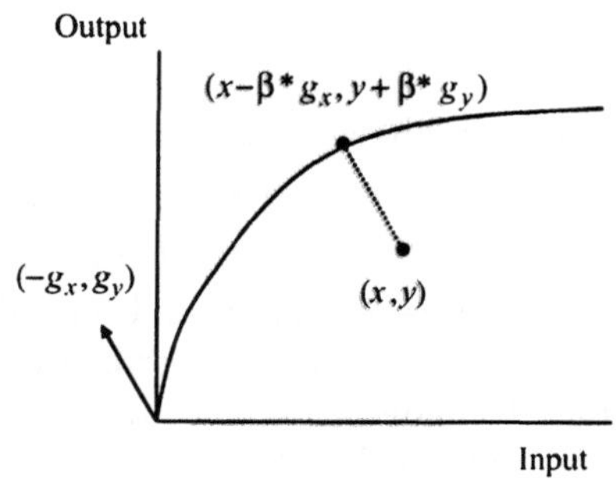

Fig. 1.

where $\beta^* = \vec{\mathbf{D}}\,(x,y;g_x,g_y)$.

There are, of course, many different implicit representations of a multi-output, muliti-input production technology. However, the directional technology distance function is particularly well-suited to the task of providing a measure of technical efficiency in the full input-output space. To see this consider some of the competing alternative measures.

The hyperbolic measure, proposed by Färe, Grosskopf, and Lovell (1985), is given by

$$F_g(x,y) = min\left\{\lambda : \left(\lambda x, \frac{y}{\lambda}\right) \in T\right\}.$$

The calculation of this hyperbolic measure is depicted in Figure 2. where $\lambda^* = F_g(x,y)$. It is possible to give this measure an economic interpretation but this is done at the expense of assuming constant returns to scale. For the details see Färe, Grosskopf, and Zaim (2002).

Another possibility is the radial measure given by

$$F_R(x,y) = \max\{\delta : (\delta x, \delta y) \in T\}.$$

The calculation of this measure is depicted in Figure 3.

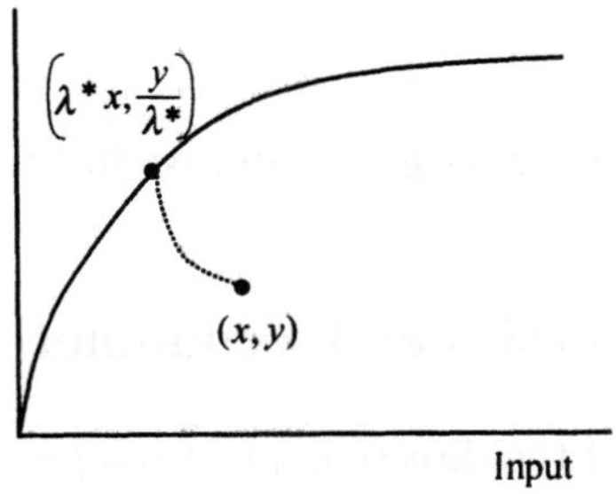

Fig. 2.

However, this measure could produce very large values (high inefficiency scores) even when (x, y) is very close to the frontier. Moreover, this measure completely breaks down under constant returns to scale.

Lemma 2.2 in Chambers, Chung, and Färe (1998) establishes that A1–A5 imply the following properties:

D1. Translation Property

$$\vec{\mathbf{D}}\,(x - \alpha g_x, y + \alpha g_y; g_x, g_y) = \vec{\mathbf{D}}\,(x, y; g_x, g_y) - \alpha \text{ for all } \alpha \in R$$

D2. g-Homogeneity of Degree Minus One

$$\vec{\mathbf{D}}\,(x, y; \lambda g_x, \lambda g_y) = \lambda^{-1}\,\vec{\mathbf{D}}\,(x, y; g_x, g_y), \lambda > 0$$

D3. Input Monotonicity

$$x' \geq x \Rightarrow \vec{\mathbf{D}}\,(x', y; g_x, g_y) \geq \mathbf{D}(x, y; g_x, g_y)$$

D4. Output Monotonicity

$$y' \geq y \Rightarrow \vec{\mathbf{D}}\,(x, y'; g_x, g_y) \leq \mathbf{D}(x, y; g_x, g_y)$$

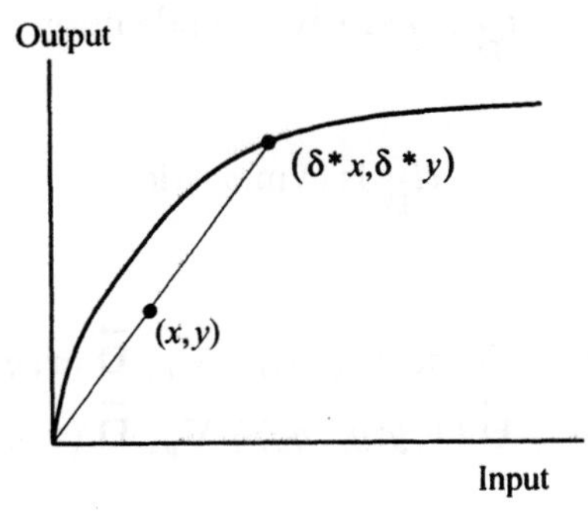

Fig. 3.

D5. Concavity

$$\vec{\mathbf{D}}\,(x, y; g_x, g_y) \text{ is concave in } (x, y)$$

2 Derivative Properties and Econometric Modelling

An econometric model of the directional technology distance function should impose properties D1–D5 listed above. This is conveniently accomplished by imposing the restrictions on the first and second derivatives of $\mathbf{D}(x, y; g_x, g_y)$ that are implied by D1–D5. These derivative conditions are given in the following lemma.

Lemma 1: Assume that $\vec{\mathbf{D}}\,(x, y; g_x, g_y)$ is twice continuously differentiable. Then D1–D5 imply that:

DD1. Translation Property

$$\nabla_x \vec{\mathbf{D}}\,(x, y; g_x, g_y) g_x - \nabla_y \vec{\mathbf{D}}\,(x, y; g_x, g_y) g_y = 1$$

DD2. g-Homogeneity of Degree Minus One

$$\nabla_{g_x} \vec{\mathbf{D}}\,(x, y; g_x, g_y) g_x + \nabla_{g_y} \vec{\mathbf{D}}\,(x, y; g_x, g_y) g_y = -\vec{\mathbf{D}}\,(x, y; g_x, g_y)$$

DD3. Input Monotonicity

$$\nabla_x \vec{\mathbf{D}}\,(x, y; g_x, g_y) \geq 0$$

DD4. Output Monotonicity

$$\nabla_y \vec{\mathbf{D}}\,(x, y; g_x, g_y) \leq 0$$

DD5. Concavity

$$H_{\vec{\mathbf{D}}} \text{ is negative semidefinite}$$

DD6. Symmetry

$$H_{\vec{\mathbf{D}}} \text{ is symmetric}$$

where

$$H_{\vec{\mathbf{D}}} = \begin{bmatrix} \nabla_{xx} \vec{\mathbf{D}}\,(x, y; g_x, g_y) & \nabla_{xy} \vec{\mathbf{D}}\,(x, y; g_x, g_y) \\ \nabla_{yx} \vec{\mathbf{D}}\,(x, y; g_x, g_y) & \nabla_{yy} \vec{\mathbf{D}}\,(x, y; g_x, g_y) \end{bmatrix}$$

is the Hessian matrix of $\vec{\mathbf{D}}$.

Proof: Differentiating (D1) with respect to α we get

$$-\nabla_x \vec{\mathbf{D}}\,(x-\alpha g_x, y+\alpha g_y; g_x, g_y)g_x + \nabla_y \vec{\mathbf{D}}\,(x-\alpha g_x, y+\alpha g_y; g_x, g_y)g_y = -1.$$

Set α equal to zero and multiply by -1 to get DD1:

$$\nabla_x \vec{\mathbf{D}}\,(x, y; g_x, g_y)g_x - \nabla_y \vec{\mathbf{D}}\,(x, y; g_x, g_y)g_y = 1.$$

D2. says that the directional technology distance function is homogeneous of degree minus one in (g_x, g_y). DD2 follows by Euler's Theorem. DD3 and DD4 follow directly from the monotonicity conditions, D3 and D4, respectively. DD5 follows directly from the concavity of $\vec{\mathbf{D}}\,(x, y; g_x, g_y)$ in (x, y) and DD6. follows from Young's Theorem. QED

Before concluding this section there is one more interesting property to explore. The profit function is defined as

$$\Pi(p, w) = \max_{x,y} \{py - wx : (x, y) \in T\} \tag{2}$$

$$= \max_{x,y} \left\{ py - wx : \vec{\mathbf{D}}\,(x, y; g_x, g_y) \geq 0 \right\} \tag{3}$$

since

$$(x, y) \in T \Leftrightarrow \vec{\mathbf{D}}\,(x, y; g_x, g_y) \geq 0. \tag{4}$$

Because of (1) and (4) we can write

$$(x, y) \in T \Leftrightarrow (x - \vec{\mathbf{D}}\,(x, y; g_x, g_y)g_x, y + \vec{\mathbf{D}}\,(x, y; g_x, g_y)g_y) \in T,$$

by the free disposability assumption. Thus, profit may be defined by the unconstrained maximization problem:

$$\Pi(p, w) = \max_{x,y} \left\{ p\left(y + \vec{\mathbf{D}}\,(x, y; g_x, g_y)g_y\right) - w\left(x - \vec{\mathbf{D}}\,(x, y; g_x, g_y)g_x\right)\right\}$$

$$= \max_{x,y} \left\{ py - wx + \vec{\mathbf{D}}\,(x, y; g_x, g_y)\,(pg_y + wg_x)\right\}$$

The first order conditions are:

$$-w + \nabla_x \vec{\mathbf{D}}\,(x, y; g_x, g_y)\,(pg_y + wg_x) = 0$$

$$p + \nabla_y \vec{\mathbf{D}}\,(x, y; g_x, g_y)\,(pg_y + wg_x) = 0$$

or

$$\frac{w}{pg_y + wg_x} = \nabla_x \vec{\mathbf{D}}\,(x, y; g_x, g_y) \tag{5}$$

$$\frac{p}{pg_y + wg_x} = -\nabla_y \vec{\mathbf{D}}\,(x, y; g_x, g_y) \tag{6}$$

These are the inverse supply and demand functions. Prices (w, p) are normalized by the number, $pg_y + wg_x$.

While this approach is efficient it does not provide an economic interpretation of the term, $pg_y + wg_x$. To provide such an interpretation we turn to a more traditional treatment of the profit maximization problem. Write the Lagrangian function for (3) as

$$L = py - wx + \lambda \vec{\mathbf{D}}\,(x, y; g_x, g_y)$$

First order conditions are:

$$\begin{aligned} L_x &= -w + \lambda \nabla_x \vec{\mathbf{D}}\,(x, y; g_x, g_y) = 0 \Rightarrow \nabla_x \vec{\mathbf{D}}\,(x, y; g_x, g_y) = \tfrac{w}{\lambda} > 0 \\ L_y &= p + \lambda \nabla_y \vec{\mathbf{D}}\,(x, y; g_x, g_y) = 0 \Rightarrow \nabla_y \vec{\mathbf{D}}\,(x, y; g_x, g_y) = \tfrac{-p}{\lambda} < 0 \end{aligned} \tag{7}$$

or

$$wg_x = \lambda \nabla_x \vec{\mathbf{D}}\,(x, y; g_x, g_y) g_x \tag{8}$$

$$pg_y = -\lambda \nabla_y \vec{\mathbf{D}}\,(x, y; g_x, g_y) g_y \tag{9}$$

Multiplying (DD1) by λ we get:

$$\lambda \nabla_x \vec{\mathbf{D}}\,(x, y; g_x, g_y) g_x - \lambda \nabla_y \mathbf{D}(x, y; g_x, g_y) g_y = \lambda$$

thus, adding (8) and (9) we get:

$$\begin{aligned} pg_y + wg_x &= \lambda \nabla_x \vec{\mathbf{D}}\,(x, y; g_x, g_y) g_x - \lambda \nabla_y \vec{\mathbf{D}}\,(x, y; g_x, g_y) g_y \\ &= \lambda \\ &\Rightarrow \lambda = pg_y + wg_x \end{aligned} \tag{10}$$

Thus, $pg_y + wg_x$ is the optimal value of the Lagrangian multiplier in the profit maximization problem. If the technology is perturbed (improved) by a small value, ε, from

$$T = \left\{ (x, y) : \vec{\mathbf{D}}\,(x, y; g_x, g_y) \geq 0 \right\}$$

to

$$T' = \left\{ (x, y) : \vec{\mathbf{D}}\,(x, y; g_x, g_y) + \varepsilon \geq 0 \right\}$$

then the firm's profit will rise and $\frac{\partial \Pi(p,w)}{\partial \varepsilon} = pg_y + wg_x$.[3]

Putting (10) into (7) and rearranging we get

$$\begin{aligned} \frac{w}{pg_y + wg_x} &= \nabla_x \vec{\mathbf{D}}\,(x, y; g_x, g_y) \\ \frac{p}{pg_y + wg_x} &= -\nabla_y \vec{\mathbf{D}}\,(x, y; g_x, g_y) \end{aligned}$$

which, of course, is the same result as (5) and (6).

[3] It is also possible to infer this result from the proof in the Appendix of Chambers, Chung, and Färe (1998).

3 Comparative Statics

In this section we show how comparative static derivatives of the input demand and the output supply functions may be expressed as functions of the first and second order derivatives of the directional technology distance function. Rearranging (5) and (6), we get

$$\nabla_x \vec{\mathbf{D}}(x,y)(pg_y + wg_x) = w \tag{11}$$

$$\nabla_y \vec{\mathbf{D}}(x,y)(pg_y + wg_x) = -p \tag{12}$$

First, differentiate (11) and (12) with respect to the input price vector, w.

$$\nabla_x \vec{\mathbf{D}}(x,y)g_x + \left[\nabla_{xx} \vec{\mathbf{D}}(x,y)\frac{\partial x}{\partial w} + \nabla_{xy} \vec{\mathbf{D}}(x,y)\frac{\partial y}{\partial w}\right](pg_y + wg_x) = 1$$
$$\nabla_y \vec{\mathbf{D}}(x,y)g_x + \left[\nabla_{yx} \vec{\mathbf{D}}(x,y)\frac{\partial x}{\partial w} + \nabla_{yy} \vec{\mathbf{D}}(x,y)\frac{\partial y}{\partial w}\right](pg_y + wg_x) = 0$$

and write the result, rearranged, n matrix notation,

$$\begin{bmatrix} \nabla_{xx} \vec{\mathbf{D}}(x,y) \; \nabla_{xy} \vec{\mathbf{D}}(x,y) \\ \nabla_{yx} \vec{\mathbf{D}}(x,y) \; \nabla_{yy} \vec{\mathbf{D}}(x,y) \end{bmatrix} \begin{bmatrix} \frac{\partial x}{\partial w} \\ \\ \frac{\partial y}{\partial w} \end{bmatrix} = \frac{1}{pg_y + wg_x} \begin{bmatrix} 1 - \nabla_x \vec{\mathbf{D}}(x,y)g_x \\ -\nabla_y \vec{\mathbf{D}}(x,y)g_x \end{bmatrix}.$$

Next, differentiate (11) and (12) with respect to output prices, p.

$$\nabla_x \vec{\mathbf{D}}(x,y)g_y + \left[\nabla_{xx} \vec{\mathbf{D}}(x,y)\frac{\partial x}{\partial p} + \nabla_{xy} \vec{\mathbf{D}}(x,y)\frac{\partial y}{\partial p}\right](pg_y + wg_x) = 0$$
$$\nabla_y \vec{\mathbf{D}}(x,y)g_y + \left[\nabla_{yx} \vec{\mathbf{D}}(x,y)\frac{\partial x}{\partial p} + \nabla_{yy} \vec{\mathbf{D}}(x,y)\frac{\partial y}{\partial p}\right](pg_y + wg_x) = -1.$$

Rearrange and write in matrix notation.

$$\begin{bmatrix} \nabla_{xx} \vec{\mathbf{D}}(x,y) \; \nabla_{xy} \vec{\mathbf{D}}(x,y) \\ \nabla_{yx} \vec{\mathbf{D}}(x,y) \; \nabla_{yy} \vec{\mathbf{D}}(x,y) \end{bmatrix} \begin{bmatrix} \frac{\partial x}{\partial p} \\ \\ \frac{\partial y}{\partial p} \end{bmatrix} = \frac{1}{pg_y + wg_x} \begin{bmatrix} -\nabla_x \vec{\mathbf{D}}(x,y)g_y \\ -1 - \nabla_y \vec{\mathbf{D}}(x,y)g_y \end{bmatrix}.$$

$$\begin{bmatrix} \nabla_{xx} \vec{\mathbf{D}}(x,y) \; \nabla_{xy} \vec{\mathbf{D}}(x,y) \\ \nabla_{yx} \vec{\mathbf{D}}(x,y) \; \nabla_{yy} \vec{\mathbf{D}}(x,y) \end{bmatrix} \begin{bmatrix} \frac{\partial x}{\partial w} \; \frac{\partial x}{\partial p} \\ \\ \frac{\partial y}{\partial w} \; \frac{\partial y}{\partial p} \end{bmatrix}$$

$$= \frac{1}{pg_y + wg_x} \begin{bmatrix} 1 - \nabla_x \vec{\mathbf{D}}(x,y) g_x & -\nabla_x \vec{\mathbf{D}}(x,y) g_y \\ -\nabla_y \vec{\mathbf{D}}(x,y) g_x & -1 - \nabla_y \vec{\mathbf{D}}(x,y) g_y \end{bmatrix}$$

$$= \frac{1}{pg_y + wg_x} \begin{bmatrix} -\nabla_y \vec{\mathbf{D}}(x,y) g_y & -\nabla_x \vec{\mathbf{D}}(x,y) g_y \\ -\nabla_y \vec{\mathbf{D}}(x,y) g_x & -\nabla_x \vec{\mathbf{D}}(x,y) g_x \end{bmatrix} \qquad \text{(using DD1.)}$$

$$= \frac{-1}{pg_y + wg_x} \begin{bmatrix} \nabla_y \vec{\mathbf{D}}(x,y) g_y & \nabla_x \vec{\mathbf{D}}(x,y) g_y \\ \nabla_y \vec{\mathbf{D}}(x,y) g_x & \nabla_x \vec{\mathbf{D}}(x,y) g_x \end{bmatrix}$$

Thus, the matrix of comparative static derivatives of the input demand and the output supply functions can be found above after we invert the Hessian matrix of the directional technology distance function. We get,

$$\begin{bmatrix} -\nabla_{ww} \Pi(p,w) & -\nabla_{wp} \Pi(p,w) \\ \\ \nabla_{pw} \Pi(p,w) & \nabla_{pp} \Pi(p,w) \end{bmatrix} = \begin{bmatrix} \frac{\partial x}{\partial w} & \frac{\partial x}{\partial p} \\ \frac{\partial y}{\partial w} & \frac{\partial y}{\partial p} \end{bmatrix}$$

$$= \frac{-1}{pg_y + wg_x} \begin{bmatrix} \nabla_{xx} \vec{\mathbf{D}}(x,y) & \nabla_{xy} \vec{\mathbf{D}}(x,y) \\ \nabla_{yx} \vec{\mathbf{D}}(x,y) & \nabla_{yy} \vec{\mathbf{D}}(x,y) \end{bmatrix}^{-1} \begin{bmatrix} \nabla_y \vec{\mathbf{D}}(x,y) g_y & \nabla_x \vec{\mathbf{D}}(x,y) g_y \\ \nabla_y \vec{\mathbf{D}}(x,y) g_x & \nabla_x \vec{\mathbf{D}}(x,y) g_x \end{bmatrix}$$

4 Functional Forms

Econometric estimation of a directional distance function requires the choice of a functional form. We will begin our discussion of this choice for the case in which $(g_x, g_y) = (1^N, 1^M)$. Chambers (1978) suggested two different functional forms in this case, namely, the *logarithmic-transcendental* and the *quadratic*. These suggestions were later validated in a paper by Färe and Lundberg (2004). They sought functional forms that satisfy the translation property, D.1, and that have a second order Taylor series approximation interpretation. A function of n variables, F, has a second order Taylor series approximation interpretation if there are real constants, $a_i, b_{jk}, i, j, k = 1, \ldots, n$ and real-valued functions ϕ and h such that

$$\phi(F(z)) = \sum_{i=1}^{n} a_i h(z_i) + \sum_{j=1}^{n} \sum_{k=1}^{n} b_{jk} h(z_j) h(z_k), \tag{13}$$

where it is assumed, without loss of generality, that $b_{jk} = b_{kj},\ j,k = 1,\ldots,n$. See Lau (1977) and Blackorby, Primont, and Russell (1978, pp. 290-296) for a further discussion.

The two functional forms that they found are the quadratic

$$T(z) = \sum_{i=1}^{N+M} a_i z_i + \sum_{j=1}^{N+M}\sum_{k=1}^{N+M} b_{jk} z_j z_k, \tag{14}$$

where $n = N+M$, $z = (x,y)$ and $T(z) = T(x,y) = D(x,y;1^N,1^M)$, and what we will call the *transcendental-exponential*

$$\begin{aligned} T(x,y) = \tfrac{1}{2\lambda}\ln\Big\{&\textstyle\sum_{i=1}^N \sum_{j=1}^N a_{ij}\exp(\lambda x_i)\exp(\lambda x_j) \\ &+\textstyle\sum_{k=1}^M \sum_{\ell=1}^M b_{k\ell}\exp(-\lambda y_k)\exp(-\lambda y_\ell) \\ &+\textstyle\sum_{i=1}^N \sum_{k=1}^M c_{ik}\exp(\lambda x_i)\exp(-\lambda y_k)\Big\}. \end{aligned} \tag{15}$$

The quadratic (14) is linear in the parameters and can be readily estimated. The transcendental-exponential (15) can be linearized in all of the parameters except for λ. Setting $\lambda = \frac{1}{2}$ and exponentiating both sides of (15) yields

$$\begin{aligned} &\exp(T(x,y)) \\ &= \textstyle\sum_{i=1}^N \sum_{j=1}^N a_{ij}\exp\left(\frac{x_i}{2}\right)\exp\left(\frac{x_j}{2}\right) + \sum_{k=1}^M \sum_{\ell=1}^M b_{k\ell}\exp\left(-\frac{y_k}{2}\right)\exp\left(-\frac{y_\ell}{2}\right) \\ &\quad+\textstyle\sum_{i=1}^N \sum_{k=1}^M c_{ik}\exp\left(\frac{x_i}{2}\right)\exp\left(-\frac{y_k}{2}\right). \end{aligned} \tag{16}$$

Equations (14) and (16) are the functional forms first suggested by Chambers (1998).

It can be verified that both (15) and (16) automatically satisfy the translation property. The quadratic functional form satisfies the translation property if the following linear parametric restrictions are imposed.

$$\sum_{i=1}^N a_i - \sum_{k=1}^M a_k = 1, \quad \sum_{j=1}^M b_{jk} - \sum_{j=1}^N b_{jk} = \sum_{k=1}^M b_{jk} - \sum_{k=1}^N b_{jk} = 0 \tag{17}$$

The restrictions in (17) will be derived in a more general setting below. Examples of the use of the quadratic functional form for directional distance functions include Färe, Grosskopf, and Weber (2001) and Färe, Grosskopf, Noh, and Weber (2005).[4]

---

[4] Actually these two papers use the directional output distance function. This entails setting $g_x = 0^N$.

We now consider any given direction vector, (g_x, g_y). Retaining our notation, $z = (x, y)$, and letting $g = (-g_x, g_y)$, the directional distance function is defined as

$$\vec{\mathbf{D}}(z; g) = \sup_{\beta} \{\beta : z + \beta g \in T\},$$

i.e., $\vec{\mathbf{D}}(z; g) = \vec{\mathbf{D}}(x, y; -g_x, g_y) = \mathbf{D}(x, y; g_x, g_y)$. In terms of $\vec{\mathbf{D}}$ the translation property is again established by

$$\begin{aligned}
\vec{\mathbf{D}}(z + \alpha g; g) &= \sup_{\beta} \{\beta : z + \alpha g + \beta g \in T\} \\
&= \sup_{\beta} \{\beta : z + (\alpha + \beta) g \in T\} \\
&= -\alpha + \sup_{\alpha+\beta} \{\alpha + \beta : z + (\alpha + \beta) g \in T\} \\
&= \vec{\mathbf{D}}(z; g) - \alpha.
\end{aligned}$$

Again, we seek functional forms that meet the Färe-Lundberg conditions, namely, 1) they satisfy the translation property and 2) they have a second-order Taylor series approximation interpretation. Any functional form that does satisfy the Färe-Lundberg conditions for any direction (g_x, g_y) must also satisfy the Färe-Lundberg conditions for the direction $(g_x, g_y) = (1^N, 1^M)$. Hence, the only candidates for such functional forms are the quadratic (14) and the transcendental exponential (15) function forms.

For the rest of this section we will be content to show that the quadratic functional form still "works" for any direction vector (g_x, g_y). We will impose the translation property on the quadratic functional form and thereby derive the restrictions imposed by the translation property. For the quadratic functional form.

$$\sum_{i=1}^{n} a_i z_i + \sum_{j=1}^{n} \sum_{k=1}^{n} b_{jk} z_j z_k$$

we want the following to hold identically for all α and for all z.

$$\begin{aligned}
&\sum_i a_i (z_i + \alpha g_i) + \sum_j \sum_k b_{jk} (z_j + \alpha g_j)(z_k + \alpha g_k) \\
&= \sum_i a_i (z_i + \alpha g_i) + \sum_j \sum_k b_{jk} \left(z_j z_k + \alpha z_j g_k + \alpha z_k g_j + \alpha^2 g_j g_k\right) \\
&= \sum_i a_i z_i + \sum_j \sum_k b_{jk} z_j z_k - \alpha
\end{aligned}$$

Cancelling common terms and factoring out the $\alpha's$ we get

$$\alpha \sum_i a_i g_i + \alpha \sum_j \sum_k b_{jk} (z_j g_k + z_k g_j) + \alpha^2 \sum_j \sum_k b_{jk} g_j g_k = -\alpha$$

or

$$\alpha\sum_i a_i g_i + \alpha\sum_j z_j \sum_k b_{jk} g_k + \alpha\sum_k z_k \sum_j b_{jk} g_j + \alpha^2 \sum_j \sum_k b_{jk} g_j g_k = -\alpha$$

Divide both sides by α to get

$$\sum_i a_i g_i + \sum_j z_j \sum_k b_{jk} g_k + \sum_k z_k \sum_j b_{jk} g_j + \alpha \sum_j \sum_k b_{jk} g_j g_k = -1 \quad (18)$$

Differentiate (18) with respect to z_l to get

$$\sum_k b_{jk} g_k + \sum_j b_{jk} g_j = 0$$

or

$$\sum_k b_{kj} g_k + \sum_j b_{jk} g_j = 0,$$

using symmetry. Hence

$$2\sum_j b_{jk} g_j = 0 \Rightarrow \sum_j b_{jk} g_j = 0.$$

We conclude that

$$\sum_k b_{kj} g_k = \sum_j b_{jk} g_j = 0 \quad (19)$$

Then (18) and (19) imply that

$$\sum_j \sum_k b_{jk} g_j g_k = 0 \text{ and hence } \sum_i a_i g_i = -1.$$

We summarize these restrictions below.

$$\sum_i a_i g_i = -1, \quad \sum_j b_{jk} g_j = \sum_k b_{jk} g_k = 0 \quad (20)$$

Now, of course, $g = (-g_x, g_y)$. If we let $(g_x, g_y) = (1^N, 1^M)$ so that $g = (-1^N, 1^M)$, then (20) becomes

$$-\sum_{i=1}^{N} a_i + \sum_{k=1}^{M} a_k = -1, \quad \sum_{j=1}^{M} b_{jk} - \sum_{j=1}^{N} b_{jk} = \sum_{k=1}^{M} b_{jk} - \sum_{k=1}^{N} b_{jk} = 0,$$

or

$$\sum_{i=1}^{N} a_i - \sum_{k=1}^{M} a_k = 1, \quad \sum_{j=1}^{M} b_{jk} - \sum_{j=1}^{N} b_{jk} = \sum_{k=1}^{M} b_{jk} - \sum_{k=1}^{N} b_{jk} = 0. \quad (21)$$

The conditions in (21) coincide with the conditions in (17).

5 Closing Remarks

In this paper we have established the derivative restrictions on the directional technology distance function that would be useful in econometric work. It was shown that the standard neoclassical comparative static analysis for a competitive firm can be easily handled with the directional technology distance function. Finally, we have briefly surveyed the functional forms that seem to be best suited for econometric estimation. There are, of course, other uses of the directional technology distance function. In addition to the previously cited papers by Färe, Grosskopf, and Weber (2001) and Färe, Grosskopf, Noh, and Weber (2005), Färe and Grosskopf (2000) show, among other things, that the directional technology distance function can be used to model plant capacity. For another example, Färe and Primont (2003) use the directional technology distance function to find conditions under which productivity indicators for each firm in an industry can be aggregated to a productivity indicator for the industry as a whole.

References

Blackorby, Charles, Daniel Primont, and R. Robert Russell, *Duality, Separability, and Functional Structure: Theory and Economic Applications*, New York: Elsevier North-Holland, 1978.

Chambers, Robert, "Input and Ouput Indicators," in Rolf Färe, Shawna Grosskopf, and R. Robert Russell, editors, *Index Numbers: Essays in Honour of Sten Malmquist*, Boston: Kluwer Academic Publishers, 1998.

Chambers, Robert, Yangho Chung, and Rolf Färe , "Profit, Directional Distance Functions, and Nerlovian Efficiency," *Journal of Optimization Theory and Applications*, **98**(2) (1998), 351–364.

Färe, Rolf, and Shawna Grosskopf, "Theory and Application of Directional Distance Functions," *Journal of Productivity Analysis*, **13**(2) (2000), 93–103.

Färe, Rolf, Shawna Grosskopf, and Osman Zaim, "Hyperbolic Efficiency and Return to the Dollar," *European Journal of Operational Research*, **136** (2002), 671–679.

Färe, Rolf, Shawna Grosskopf, Dong-Woon Noh, and William Weber, "Characteristics of a Polluting Technology: Theory and Practice," *Journal of Econometrics* **126** (2005), 469–492.

Färe, Rolf, Shawna Grosskopf, and William Weber, "Shadow Prices of Missouri Public Conservation Land," *Public Finance Review*, **29**(6) (2001), 444–460.

Färe, Rolf, and Anders Lundberg, "Parameterizing the Shortage Function," unpublished paper, 2004.

Färe, Rolf and Daniel Primont, "Luenberger Productivity Indicators: Aggregation Across Firms", forthcoming, *Journal of Productivity Analysis*, 2003.

Lau, Lawrence J., "Complete Systems of Consumer Demand Functions Through Duality," in Michael D. Intriligator, editor, *Frontiers of Quantitative Economics*, Volume IIIA, Amsterdam: North-Holland, 1977.

Luenberger, David G., "New Optimality Principles for Economic Efficiency and Equilibrium," *Journal of Optimization Theory and Applications*, **75**(2) (1992), 221–264.
Luenberger, David G., Microeconomic Theory, New York: McGraw-Hill, 1995.

Synergistic Mergers in an Agency Context: An Illustration of the Interaction of the Observability Problem and Synergistic Merger

Tim S. Campbell[1] and Anthony M. Marino[2]*

[1] Department of Finance and Business Economics, Marshall School of Business, University of Southern California tcampbell@marshall.usc.edu
[2] Department of Finance and Business Economics, Marshall School of Business, University of Southern California amarino@marshall.usc.edu

Summary. This paper formulates a simple agency problem in a single division firm and has that firm merge with another firm having the same agency problem. The merger creates synergy, but it also causes the principal to lose information in observing the agent's performance. We call the latter problem the observability problem associated with merger. We focus on the interaction of these two by-products of merger and study their effects on the firm's agency contract and profit. A key point is that many of the beneficial effects that we would associate with the presence of synergy can be undone by the observability problem, so that the synergistic benefits of merger can be misgauged, if the observability problem is ignored. Two empirically testable implications arise. First, if the post merger contract is less sensitive, then the observability problem is essentially nonexistent and the merger is profitable. Second, if the post merger contract is very sensitive, then synergy is swamping the observability problem and the merger is profitable.

1 Introduction

The economics literature has provided a variety of motivations for mergers. A first key motive in horizontal mergers is the creation of market power and the associated value that comes along with such power. (See Stigler (1950) for an early discussion.) A second related set of motives might be called technological in nature. The merger of two firms can create cost savings through a variety of sources. Merger can eliminate redundant facilities such as overlapping bank ATM's. It can also induce more efficient use of support functions, such as accounting and marketing, and more efficient use of fixed inputs (e.g., common pooling of fixed inputs and elimination of redundancy.) The merger

* The authors benefited from discussions with Tom Gilligan, Tracy Lewis, John Matsusaka, and Jan Zabojnik. An anonymous referee gave beneficial comments. This research was supported by the Marshall General Research Fund.

of two firms can lead to sharing of previously private information and ideas. Learning might take place among the employees of one merged firm as they associate with their counterparts from the other merged firm. A third key set of motivations given for merger is founded on the notion that a manager's incentive to maximize his own well being may not lead to value maximization for the firm's shareholders. The manager may derive utility from pure empire building. (See, for example, Baumol (1967) and Mueller (1969)). Alternatively, more acquisitions might allow the manager to invest in assets whose returns are dependent on the manager's private information so as to entrench himself within the company. (Shleifer and Vishney, 1989). Further, the tendency for managers to overestimate their own ability can lead them to over estimate the future performance of acquired firms (Roll, 1986).

We focus on the first two motives and term these rationalizations for merger as general "synergy". While many merger and acquisition decisions are justified based on the synergy they are expected to generate, curiously, subsequent divestitures of businesses are also often justified on the basis that they did not generate sufficient synergy.[3] Moreover, the frequency of divestitures of initial acquisitions is quite large. Kaplan and Weisbach (1992) report that, for a sample of large acquisitions between 1971 and 1982, almost 44% of the acquirers had divested their previous target by 1989. In addition, a now extensive applied management literature emphasizes the need for a systematic process for generating synergies.[4] A failure to implement such a process effectively can undermine the anticipated synergies in an acquisition and ultimately lead to divestiture. Clearly, synergy is sufficiently hard to estimate, ex ante, and hard to deliver, ex post, that the search for synergy in the business community appears to involve a fair amount of experimentation. Errors in this synergy prediction and implementation process could account for the large number of failed mergers, or it could be that one of the above self-interest motives for merger is the reason that a merger turned out to be unprofitable. We want to examine a different problem arising in the process of synergy prediction and implementation.

A potential stumbling block which could make the successful realization and correct prediction of synergy difficult is that seemingly simple forms of synergy; arising from enhanced revenues, reduced redundancy, and lower costs; must be realized in an agency context. The common pooling and intermeshing of two firm's resources which create synergy under merger, can also make it more difficult for the principal of a firm to observe the separate performances of the agents in the merged organization. We call the latter problem the performance observability problem created by mergers.

This paper will focus on the interaction of the performance observability problem and the creation of synergy as a result of merger, and it will study the effects of this interaction on the endogenously optimal agency contact

[3] See Cusatis et al. (1993).

[4] See, for example, Goold and Campbell (1998).

before and after merger. Our goal will be to outline the effects of synergy, the observability problem and the joint presence of both phenomena on the optimal agency contract and the equilibrium of the firm. We will show that many of the beneficial effects resulting from synergy may be undone by the observability problem and we will develop testable implications regarding the contract sensitivity (the gradient of the pay-performance relationship) and the expected compensation of the agent in the post merger contract.

The idea that the performance of individual business units may be difficult to measure in a multi-divisional business firm and that this measurement problem may stem from the organization of the firm is not new. Williamson (1985) emphasized the importance of the "power of incentives" in explaining organizational structure of firms. In particular, that merger might result in lower powered incentives. In addition, Hermalin and Katz (1996) distinguish between the risk reduction effects and the informational effects of diversification. They argue that the value of diversification in an agency setting derives from its effects on the principal's information concerning the agent's actions, rather than solely from its effects on risk. They demonstrate that diversification can endogenously increase or decrease the principal's information about the agent's actions, thus, diversification can raise or lower agency cost.[5] By assuming that merger eliminates some of the principal's information, our analysis is similar in spirit to that of Hermalin and Katz.

We specify a simple discrete-outcome agency model where an agent exerts unobservable effort to increase the probability of a high return. The agency cost derives from a limited liability constraint on the agent. Synergistic gains from merger of two firms arise because effort exerted by the agent in each of two firms is assumed to proportionally increase the probability of generating a high return in the other firm. When two firms with similar agency problems merge to achieve synergy, information on the returns on the individual businesses is assumed to be lost in that the principal is able to observe only aggregate performance as opposed to individual performance after merger.

After presenting the model in Section 2a, we consider the observability problem without synergy in Section 2.b. We find that merger with the observability problem (but without synergy) increases the optimal contract's marginal compensation for good performance, but at the same time reduces the probability the agent will be rewarded for a good performance, thus making changes in the agent's expected compensation indeterminate. Merger with the observability problem always increases the sensitivity of the agency contract, decreases the firm's value and decreases the equilibrium effort of the agent. Section 3a considers merger with synergy but without the observability

[5] Their analysis is addressed to the literature that argues that agency considerations can lead to firm diversification. Diamond and Verrecchia (1982), Marshall (1984), and Aron (1988) each has a different model of the beneficial effects of diversification and the resultant risk reduction in the agency problem.

problem, and we find that the effects on the agency contract; effort and profit are exactly the opposite of those of the observability problem, except that with synergy alone, the expected payment to the agent must rise. In Section 3.b we study the effects of the opposing forces of synergy and the observability problem on the incentive contract. We find that the magnitude of synergy must be greater than a certain positive threshold so as to swamp the observability problem and make merger profitable. In this case, merger results in a more sensitive agency contract. However, the impact on expected costs, the agent's effort and expected profit depend on the trade-off between the level of synergy and the observability problem.

An empirically testable implication of this analysis is that if, after merger, the agent's contract becomes less sensitive, then the observability problem is essentially nonexistent and we would expect the merger to be profitable. The lesser is the degree of sensitivity of the post merger contract the greater is the degree of profitability of the merged firms. A further empirical implication is that if the contract, after merger, is more sensitive and the expected compensation of the agent is greater, then synergy is swamping the observability problem and the merger is profitable. A general implication is that any ex ante quantification of potential synergies or post-merger attempts to deliver synergies should take into account the agency costs and contracting implications of any observability problem created by the merger.

2 The Agency and the Observability Problems

2.1 The Single Division Agency Problem

Consider a hidden action agency problem, where a principal has control over a firm, but the firm requires the services of an agent whose effort is unobservable. Let e denote the agent's effort and its cost to the agent, and suppose that there are three possible cash flows for the firm:

$H > M > L$, where $\text{Prob}(H) \equiv r$, $\text{Prob}(M) \equiv p(e)$, and $\text{Prob}(L) \equiv 1-r-p(e)$.

The high cash flow occurs with an exogenous probability and the probabilities of the medium and the low cash flows are functions of the agent's effort.[6] Greater effort by the agent increases the probability of the medium cash flow and decreases the probability of the low cash flow. We assume

$$\text{A.1. } p' > 0,\ p'' < 0.$$

[6] We did not use the more convenient two-outcome model, where performance can take on the values H or L, because the performance observability problem unravels in this version. The principal can attain the same second best as in the single division problem by making a positive payment in the event of the outcome H for each division.

The principal designs a contingent payment scheme for the agent, under the assumption that the agent and the principal are risk neutral. In the event of a performance $i \in \{H, M, L\}$, the principal pays C^i. Also, assume that the agent has limited liability, so that the principal can not issue negative contingent payments. In the present risk neutral environment, there is no agency problem and the principal can implement the first best when there are no lower bounds on the C^i. Let the agent have a market wage of w. The agent's expected payoff is given by

$$rC^H + pC^M + (1 - r - p)C^L - e.$$

Given a compensation vector from the principal, the agent's optimal effort is determined by solving

$$p'(e)(C^M - C^L) - 1 = 0. \tag{1}$$

Employment will be desirable to an agent with reservation wage w if

$$rC^H + pC^M + (1 - r - p)C^L - e - w \geq 0. \tag{2}$$

Equations 1 and 2 are the incentive compatibility (IC) and participation constraints, and these along with the limited liability constraints $C^i \geq 0$ define the constraints for the principal's maximization problem. In the present risk neutral environment, there is no agency problem and the principal can implement the first best when there are no lower bounds on the C^i through limited liability. This is critical for a second best in that the principal could generate first best effort through the (IC) constraint by raising C^M and lowering say C^H sufficiently to meet the participation constraint with equality. That is, if the participation constraint is binding and the limited liability constraints are not, the principal keeps the entire surplus (the agent retains no rent) and achieves the first best. If the participation constraint is binding (the agent has no rent) and some of the limited liability constraints are binding and some are not, then we have a knife edge solution which may or may not be the first best. We then want to only consider second best solutions where at least one limited liability constraint is binding and the participation constraint is nonbinding (the agent keeps some rent). We posit a fairly standard sufficiency condition to guarantee that the latter is true. Note that through the (IC), $C^M = 1/p'(e) + C^L \geq 1/p'(e)$, so that $p(e)C^M \geq p(e)/p'(e)$. It follows that the participation constraint is nonbinding if $p(0)/p'(0) > w$, by $p(e)C^M - e \geq p(e)/p'(e) - e$, the fact that the function $(p/p' - e)$ is increasing, and that $rC^H, (1 - r - p)C^L \geq 0$. That is, the lowest level of effort generates a large enough expected net return to exceed the outside wage.[7] We assume the analogue to this assumption in all of the problems to follow. Under this assumption, the principal's optimum is characterized as in the following (All proofs are provided in the Appendix).

[7] See Levitt and Synder (1997) for an identical assumption.

Lemma 1. *In equilibrium, only C^M is positive. Expected cost is given by $pC^M = p/p'$ and equilibrium effort is defined by*

$$p'(e^s)(M-L) = 1 - p''(e^s)p(e^s)/(p'(e^s))^2 \equiv z(e) > 1. \quad (3)$$

In what follows we will think of the function p/p' as the firm's equilibrium cost function and define marginal cost as

$$z(e) = 1 - p''p/(p')^2.$$

We will assume that marginal cost is increasing in e

$$\text{A.2} z'(e) = -\{(p'''p + p'p'')(p')^2 - 2(p')(p'')(p''p)\}/(p')^4 > 0.$$

For A.2 to be true, it suffices that $p''' \geq 0$, although this is not a necessary condition.

As expected, only the highest discretionary performance receives a positive payment in equilibrium. Condition 3 equates the marginal benefit of effort with its marginal cost. We note that marginal cost is greater than unity, and the first best marginal cost is equal to unity. Using the results of Lemma 1, we can rewrite the principal's problem as

$$\underset{\{e\}}{Max}\ rH + pM + (1-r-p)L - p/p'. \quad (4)$$

Problem 4 has a first order condition identical to 3. Let $\pi(e) \equiv rH + pM + (1-r-p)L - p/p'$. The equilibrium is illustrated in Figure 1, where we also illustrate the first best effort as e^f defined by $p'(e^f)(M-L) = 1$. It is clear that $e^f > e^s$.

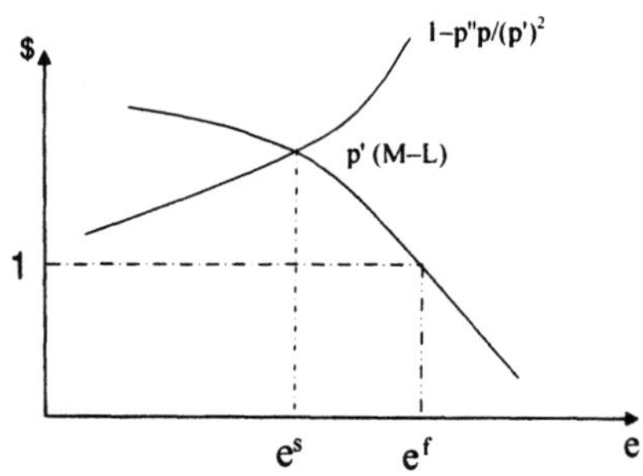

2.2 The Observability Problem in a Multidivisional Firm

Next, let the single division firm merge with another identical firm. The merger creates a new firm with two agents and one principal. Initially, we assume that there is no synergy. The merger is costly due to the fact that the principal is not as well informed about the individual performance of the agents in the two separate divisions. This section isolates the cost associated with the performance observability problem. Let us take the simplest version of such a story and assume that, as a result of the merger, the principal can no longer observe a single agent's performance, but, instead, can only observe aggregate performance.[8] We assume

$$\text{A.3. } 2M = H + L.$$

Assumption A.3 makes it impossible for the principal to distinguish between two middle outputs and a high and a low output. Table 1 summarizes the outcomes that can be observed by the principal and the associated contingent payments.

Set of Outcomes	Payment
HL, LH, or MM	C^*
MH or HM	$C^{M,H}$
LM or ML	$C^{L,M}$
HH	C^H
LL	C^L

We wish to formulate and solve the new agency problem with merger and unobservability.

Let p_i denote $p(e_i)$. Then a single agent's welfare can be written as

$$C = rrC^H + (1 - r - p_1)(1 - r - p_2)C^L + (rp_1 + rp_2)C^{M,H} + [(1 - r - p_1)p_2 + (1-r-p_2)p_1]C^{L,M} + [r(1-r-p_2)+(1-r-p_1)r+p_1p_2]C^* - e_i. \quad (5)$$

If each agent acts as a Nash player, then he will maximize welfare over a choice of e_i, assuming that the other agent's effort is given. For example, agent 1 has the incentive compatibility constraint

$$\partial C/\partial e_1 = -p_1'(1 - r - p_2)C^L + p_1'rC^{M,H} + [-p_1'p_2 + p_1'(1 - r - p_2)]C^{L,M} + [-p_1'r + p_1'p_2]C^* - 1 = 0. \quad (6)$$

If we again assume that the relevant participation constraint is nonbinding, then we can summarize the solution to the principal's problem in

[8] The most reasonable justification for this assumption relies on an additional assumption that the return generated by a division is, in part, the current cash flow and, in part, the expectation of future cash flows. Then, even if current cash flows can be observed at the level of each division, the only objective measure of the current value of future cash flows is the firm's current stock price. However, the merged firm only has one stock price pertaining to future cash flows from both divisions. Hence, a measure of present value of future cash flows is not directly observable at the level of the individual division.

Lemma 2. *Only one of C^* and $C^{M,H}$ can be optimally positive in equilibrium, with* Prob(C^*) • $C^* = [2r(1\text{-}r\text{-}p) + p^2]/[(p\text{-}r)p']$ *and* Prob($C^{M,H}$)• $C^{M,H} = 2p/p'$. *The optimal positive payment is the* $\min\{2p/p', [2r(1\text{-}r\text{-}p) + p^2] / [(p - r)p']\}$.

Depending on parameter values, either payment contingency presented in Lemma 2 can be optimal. However, we wish to focus on the payment $C^{M,H}$ because of its simplicity. In what follows, we assume that the parameters of the model are such that $C^{M,H}$ is optimal. A sufficiency condition for $C^{M,H}$ to be optimal is

$$\text{A.4 } [2(r - r^2)]^{1/2} > p(e), \text{ for all } e.$$

The principal's problem can now be written in a very simple reduced form. Define

$$\pi(e_1, e_2) = 2rH + \Sigma p_i M + \Sigma(1 - r - p_i)L - (p_1 + p_2)/p_1' - -(p_1 + p_2)/p_2'. \tag{7}$$

Then the principal's problem is to $\underset{\{e_1,e_2\}}{Max}\ \pi(e_1,e_2)$, and the first order condition for e_1 is

$$\partial\pi/\partial e_1 = p_1'(M - L) - [(p_1')^2 - p_1''(p_2 + p_1)]/(p_1')^2 - p_1'/p_2' = 0. \tag{8}$$

The first order condition for e_2 is symmetric. Equalizing the e_i, we have that

$$p'(e^m)(M - L) = 2[1 - p(e^m)p''(e^m)/(p'(e^m))^2] = 2z(e^m) \tag{9}$$

describes the optimal e_i for each division.

The effect of merging the two firms and introducing the observability problem is apparent from equations (3) and (9). The observability problem has forced the optimal incentive contract to lump the reward for good performance into a public good performance versus a private one. In this sense, it has lowered the power of the incentive contract. The effect is to double both the total and the marginal costs of eliciting effort, at a given effort level. It is clear that equilibrium effort is less in each division of the merged firm, due to this fact. That is, $e^s > e^m$. Further, it is clear that the profit of a single division of the merged firm, $.5\pi(e,e)$, is strictly less than that of a single division firm for all levels of e. Let $.5\pi(e,e) \equiv \pi^m(e)$. We have

$$\pi^m(e) = rH + pM + (1 - r - p)L - 2p/p'$$
$$< rH + pM + (1 - r - p)L - p/p' = \pi(e), \text{ for all } e.$$

It follows that by $e^s > e^m$ and each of $\pi^m(e,)$ and $\pi(e)$ strictly concave, $\pi^m(e^m) < \pi(e^s)$. Thus, as one would expect, it is not optimal for the firms to merge, if there is an observability problem without compensating synergy. We consider this as a benchmark case only.

We want to examine how the optimal agency contract has changed as the result of merger and the unobservability problem. First consider the magnitude of the probability of a good performance at a given effort level. In a single division firm, the probability of a good performance is p, whereas in a merged firm, this probability is 2rp. For feasibility we require that $2rp < 1$ for all e. Therefore, we must assume

$$\text{A.5 } r < 1/2.$$

Under A.5, $p > 2rp$, for all e, and, in particular, $e^s > e^m$, implies $p(e^s) > 2rp(e^m)$. The effect of the observability problem is to lower the equilibrium probability of a good performance.

Next, define the *sensitivity* of the incentive contract as the magnitude of the payment for a good (discretionary) performance, in equilibrium. In this model, sensitivity is a measure of the "gradient" of the contact, because the difference between the optimal positive payment (C^M or $C^{M,H}$) and zero is the incremental benefit for a good performance. Intuition would suggest that merger would dictate that the incentive contract become more sensitive in the presence of lower powered incentives. However, this simple logic presumes a constant level of equilibrium effort and effort is of course endogenous to the contract. The unobservability problem has in fact lowered equilibrium effort by raising its marginal cost. From the above analysis, our question is formalized as

$$C^{M,H} \gtrless C^M \text{ if } p'(e^s)/p'(e^{m*}) \gtrless r, \text{ where } p'(e^s)/p'(e^{m*}) \in (0,1). \tag{10}$$

Proposition 1 summarizes our results.

Proposition 1. *In the presence of the observability problem, merger always results in a more sensitive incentive contract, which has a lower probability of a good performance by the agent. The agent's expected compensation before and after merger can rise or fall. The principal's profit must fall after merger, as does the agent's effort level.*

Proposition 1 confirms our intuition that merger with the unobservability problem results in an optimal contract with a greater incremental benefit for a good performance. However, because the equilibrium probability of a good performance must fall, the effect on the agent's expected payment is indeterminate.

3 Synergy in an Agency Context

In this section, we introduce synergy into the two-division agency model. We modify the model so that probability of the return M in the ith division is equal to $sp(e_i)$, where $s > 1$ is a parameter reflecting the amount of external synergy for division i, emanating from the other division, $j \neq i$. That is $s > 1$, if $e_{j \neq i} > 0$.[9] Because firms and divisions are assumed to be identical, s is the same across divisions. To better understand the impact of synergy, we will first consider the effect of synergy alone on the incentive contract. That is, will begin by assuming that the observability problem does not exist.

3.1 Merger with Synergy Alone

Without the observability problem, the single division firm and a single division of the merged firms have identical incentive contracts, in the sense that an agent is paid when performance M is observed. Let C^{M*} be the payment to an agent in a single division of the merged firms. In equilibrium, this payment is given by $C^{M*} = 1/sp'$ and expected cost is $sp/sp' = p/p'$. The equilibrium profit of a single division of the merged firms is

$$\pi^m(e) = rH + (1-r)L + sp(M-L) - p/p',$$

so that equilibrium effort in each division is given by the condition

$$sp'(e^m)(M-L) = z(e^m). \tag{11}$$

To economize on notation, we have used the same symbol for equilibrium effort and profit of a division of the merged firm. Comparing (11) and (3), it is immediate that $e^s < e^m$. Synergy has raised the benefit of effort without affecting its cost. Thus, equilibrium effort use increases. Because $e^m > e^s$ and each of $\pi^m(e)$ and $\pi(e)$ is strictly concave in e, it is clear that merger with synergy increases equilibrium profit, $\pi^m(e^m) > \pi(e^s)$. Further, because the expected cost function is the same before and after merger and effort after merger is greater, expected costs rise.

The probability of payment $C^{M*}$is sp, so that, by $s > 1, sp > p$, for all e. In particular, because $e^m > e^s$, $sp(e^m) > p(e^s)$. Merger with synergy raises the probability of a good performance in equilibrium.

Finally, let us consider the sensitivity of the contract before and after merger. We must compare $C^{M*} = 1/sp'(e^m)$ with $C^M = 1/p'(e^s)$. Clearly,

$$C^{M*} \gtreqless C^M \text{ as } \frac{p'(e^s)}{p'(e^m)} \gtreqless s, \tag{12}$$

where $p'(e^s)/p'(e^m) > 1$, by p' decreasing and $e^m > e^s$. We have

[9] This is a simple formulation of a beneficial externality between divisions. More general formulations are of course possible, but our intent is to present a simple and tractable illustration of the interaction of synergy and the observability problem.

Proposition 2. *Merger with synergy and without the observability problem always results in a less sensitive incentive contract, which has a greater probability of a good performance by the agent in equilibrium. The sensitivity of the optimal contract is decreasing in the synergy parameter. The principal's expected profit, the expected compensation to the agent and the agent's effort all rise after merger.*

Synergy alone has the opposite effects on the incentive contract as does the observability problem. The exception is that synergy with merger raises the agent's expected compensation whereas this effect is uncertain under the observability problem alone.

3.2 Merger with Synergy and the Observability Problem

Let us begin by considering a single representative agent's compensation under the observability problem and synergy. This is given by

$$C = rrC^H + (1 - r - sp_1)(1 - r - sp_2)C^L + [r(sp_1) + r(sp_2)]C^{M,H}$$
$$+[(1 - r - sp_1)(sp_2) + (1 - r - sp_2)(sp_1)]C^{L,M}$$
$$+[r(1 - r - sp_2) + r(1 - r - sp_1) + (sp_1)(sp_2)]C^* - e_i. \quad (13)$$

Using the same logic as in the model without synergy, we have that all payments except for $C^{M,H}$ and C^* must be zero in equilibrium. However, we again assume that the parameters are such that only $C^{M,H}$ can be positive. It suffices that

$$\text{A.6 } (s)^{-1}[2(r - r^2)]^{1/2} > p(e), \text{ for all } e,$$

hold. It is clear that A.6 implies A.4, given $s > 1$. For agent one, the reduced form incentive compatibility constraint now reads

$$rsp'_1C^{M,H} - 1 = 0. \quad (14)$$

The expected payment to agent one is then $[r(sp_1) + r(sp_2)]/(rsp'_1) = (p_1 + p_2)/(p'_1)$. Agent two's expected payment is symmetric. Using the same logic as in the problem without synergy, we can write the principal's problem as

$$\pi(e_1, e_2) = 2rH + 2(1 - r)L + \Sigma(sp_i)(M - L) - \Sigma(p_1 + p_2)/(p'_i). \quad (15)$$

The principal then sets

$$\partial\pi/\partial e_1 = (sp'_1)(M - L) - \{[(p'_1)^2 - (p''_1)(p_1 + p_2)]/(p'_1)^2\}$$
$$+ (p_1')/(p_2') = 0. \quad (16)$$

The first order condition for e_2 is symmetric. Equalizing the e_i, we can write this condition as

$$sp'(e^m)(M - L) - 2z(e^m) = 0. \tag{17}$$

Equation (17) describes the optimal effort choice for each division, denoted e^m.

Synergy has changed the firm's reduced form profit function in a way that it increases the net benefit of effort in each division. Equalizing the e_i, we can write the reduced form profit of a single division and compare this to the case of no synergy as follows:

$$\pi^m(e) = rH + spM + (1 - r - p)L - 2p/p' > rH + pM + (1 - r - p)L - 2p/p',$$

for all e. The new marginal benefit of effort is increased due to synergy as shown in (14) or alternatively the effective marginal cost of effort has been reduced. The observability problem has then been dampened.

The equilibrium amount of effort chosen by a division of a merged firm with synergy can be compared to that of a single division firm. Whether effort under unobservability and synergy is less or greater depends on the magnitude of that synergy. From (17), the marginal benefit of effort can be written as p'(e)(M-L) and its effective marginal cost is $(2/s)z(e^m)$. The observability problem has doubled effort's marginal cost and synergy reduces this effect. Whether effort's effective marginal cost is greater or less after merger as opposed to pre-merger, depends on whether s is less or greater than 2. Because the above marginal benefit of effort is the same before and after merger, we have

$$e^m \gtreqless e^s \text{ if } s \gtreqless 2, \text{ where } s > 1. \tag{18}$$

Next, consider how merger with synergy affects the sensitivity and the probability of a good performance by the agent. The effect on sensitivity of the contract is described by the condition

$$C^{M,H} \gtreqless C^M \text{ if } p'(e^s)/p'(e^m) \gtreqless sr. \tag{19}$$

The probability of the payment $C^{M,H}$ is 2rsp. For the latter to be less than unity for all e, we assume, for feasibility,

A.7 2 sr < 1.

Given that $s > 1$, A.7 implies that $r < 1/2$. For feasible parameter values, the combination of the observability problem and synergy results in $2rsp < p$, for all e. If $s \in (1, 2]$, then we saw, from (18), that $e^s \geq e^m$. For this case, it follows that $2rsp(e^m) < p(e^s)$, and the probability of good performance by the agent is decreased by merger. On the other hand, using the same logic, if $s > 2$, then $e^m > e^s, p(e^m) > p(e^s)$, and it is unclear whether the probability of a good performance by the agent is increased or decreased by merger. We have

Proposition 3. *(i) In the presence of the observability problem, merger always results in a more sensitive incentive contract, regardless of the level of synergy.*

(ii) The equilibrium probability of a good performance by the agent is less after merger, if synergy does not swamp the unobservability problem ($s \in (1,2]$). In this case, the equilibrium effort of the agent satisfies $e^m \leq e^s$ as s is ≤ 2, and the expected compensation to the agent can rise or fall after merger.

(iii) The effect of merger on the probability of a good performance by the agent is indeterminate, if the level of synergy is sufficient to swamp the observability problem ($s > 2$). For $s > 2$, merger results in an increase in the agent's effort and his expected compensation, and each of these equilibrium values as well as the sensitivity of the optimal contract is increasing in the synergy parameter.

Our final result is concerned with the profitability of merger for the case where the observability problem and synergy coexist.

Proposition 4. *If the observability problem is present, there exists a feasible value of the synergy parameter $s^m \in (1,2)$ for which merger is minimally profitable. That is, $\pi^m(e^m) \geq \pi(e^s)$ for $s \geq s^m$ and conversely for $s < s^m$.*

Concluding Remarks

Synergistic merger has the effects of increasing profit, increasing the agent's expected compensation, increasing the agent's effort, and decreasing the sensitivity of the optimal incentive contract. However, the observability problem reverses all but one of these effects (The impact on the agent's expected compensation is uncertain.) When we combine synergistic merger with the observability problem, we place greater requirements on the level of synergy for there to be profitable merger. Many of the above intuitive effects of synergistic merger are dampened. For synergistic merger to raise profit, increase the agent's effort and increase the agent's expected compensation, synergy must be of sufficient magnitude to overcome the observability problem. Ignoring the latter problem can lead to an over estimate of the benefits of merger.

Finally, Propositions 1 through 3 can be used to arrive at two empirically testable predictions. First, if the post merger contract is less sensitive, then the observability problem is essentially nonexistent and we would expect the merger to be profitable. A second empirical implication is that if the contract after merger is more sensitive and the expected compensation of the agent is greater, then synergy is overcoming the observability problem and the merger should be a profitable one.

Appendix

Proof of Lemma 1: Since equal contingent payments apply to both agents, in equilibrium $e_1 = e_2$. Then, the first order conditions for the principal's choice of contingent payments are as follows:

$$-r + \gamma^H = 0 \Rightarrow \gamma^H > 0 \text{ and } C^H = 0. \tag{i}$$

$$-(1 - r - p) - \mu p' - \gamma^L = 0. \tag{ii}$$

$$-p + \mu p' + \gamma^M = 0. \tag{iii}$$

We know that from the incentive compatibility constraint, it must be that $C^M > C^L = 0$. Thus, from (iii), $\gamma^M = 0$ and $\mu = p/p' > 0$. Whence, (ii) implies that $C^L = 0$. From the incentive compatibility constraint, $C^M = 1/p'$, so that the principal's expected cost is p/p'. The principal's first order condition for effort is $p'(M - L) - p'C^M + \mu p''C^M = 0$. Substituting $\mu = p/p'$ and $p'C^m = 1$ from the incentive compatibility constraint, we have that the equilibrium e is defined by $p'(M - L) = 1 - p''p/(p')^2 > 1.||$

Proof of Lemma 2: Because both divisions are identical, we can consider the first order conditions for agent one and use symmetry to determine those of agent two.

$$C^H : -rr + \gamma^H = 0 \Rightarrow \gamma^H > 0 \text{ and } C^H = 0.$$

$$C^L : -(1 - r - p_1)(1 - r - p_2) - p_1'(1 - r - p_2) + \gamma^L = 0 \Rightarrow \gamma^L > 0 \text{ and } C^L = 0.$$

$$C^{L,M} : -[(1 - r - p_1)p_2 + p_1(1 - r - p_2)] + \mu_1 p_1'(1 - r - 2p_2) + \gamma^{L,M} = 0.$$

$$C^* : -[r(1 - r - p_2) + (1 - r - p_1)r + p_1 p_2] + \mu_1 p_1'(p_2 - r) + \gamma^* = 0.$$

$$C^{M,H} : -(rp_1 + rp_2) + \mu p_1' r + \gamma^{M,H} = 0.$$

Above, we have shown that C^H and C^L are optimally zero. Next, we consider the remaining payments. First consider $C^{L,M}$. If $(1 - r - 2p_2) \leq 0$ then from the above first order condition $\gamma^{L,M} \sim> 0$ and $C^{L,M} = 0$. Next suppose that $(1 - r - 2p_2) > 0$. Then we have that

$$[(1 - r - p_1)p_2 + p_1(1 - r - p_2)]/[p_1'(1 - r - 2p_2)] \geq \mu/(1 - \lambda).$$

Noting that in equilibrium $p_1 = p_2$ this condition can be written as

$$2p(1 - r - p)/[p'(1 - r - 2p)] \geq \mu/(1 - \lambda).$$

From the first order condition for $C^{M,H}$ we have

$$2p/p' \geq \mu/(1 - \lambda).$$

However,

$(1-r-p)/[(1-r-2p)] > 1$, so that $2p(1-r-p)/[p'(1-r-2p)] > \mu/(1-\lambda)$.

It follows that $C^{L,M} = 0$. We can conclude that only C^* and $C^{M,H}$ can be positive.

Let us focus on the possible positive payments. The first order conditions for these payments can be written as

$$C* : [2r(1-r-p)+p^2]/[(p-r)p'] \geq \mu/(1-\lambda)$$

with strict inequality implying $C^* = 0$.

$$C^{M,H} : 2p/p' \geq \mu/(1-\lambda) \text{ with strict inequality implying } C^{M,H} = 0.$$

It follows that the positive payment is the $\min\{2p/p', [2r(1-r-p)+p^2]/[(p-r)p']\}$.||

Proof of Proposition 1: From (10) we need to show that $p'(e^s)/p'(e^m) > r$. Using the FOC to optimal effort choice, we can rewrite this condition as $TRIALRESTRICTION$ We have that $e^s > e^m$ and that z is nondecreasing. Further, from feasibility, $r < 1/2$. We have $TRIALRESTRICTION$ Whence, $C^{M,H} > C^M$.

All that remains to be shown is that the principal's expected payment can rise or fall under merger. To see this, consider an example. Let $p = 1-\exp(-e)$ and define $(M-L) \equiv \Delta$. Before merger, expected compensation is $p(e^s)/p'(e^s) = \exp(e^s)-1$, where $e^s = .5(\ln \Delta)$. After merger, expected compensation is $p(e^m)/p'(e^m) = 2[\exp(e^m) - 1]$, where $e^m = .5\ln(\Delta/2)$. Thus, we compare pre-merger expected cost $\exp(.5(\ln\Delta)) - 1$ to post merger expected cost $2[\exp(.5\ln(\Delta/2)) - 1]$. If $\Delta = 6$, then post-merger expected cost is greater. If $\Delta = 5$, then the opposite is true. In each of these cases if $r = .3$, then all of our assumptions are met. ||

Proof of Proposition 2: Using condition (12), we need to show $p'(e^s)/sp'(e^m) < 1$. Substituting from condition (11), this becomes $z(e^s)/z(e^m) < 1$. Given A.2, z is increasing in e. Further, $e^s < e^m$. It follows that $z(e^s)/z(e^m) < 1$, and that this ratio is decreasing in s. Because p/p' is an increasing function, $e^m > e^s$ implies that the expected compensation to the agent is greater after merger. ||

Proof of Proposition 3: First suppose that $s \in (1,2)$. Using condition (17) and condition (19), $C^{M,H} > C^M$ if $z(e^s)/2z(e^m) > r$. Because $e^s > e^m$ and z is increasing, $z(e^s) > z(e^m)$. Thus, $z(e^s)/2z(e^m) > 1/2 > r$.

Next, suppose that $s \geq 2$. From (18), $e^m \geq e^s$. Using (19), $C^{M,H} > C^M$, if $p'(e^s)/p'(e^m) > sr$. If $e^m \geq e^s$, then because p' is positive and decreasing, $p'(e^s)/p'(e^m) \geq 1 > sr$. The ratio $p'(e^s)/p'(e^m)$ is increasing in s. Thus, sensitivity and effort in the merged firm become greater as s increases.

All that remains to be considered is the impact of merger on expected costs of the principal. If $s \leq 2$, then while sensitivity increases with merger, effort and the probability of a good performance decrease. We can use the example used in the proof of Proposition 1, to show that the expected payment to the principal can rise or fall. With synergy, expected cost before merger is $\exp(.5(\ln \Delta)) - 1$ and expected cost after merger is $2[\exp(.5\ln(s\Delta/2)) - 1]$. For $s = 1.1$, post merger expected cost is less if $\Delta = 3$, but it is greater if $\Delta = 5$. In each of these cases, if $r = .4$, the assumptions of our model hold. If $s > 2$, then expected cost in the merged firm is greater after merger, because $s > 2$ implies that $e^m > e^s$. By $2p/p' > p/p'$, for all e, and by p/p' increasing, it follows that $2p(e^m)/p'(e^m) > p(e^s)/p'(e^s)$. Further, it is clear that as synergy increases expected costs become greater in the merged firm.||

Proof of Proposition 4: Using the envelope theorem, we find that $d\pi^m(e^m(s))/ds = p(e^m)(M - L) > 0$. The function $\pi^m(e^m(s))$ is then increasing and continuous in s, while $\pi(e^s)$ is invariant with respect to s. If we can show that $\exists$ a feasible s at which $\pi^m(e^m(s)) < \pi(e^s)$ and a feasible s at which the converse holds, then, by the intermediate value theorem for continuous functions, there is an s* such that $\pi^m(e^m(s*)) = \pi(e^s)$. Further, for $s < s*$, it would be true that $\pi^m(e^m(s)) < \pi(e^s)$, while, for s > $s*$, we would have that $\pi^m(e^m(s)) > \pi(e^s)$.

Set $s = 1$ in the merged firm. Then $\pi^m(e) > \pi(e)$, for all e. It is further true that $e^s > e^m$ and each of these functions is strictly concave in e. Thus, for $e \in [e^m, e^s]$, $\pi^m(e)$ is decreasing in e, while $\pi(e)$ is increasing in e. It follows that $\pi^m(e^m(s)) < \pi(e^s)$.

For each e, take the difference $\pi^m(e) - \pi(e) = p(e)(s-1) - p/p'$. Let $\hat{e}$ be the e which sets this differences to zero. We have $(s-1)(M-L) = 1/p'(\hat{e})$. the function $1/p'(e)$ is strictly increasing in e. Thus, for $e > \hat{e}, \pi^m(e) < \pi(e)$, and, for $e < \hat{e}, \pi^m(e) > \pi(e)$.

Set $s = 2$, Then $e^m = e^s$. $e^s = e^m$ is defined by $(M - L) = z(1/p')$, with $z > 1$, for all e. e^ is defined by $(M - L) = 1/p'$, in this case. By $z > 1$ and $1/p'$ increasing, e^ $> e^s = e^m$. Thus, it follows that $\pi^m(\mathrm{e}^m(\mathrm{s})) > \pi(\mathrm{e}^s)$. The point s* then exists and the result holds. ||

References

Aron, D. J., "Ability, Moral Hazard, Firm Size, and Diversification", *Rand Journal of Economics*, **19**(1) (1988), 72–87.

Baumol, W. J., *Business Behavior, Value and Growth.* New York: Harcourt, Brace and World, 1967.

Cusatis, P. J., J. A. Miles and J. R. Woolridge , "Restructuring through Spin-offs", *Journal of Financial Economics*, **33**(3) (1993), 293–311.

Diamond, D. W. and R. E. Verrecchia, "Optimal Managerial Contracts and Equilibrium Security Prices", *The Journal of Finance*, **37** (1982), 275–288.

Michael Goold and Andrew Campbell, "Desperately Seeking Synergy," *Harvard Business Review*, **76**(5) (1998), 130–143.

B.E. Hermalin and M.L. Katz, Corporate Diverisification and Agency, September 1996.

Kaplan, S. N. and M. S. Weisbach, "The Success of Acquisitions: Evidence from Divestitures", Journal of Finance, **47**(1) (1992), 107,138.

Levitt, S. D. and C. M. Synder, "Is NoNews Bad News? Information Transmission and the Role of Early Warning in the Principal-Agent Model", *Rand Journal of Economics*, **28**(4) (1997), 641–661.

Marshall, W. J., J.B. Yawitz and E. Greenberg, "Incentives for Diversification and the Structure of the Conglomerate Firm", *Southern Economic Journal*, **51** (1985), 1–23.

R. H. McGuckin and S.V. Nguyen, On Productivity and Plant Ownership Change: New Evidence from the Longitudinal Research Database, *Rand Journal of Economics*, **26**(2) (1995), 257–276.

Mueller, D. C., "A Theory of Competitive Mergers", *Quarterly Journal of Economics*, **83** (1969), 643–659.

Roll, R., "The Hubris Hypothesis of Corporate Takeovers", *Journal of Business*, **59** (1986), 197–216.

Shleifer, A. and Vishny, R. W., "Management Entrenchment: The Case of Manager Specific Investments," *Journal of Financial Economics*, **25** (1989), 123–139.

Stigler, G. J., "Monopoly and Oligopoly by Merger," *American Economic Review*, **40** (1950), 23–34.

Williamson, O. E., *The Economic Institutions of Capitalism.* New York: The Free Press, 1985.

The Le Chatelier Principle in Data Envelopment Analysis

W. Erwin Diewert[1] and M. Nimfa F. Mendoza[2]

[1] Department of Economics, University of British Columbia, Vancouver, B.C., Canada, V6T 1Z1. diewert@econ.ubc.ca

[2] School of Economics, University of the Philipines-Diliman, Manila, The Philippines. nimfa.mendoza@up.edu.ph

Summary. The paper gives a brief review of the nonparametric approach to efficiency measurement or Data Envelopment Analysis as it is known in the operations research literature. Inequalities are derived between the efficiency measures when different assumptions are made on the technology sets or on the behavior of managers. Of particular interest is the derivation of a Le Chatelier Principle for measures of allocative inefficiency. Finally, the various inequalities are illustrated using some Canadian data, which is also used to compare DEA methods for measuring the relative efficiency of production units with more traditional index number methods.

Key words: efficiency measurement, data envelopment analysis, Le Chatelier Principle, productivity, nonparametric measurement of technology, index numbers.

Classification code: C14, C43, C61, D61

1 Introduction

Data Envelopment Analysis or (DEA) is the term used by Charnes and Cooper (1985) and their co-workers to denote an area of analysis which is called the nonparameteric approach to production theory[3] or the measurement of the efficiency of production[4] by economists.

In section 2, we will provide an introduction to the theory of benchmarking and the measurement of relative efficiency of production units. Section 3 develops measures of relative efficiency that use only quantity data. These measures are particularly useful in the context of measuring the efficiency of government owned enterprises or units of the general government sector that

[3] See Hanoch and Rothschild (1972), Diewert (1981), Diewert and Parkan (1983) and Varian (1984). It should be noted that in recent times, the term "nonparametric approach to production theory" has sometimes included index number methods for defining the relative efficiency of production units.

[4] See Farrell (1957), Afriat (1972), Färe and Lovell (1978), Färe, Grosskopf and Lovell (1985) and Coelli, Prasada Rao and Battese (1997). The last two books provide a good overview of the subject.

deliver services to the public for free or for prices that do not reflect costs of production. Efficiency measures that use only quantity data (and not price data) are also useful in the regulatory context[5] Section 4 develops measures of relative efficiency for production units in the same industry where reliable price and quantity data are available for the units in the sample. Section 5 notes some relationships between the various efficiency measures developed in the previous two sections. In particular, an efficiency measurement analogue to Samuelson's (1947; 36–39) Le Chatelier Principle is developed in section 5.

Mendoza (1989) undertook an empirical comparison of 3 different methods for measuring productivity change in the context of time series data for Canada. The 3 different methods of comparison she considered were: (i) a nonparametric or DEA method; (ii) traditional index number methods and (iii) an econometric method based on the estimation of a unit profit function[6] In section 6 we will compare the DEA and index number approaches to efficiency measurement using some more recent aggregate Canadian data and we also illustrate the theoretical Rules developed in previous sections.

Drawing on the empirical and theoretical results reviewed in the previous sections, in section 7 we compare the advantages and disadvantages of DEA methods for measuring the relative efficiency of production units with the more traditional index number and econometric methods.

2 An Introduction to the Nonparametric Measurement of Efficiency

The basic idea in the case of similar firms producing one output and using 2 inputs is due to Farrell (1957; 254). Let there be K firms, denote the output of firm k by $y^k \geq 0$ and denote the amounts of inputs 1 and 2 used by firm k by $x_1^k \geq 0$ and $x_2^k \geq 0$ respectively, for $k = 1,2,\ldots, K$. Calculate the *input-output coefficients* for each firm defined by x_1^k/y^k and x_2^k/y^k for $k = 1, 2, \ldots$, K. Now plot these pairs of input output coefficients in a two dimensional diagram as in Figure 1 where we have labeled these pairs as the points P^1, $P^2, \ldots$, P^5 (so that $k = 5$).

The convex hull of the 5 data points $P^1, \ldots$, P^5 in Figure 1 is the shaded set: it is the set of all non-negative weighted averages of the 5 points where the weights sum up to 1. The convex free disposal hull of the original 5 points is the shaded set plus all of the points that lie to the north and east of the shaded

[5] See Diewert (1981).

[6] For material on variable and unit profit functions, see Diewert (1973) (1974) and Diewert and Wales (1992). Coelli, Prasada Rao and Battese (1997) also compared the three approaches to the measurement of efficiency. Balk (1998; 179–209) also compared the three approaches. Diewert (1980) was perhaps the first to contrast the three approaches and he also included a fourth approach: the Divisia approach. The index number approach was reviewed in detail by Diewert and Nakamura (2003).

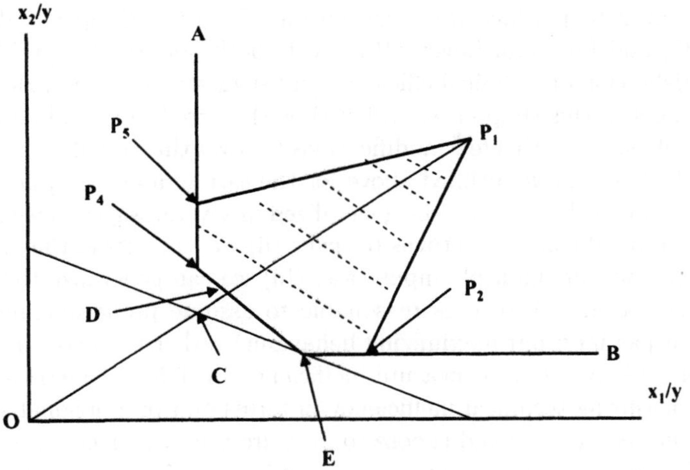

set. Farrell took the boundary or frontier of this set as an approximation to the unit output isoquant of the underlying production function[7] In Figure 1, this frontier set is the piecewise linear curve AP^4P^3B. The *Farrell technical efficiency* of the point P^1 was defined to be the ratio of distances OD/OP^1, since this is the fraction (of both inputs) that an efficient firm could use to produce the same output as that produced by Firm 1. A point Pi is regarded as being *technically efficient* if its technical efficiency is unity.

Farrell (1957; 254) noted the formal similarity of his definition of technical efficiency to Debreu's (1951) coefficient of resource utilization.

Farrell (1957; 255) also defined two further efficiency concepts using a diagram similar to Figure 1. Suppose Firm 1 faced the fixed input prices w_1 and w_2 for the two inputs. Then we could form a family of isocost lines with slope w_1/w_2 and find the lowest such isocost line that is just tangent to the free disposal convex hull of the 5 points. In Figure 1, this is the line CE which is tangent to the point P^3. Farrell noted that even if the point P^1 were shrunk in towards the origin to end up at the technically efficient point D, the resulting point would still not be the cost minimizing input combination (which is at P^3). Thus Farrell defined the *price efficiency* of P^1 as the ratio of distances OC/OD. Finally, Farrell (1957; 255) defined the *overall efficiency* of Firm 1 as the ratio of distances OC/OP^1. This measure incorporates both technical and allocative inefficiency. A point Pi is *overall efficient* if its overall efficiency is unity.

There is a problem with Farrell's measure of technical efficiency: Farrell's definition makes the points P^2 and P^5 in Figure 1 technically efficient when it seems clear that they are not: P^2 is dominated by P^3 which uses less of input 1 to produce the same output and P^5 is dominated by P^4 which uses

---

[7] Farrell (1957; 254) was assuming constant returns to scale in this part of his paper.

less of input 2 to produce the same output. Charnes, Cooper and Rhodes (1978; 437) and Färe and Lovell (1978; 151) both noticed this problem with Farrell's definition of technical efficiency and suggested remedies. However, in the remainder of this chapter we will stick with Farrell's original definition of technical efficiency, with a few modifications to cover the case of many outputs.

Farrell's basic ideas outlined above for the case of a one output, constant returns to scale technology can be generalized in several ways: (i) we can relax the assumption of constant returns to scale; (ii) we can extend the analysis to the multiple output, multiple input case; (iii) we can generalize the analysis to cover situations where it is reasonable to assume profit maximizing behaviour (or partial profit maximizing behaviour) rather than cost minimizing behaviour and (iv) we can measure inefficiency in different metrics (i.e., instead of measuring technical inefficiency in terms of a proportional shrinkage of the input vector, we could choose to measure the inefficiency in terms of a basket of outputs or a basket of outputs and inputs). Drawing on the work of Mendoza (1989) and others, we shall indicate how the above generalizations (i)–(iii) can be implemented for the case of technologies that produce only 2 outputs and utilize only 2 inputs. The generalization to many outputs and inputs is straightforward. Section 3 below covers approaches that use only quantity data while section 4 describes approaches that utilize both price and quantity data. Section 5 draws on the results of the previous two sections and notes some interesting general relationships between various measures of efficiency loss. Of particular interest is a Le Chatelier Principle for measures of allocative inefficiency.

3 Efficiency Tests Using Only Quantity Data

3.1 The Case of a Convex Technology

Suppose that we have quantity data on k production units that are producing 2 outputs using 2 inputs. Let $y_m^k \geq 0$ denote the amount of output m produced by each production unit (or firm or plant) j for $m = 1, 2$, and let $x_n^k \geq 0$ denote the amount of input n used by firm k for $n = 1, 2$ and $k = 1, 2, \ldots, K$.

We assume that each firm has access to the same basic technology except for efficiency differences. An approximation to the basic technology is defined to be the convex free disposal hull of the observed quantity data $\{(y_1^k, y_2^k, x_1^k, x_2^k) : k = 1, \ldots, K\}$. This technology assumption is consistent with decreasing returns to scale (and constant returns to scale) but it is *not* consistent with increasing returns to scale.

It is necessary to specify a *direction* in which possible inefficiencies are measured; i.e., do we measure the inefficiency of observation i in terms of output m or input n or some combination of outputs and inputs? Mendoza's (1989) methodology allowed for an arbitrary efficiency direction[8] but for simplicity,

[8] See Mendoza (1989; 25–30).

we will restrict ourselves to the Debreu (1951)–Farrell (1957) direction; i.e., we shall measure the inefficiency of observation i by the smallest positive fraction δ_i^* of the ith input vector (x_1^i, x_2^i) which is such that $\{(y_1^k, y_2^k, \delta_i^* x_1^k, \delta_i^* x_2^k)$ is on the efficient frontier spanned by the convex free disposal hull of the k observations. If the ith observation is efficient relative to this frontier, then $\delta_i^* = 1$; the smaller δ_i^* is, then the lower is the efficiency of the ith observation. The number δ_i^* can be determined as the optimal objective function of the following linear programming problem[9]:

$$\begin{aligned}\delta_i^* = min_{\delta_i \geq 0, \lambda_1 \geq 0, \ldots, \lambda k \geq 0}\{\delta_i : \textstyle\sum_{k=1}^K y_1^k \lambda_k \geq y_1^i ; \sum_{k=1}^K y_2^k \lambda k \geq y_2^i ;\\ \textstyle\sum_{k=1}^K x_1^k \lambda_k \leq \delta_i x_1^i ; \sum_{k=1}^K x_2^k \lambda_k \leq \delta_i x_2^i ;_{k=1}^K \lambda_k = 1\}.\end{aligned} \tag{1}$$

Thus we look for a convex combination of the K data points that can produce at least the observation i combination of outputs (y_1^i, y_2^i) and use only δ_i times the observation i combination of inputs (x_1^i, x_2^i). The smallest such δ_i is δ_i^*.

The linear programming problems (1) are run for each observation i and the resulting $\delta_i^* \geq 0$, serves to measure the relative efficiency of observation i; if $\delta_i^* = 1$, then observation i is efficient. At least one of the J observations will be efficient.

We turn now to the corresponding linear program that tests for efficiency under the maintained hypothesis that the underlying technology is subject to constant returns to scale (in addition to being convex).

3.2 The Case of a Convex, Constant Returns to Scale Technology

In this case, the approximation to the underlying technology set is taken to be the free disposal hull of the convex cone spanned by the K data points. The efficiency of observation i is measured by the positive fraction δ_i^{**} of the ith input vector (x_1^i, x_2^i) which is such that $(y_1^k, y_2^k, \delta_i^{**} x_1^k, \delta_i^{**} x_2^k)$ is on the efficient frontier spanned by the conical convex free disposal hull of the K observations. The efficiency of the ith observation relative to this technology set can be calculated by solving the following linear program:

$$\begin{aligned}\delta_i^{**} = min_{\delta_i \geq 0, \lambda_1 \geq 0, \ldots, \lambda_K \geq 0}\{\delta_i \text{ subject to: } \textstyle\sum_{k=1}^K y_1^k \lambda_k \geq y_1^i ; \sum_{k=1}^K y_2^k \lambda_k \geq y_2^i ;\\ \textstyle\sum_{k=1}^K x_1^k \lambda_k \leq \delta_i x_1^i ; \sum_{k=1}^K x_2^k \lambda_k \leq \delta_i x_2^i ; \}.\end{aligned} \tag{2}$$

Note that the LP (2) is the same as (1) except that the constraint $\sum_{k=1}^K \lambda_k = 1$ has been dropped. Thus the optimal solution for (1) is feasible

[9] See Mendoza (1989; 30) for a general version of Test 1. The use of linear programming techniques to calculate nonparametric efficiencies was first suggested by Hoffman (1957; 284) and first used by Farrell and Fieldhouse (1962). Related tests are due to Afriat (1972; 571) and Diewert and Parkan (1983; 141).

for (2) and thus $\delta_i^{**} \leq \delta_i^*$; i.e., the constant returns to scale measure of efficiency for observation i will be equal to or less than the convex technology measure of inefficiency for observation i.

We turn now to models that are consistent with increasing returns to scale.

3.3 Quasiconcave Technologies

We first need to define what we mean by a production possibilities set $L(y_1)$ that is conditional on an amount y_1 of output 1. Let S be the set of feasible outputs and inputs. Then $L(y_1)$ is defined to be the set of (y_2, x_1, x_2) such that $(y1, y_2, x_1, x_2)$ belongs to S; i.e., $L(y_1)$ is the set of other outputs y_2 and inputs x_1 and x_2 that are consistent with the production of y_1 units of output 1. We assume that the family of production possibilities sets $L(y_2)$ has the following three properties: (i) for each $y1 \geq 0$, $L(y_1)$ is a closed, convex set[10] (ii) if $y_1' \leq y_1''$, then $L(y_1)$ is a subset of $L(y_1)$ and (iii) the sets $L(y_1)$ exhibit free disposal.

For each observation i, define the following set of indexes:

$$I_1^i \equiv \{k : y_1^k \geq y_1^i, k = 1, 2, \ldots, K\}; \tag{3}$$

i.e., I_1^i is the set of observations k such that the amount of output 1 produced by observation k is equal to or greater than the amount of output 1 produced by observation i. Note that observation i must belong to I_1^i.

Given our assumptions on the underlying technology, it can be seen that the free disposal convex hull of the points $(y_2^j, x_1^j, x_2^j), j \in I_1^i$, forms an approximation to the set $L(y_1^i)$. The frontier of this set is taken to be the efficient set. As usual, we measure the efficiency of observation i by the positive fraction δ_i^{**} of the ith input vector (x_1^i, x_2^i) which is such that $\{(y_2^k, \delta_i^{**} x_1^k, \delta_i^{**} x_2^k)$ is on the efficient frontier defined above. The number can be calculated by solving the following linear program[11]:

$$\begin{aligned} \delta_i^{**} = min_{\delta_i \geq 0, \lambda_1 \geq 0, \ldots, \lambda_K \geq 0} \{\delta_i : \textstyle\sum_{k \in I_i^i} y_2^k \lambda_k \geq y_2^i; \sum_{k \in I_i^i} x_1^k \lambda_k \leq \delta_i x_1^i; \\ \textstyle\sum_{k \in I_i^i} x_2^k \lambda_k \leq \delta_i x_2^i; \sum_{k \in I_i^i} \lambda_k = 1\} \quad . \end{aligned} \tag{4}$$

On the left hand side of each constraint in (4), the indexes k must belong to the index set I_1^i defined by (3) above.

---

[10] If we represent the underlying technology by means of the production function $y_1 = f(y_2, x_1, x_2)$, assumption (i) implies that f is a quasiconcave function.

[11] See Mendoza (1989; 54) for a general version of (4) which she called Test 3. The one output quasiconcavity test is due to Hanoch and Rothschild (1972; 259–261). Diewert (1980; 264)(1981) and Diewert and Parkan (1983; 140) developed alternative methods for dealing with a quasiconcave technology but the present method seems preferable.

Denote the optimal k for (4) above by λ_k^{***} for $k \in I_1^i$. By the last constraint in (4), we have

$$\sum_{k \in I_i^i} \lambda_k^{***} = 1; \tag{5}$$

Using definition (3), $\lambda_k^{***} \geq 0$ and (5), it can be seen that

$$\sum_{k \in I_i^i} y_1^k \lambda_k \geq y_1^i. \tag{6}$$

Using (1), (4) and (6), we see that the optimal solution for (4) is feasible for (1) and thus we must have $\delta_i^* \leq \delta_i^{***}$. Recall that we showed that $\delta_i^{**} \leq \delta_i^*$ and so we have

$$0 \leq \delta_i^{**} \leq \delta_i^* \leq \delta_i^{***}. \tag{7}$$

Thus the efficiency measures generally *increase* (or remain constant) as we make *weaker* assumptions on the underlying technology: the biggest efficiency measure δ_i^{***} corresponds to a quasiconcave (in output 1)[12] technology, the next measure δ_i^* corresponds to a convex technology, and the smallest efficiency measure δ_i^{**} corresponds to a constant returns to scale convex technology.

In definition (3) and in the LP (4), output 1 was singled out to play a special role. Obviously, analogues to (3) and (4) could be constructed where output 2 played the asymmetric role. In this latter case, the underlying technological assumption is that the $y_2 = f(y_1, x_1, x_2)$ production function is quasiconcave. This is a somewhat different technological assumption than our initial one, but both assumptions are consistent with an increasing returns to scale technology[13].

The last paragraph raises two questions:

- What is the motivation for imposing quasiconcavity on all of the inputs and all but one of the outputs?
- How exactly is the researcher to choose which output is to be singled out to play an asymmetric role in the above efficiency measure?

These are difficult to answer questions. In the one output, many input context, we routinely assume quasiconcave technologies, at least in part, because a non quasiconcave technology cannot be identified using observable price and quantity data if producers are competitively minimizing costs. If we carry this line of reasoning over to the case of many outputs, then if the production units in the relevant peer group are competitively minimizing costs and competitively selling all of their outputs except one, then that non competitively supplied

[12] Thus δ_i^{***} should be more accurately denoted by δ_{i1}^{***} in order to indicate that we are assuming quasiconcavity with respect to output 1.

[13] Mendoza's (1989; 54) Test 3 can also be modified to model quasiconcave technologies of the form $x_1 = g(y_1, y_2, x_2)$, where g is now a factor requirements function.

output should be singled out in the above test to play the asymmetric role. However, strictly speaking, under these hypotheses, we should move on to the tests for efficiency in subsequent sections, where we assume some form of competitive pricing behavior. In general, we cannot offer definitive advice on which output should be singled out to play an asymmetric role in the above efficiency test: the researcher will perhaps have to rely on engineering considerations to single out the output which is most likely to be subject to increasing returns to scale or perhaps just pick the most important output (in terms of market share) as the numeraire output.

This completes our overview of nonparametric efficiency tests that involve the use of quantity data. We now turn to tests that involve both price and quantity data so that overall efficiency measures can be constructed in place of the technical efficiency measures of this section.

4 Efficiency Tests Using Price and Quantity Data

4.1 The Convex Technology Case

We make the same assumptions on the underlying technology as in section 3.1 above. However, we now assume that each producer may be either minimizing cost or maximizing profits[14] We consider each case in turn.

Case (i): Cost Minimization:

We assume that producer k faces the input prices (w_1k, w_2k) for the two inputs. To determine whether producer i is minimizing cost subject to our convex technology assumptions, we solve the following linear program[15]:

$$min_{\delta_i \geq 0, \lambda_1 \geq 0, \ldots, \lambda_K \geq 0} \{ w_1^i (\sum_{k=1}^{K} x_1^k \lambda_k) + w_2^i (\sum_{k=1}^{K} x_2^k \lambda_k) : \sum_{k=1}^{K} y_1^k \lambda_k \geq y_1^i;$$

$$\sum_{k=1}^{K} y_2^k \lambda_k \geq y_2^i; \sum_{k=1}^{K} \lambda_k = 1 \} \tag{8}$$

$$\equiv \epsilon_i^* [w_1^i x_1^i + w_2^i x_2^i]. \tag{9}$$

The meaning of (9) is that we define the overall efficiency measure ϵ_i^* for observation i by equating (9) to the optimized objective function in (8). If we set $\lambda_i = 1$ and the other $\lambda_k = 0$, we have a feasible solution for (8) which yields a value of the objective function equal to $w_1^i x_1^i + w_2^i x_2^i$. Thus $0 < \epsilon_i^* \leq 1$. The number ϵ_i^* can be interpreted as the fraction of (x_1^i, x_2^i) which is such that

[14] In contrast to the technical efficiency measures defined in section 2 where at least one observation had to be efficient (with an efficiency score of 1), in this section, it can be the case that no observation is efficient.

[15] See Mendoza (1989; 67) for a general version of (8) which she called Test 4.

$\epsilon_i^*(x_1^i, x_2^i)$ on the minimum cost isocost line for observation i; i.e., ϵ_i^* is an analogue to the overall efficiency measure OC/OP[1] which occurred in Figure 1. Comparing (1) and (8), it can be seen that the optimal λ_k^* solution for (1) is a feasible solution for (8) and thus:

$$0 < \epsilon_i^* \le \delta_i^*. \tag{10}$$

The second inequality in (10) simply reflects the fact that overall efficiency ϵ_i^* is equal to or less than technical efficiency δ_i^* (recall Figure 1 again).

Case (ii):Profit Maximization:

We now assume that firm i also faces the positive output prices (p_1^i, p_2^i) for the two outputs. To determine whether producer i is maximizing profits subject to our convex technology assumptions; we solve the following linear program[16]:

$$max_{\lambda_1 \ge 0, \ldots, \lambda_K \ge 0}\{\sum_{m=1}^{2} p_m^i(\sum_{k=1}^{K} y_m^k \lambda_k) - (\sum_{k=1}^{K} x_n^k \lambda_k) : \sum_{k=1}^{K} \lambda_k = 1\} \tag{11}$$

$$\equiv p_1^i y_1^i + p_2^i y_2^i - \alpha_i^*[w_1^i x_1^i + w_2^i x_2^i]. \tag{12}$$

Equating (11) to (12) defines the efficiency measure α_i^* for observation i. If we set $\lambda_i = 1$ in (11) and the other $\lambda_k = 0$, we obtain a feasible value for the objective function equal to $p_1^i y_1^i + p_2^i y_2^i - [w_1^i x_1^i + w_2^i x_2^i]$. Thus $\alpha_i^* = 1$. If $\alpha_i^* = 1$, then observation i is efficient relative to our assumptions on the technology and relative to the hypothesis of complete profit maximization. The interpretation of α_i^* is similar to that of ϵ_i^* defined above by (9).

It can be seen that the optimal $\lambda_k^* = 0$ solution to (8) is feasible for (11). Using this fact and the inequalities in (8), we have[17]

$$\alpha_i^* \le \delta_i^*. \tag{13}$$

Thus when we assume that the underlying technology set is convex and calculate the efficiency of observation i, ϵ_i^*, under the assumption of cost minimizing behavior and compare this efficiency level to the relative efficiency of observation i, α_i^*, calculated under the assumption of profit maximizing behavior, we find that the relative efficiency level under the profit maximizing assumption will be equal to or less than the relative efficiency level under the cost minimizing assumption.

We now turn to the corresponding linear programs that test for the efficiency of observation i under the maintained hypothesis that the underlying technology is subject to constant returns to scale.

---

[16] This is Mendoza's (1989; 88) Test 7. It is also a special case of her Test 4. Since there is only one constraint in the problem, the solution to (11) is $max_k \sum_{m=1}^{2} p_m^i y_m^i - \sum_{n=1}^{2} w_n^i x_n^i; k = 1, 2, \ldots, K$. For related tests, see Afriat (1972; 594) for the single output case and Hanoch and Rothschild (1972; 268–270) and Diewert and Parkan (1983; 151) for the multiple output case.

[17] Mendoza (1989; 76–77) showed this.

4.2 The Convex Conical Technology Case

Case (i): Cost Minimization:

Guided by the results of section 3.2, it can be seen that all we have to do is to drop the constraint $\sum_{k=1}^{K} \lambda_k = 1$ from (8). The resulting optimized objective function is set equal to $\epsilon_i^{**}[w_1^i x_1^i + w_2^i x_2^i]$. Since the new LP has one less constraint than (8), it will generally attain a smaller optimized objective function and so ϵ_i^{**} will generally be smaller than ϵ_i^*; i.e.,

$$\epsilon_i^{**} \leq \epsilon_i^*. \tag{14}$$

By comparing the new LP to (2), we can also show

$$\delta_i^{**} \geq \epsilon_i^{**}. \tag{15}$$

The inequality (14) shows that making *stronger* assumptions on the underlying technology tends to *decrease* the efficiency measure; i.e., the constant returns to scale measure of the efficiency of observation i, ϵ_i^{**}, will be equal to or less that the convex technology measure of the efficiency of observation i,ϵ_i^*. The inequality (15) shows that assuming cost minimizing behaviour tends to decrease the efficiency of observation i, ϵ_i^{**}, compared to the measure of technical efficiency that we obtained earlier for observation i, δ_i^{**}.[18].

Case (ii): Profit Maximization:

As in section 2.2, we could approximate the underlying technology set by the free disposal hull of the convex cone spanned by the K data points. To determine whether observation i is on the frontier of this set, we could attempt to solve the LP problem (11) after dropping the constraint $\sum_{k=1}^{K} \lambda_k = 1$. Unfortunately, the resulting optimal objective function is either 0 or plus infinity. Hence a different approach is required.

In order to obtain an operational approach, we consider a *conditional profit maximization problem* in place of the full profit maximization problem that appears in the objective function of (11); i.e., we allow firm i to maximize profits but we assume that the level of one input is *fixed* in the short run. Thus if the fixed input is input 2, to determine whether producer i is maximizing (variable) profits subject to our convex, conical technology assumptions, we solve the following linear programming problem[19]:

$$max_{\lambda_1 \geq 0 \lambda_2 \geq 0, \ldots, \lambda_K \geq 0} \{ \sum_{m=1}^{2} p_m^i (\sum_{k=1}^{K} y_m^k \lambda_k) - \sum_{n=1}^{2} w_n^i (\sum_{k=1}^{K} x_1^k \lambda_k) : \sum_{k=1}^{K} x_2^k \lambda_k \leq x_2^i \} \tag{16}$$

[18] These results and the appropriate general test may be found in Mendoza (1989; 78), which she called Test 5.

[19] The constraint in (16) will hold as an equality in the optimal solution. Hence the nonnegative λ_k^* which solve (16) serve to define a weighted combination of the K data points which uses the observation i amount of input 2, x_2^i, and maximizes profits at the prices of observation i.

$$= max_k\{[\sum_{m=1}^{2} p_m^i y_m^k - (\sum_{n=1}^{2} w_n^i x_1^k)][x_2^i/x_2^k] : k = 1, 2, , K\}^{20} \quad (17)$$

$$\equiv p_1^i y_1^i + p_2^i y_2^i - \alpha_i^{**}[w_1^i x_1^i + w_2^i x_2^i] \quad (18)$$

where (18) serves to define the observation i efficiency measure α_i^{**}. Note that $\lambda_i^{**} = 1$ and the other $\lambda_k = 0$ is a feasible solution for (16) and this implies that $\alpha_i^{**} \leq 1$.[21].

The simple maximization problem defined by (17) can be written in the following instructive way:

$$\begin{aligned} &max_k\{[\textstyle\sum_{m=1}^{2} p_m^i y_m^k - (\sum_{n=1}^{2} w_n^i x_1^k][x_2^i/x_2^k] : k = 1, 2, \ldots, K\} \\ &= x_2^i max_k\{\textstyle\sum_{m=1}^{2} p_m^i [y_m^k/x_2^k] - (\sum_{n=1}^{2} w_n^i [x_n^k/x_2^k]) : k = 1, 2, \ldots, K\}. \end{aligned} \quad (19)$$

Note that the points $[y_1^k/x_2^k, y_2^k/x_2^k, x_1^k/x_2^k, x_2^k/x_2^k] = [y_1^k/x_2^k, y_2^k/x_2^k, x_1^k/x_2^k, 1]$ are feasible output and input vectors under our constant returns to scale assumption but where the amount of input 2 is fixed at the level 1. Thus the maximization problem in (19) scales each observed output-input vector k so that the resulting scaled last input level is equal to 1 and then we take the output and input prices faced by production unit i, $[p_1^i, p_2^i, w_1^i, w_2^i]$, evaluate unit profits at these prices for each scaled output-input vector k, $p_1^i[y_1^k/x_2^k] + p_2^i[y_2^k/x_2^k] - w_1^i[x_1^k/x_2^k] - w_2^i[x_1^k/x_2^k]$, take the maximum over k of these hypothetical profits and then scale the resulting hypothetical profits by the observation i level of the "fixed" input, which is equal to x_2^i.

Comparison of (2) and (16) shows that the optimal solution to (2) generates a feasible solution for (16) and thus

$$\delta_i^{**} \geq \alpha_i^{**}; \quad (20)$$

i.e., the observation i technical efficiency measure δ_i^{**} is always equal to or greater than the overall observation i (conditional on input 2) profit maximization efficiency measure α_i^{**}.

Since the LP problem (16) does not simply drop the constraint $\sum_{k=1}^{K} \lambda_k = 1$, the single constraint in the convex technology LP problem (11), we cannot develop an inequality between the solution to (16) and the solution to (11). However, since both problems use *all* of the price and quantity data pertaining to the K observations, typically the solutions to (11) and (16) will be similar in that the efficiencies generated by these models will tend to be much lower than the technical efficiencies generated by the models presented in section 3.

---

20 We require $x_2^k > 0$ for $k = 1, 2, \ldots, K$ in order to derive (17) from (16).

21 A sufficient condition to ensure that the solution to (16) is finite is $x_2^k > 0$ for $k = 1, \ldots, K$.

4.3 The Quasiconcave Technology Case

We consider only the cost minimization case[22]

We make the same technology assumptions as were made in section 3.3. Recall the index set I_1^i defined by (3). To determine whether producer i is minimizing cost subject to our quasiconcave technology in output 1 assumption, we solve the following linear program:

$$min_{\lambda_1 \geq 0 \lambda_2 \geq 0, \ldots, \lambda_k \geq 0}\{w_1^i(\textstyle\sum_{k \in I_1^i} x_1^k \lambda_k) + w_2^i(\sum_{k \in I_1^i} x_2^k \lambda_k) : \sum_{k \in I_1^i} y_2^k \lambda_k \geq y_2^i; \sum_{k \in I_1^i} \lambda_k = 1\} \quad (21)$$

$$\equiv \epsilon_i^{***}[w_1^i x_1^i + w_2^i x_2^i]. \quad (22)$$

As usual, ϵ_i^{***} is our measure of overall efficiency for observation i under our present assumptions on the technology and on the producer's behaviour. Since the index i belongs to the index set I_1^i (recall (3)), it can be seen that $\lambda_i = 1$ and the other $\lambda_k = 0$ is feasible for the LP(21) and gives rise to the feasible value for the objective function equal to $w_1^i x_1^i + w_2^i x_2^i$. Thus $\epsilon_i^{***} \leq 1$. It is also possible to see that the optimal δ_i^{***}, λ_i^{***} solution to (4) is a feasible ϵ_i,λ_k solution for (21). Thus

$$0 \leq \epsilon_i^{***} \leq \delta_i^{***}; \quad (23)$$

i.e., the (quasiconcave in output 1) cost minimizing overall efficiency for observation i, ϵ_i^{***}, will be equal to or less than the corresponding (quasiconcave in output 1) technical efficiency loss for observation i, δ_i^{***}.

Comparing (21) with (8) and using the definition of the index set I_1^i (recall (3)), it can be seen that the optimal λ_i^{***}, ϵ_i^{***} solution for (21) is a feasible solution for (8[23] Thus

$$\epsilon_i^{***} \geq \epsilon_i^*; \quad (24)$$

i.e., the observation i efficiency measure assuming a quasiconcave technology and cost minimizing behaviour ϵ_i^{***} will be equal to or greater than the observation i efficiency measure assuming a convex technology and cost minimizing behaviour ϵ_i^*.

5 Relationships between the Efficiency Measures

The inequalities derived in the previous two sections can be summarized by two rules. Note that all efficiency measures are measured in the same metric.

Rule 1: The nonparametric efficiency measures tend to *fall* as we make more restrictive technological assumptions; i.e., the quasiconcave technology

---

[22] Mendoza (1989; 83) considered more general cases in her Test 6.

[23] Using definition (3), $\lambda_i^{***} \geq 0$ and (5), it can be seen that $\sum_{k \in I_1^i} y_1^k \lambda_k^{***} \geq y_1^i$.

efficiency measure will be equal to or greater than the corresponding convex technology efficiency measure which in turn will be equal to or greater than the corresponding convex conical technology loss measure.

Rule 2: The nonparametric efficiency measures tend to *fall* as we assume optimizing behaviour over a larger number of goods; i.e., the technical efficiency measure will be equal to or greater than the corresponding cost minimizing efficiency measure which will be equal to or greater than the corresponding profit maximizing efficiency measure. This is Mendoza's (1989; 76–77) Le Chatelier Principle for measures of allocative efficiency.

We illustrate some of the above points using some Canadian data in the following section.

6 An Empirical Comparison of Alternative Efficiency Measures for Canada

We use National Accounts and OECD data for Canada for the years 1980-2004 in order to illustrate the above programs[24] Producer data on three (net) outputs and two primary inputs are used. The three net outputs are: domestic output, y_1 (C + G + I); exports, y_2; and minus imports, y_3. The two primary inputs are: labour, x_1 and reproducible capital, x_2. These data are listed in Table 1. The corresponding producer prices, p_1, p_2, p_3 for net outputs and w_1 and w_2 for primary inputs are listed in Table 2[25].

The tests for technical efficiency of each observation, (1) and (2) in sections 3.1 and 3.2, were run using the quantity data listed in Table 1 above[26] The relative technical efficiencies of the year i observation assuming a convex technology set, δ_i^*, and assuming a convex, constant returns to scale technology set, δ_i^{**}, are listed in Table 3 below. The cost minimization relative efficiencies ϵ_i^* defined by (8) and (9) in section 4.1 for the case of a convex technology and ϵ_i^{**} defined in section 4.2 for the case of a convex, constant returns to scale technology are also listed in Table 3 below. The profit maximization relative efficiencies α_i^* defined by (11) and (12) in section 4.1 for the case of a convex technology and α_i^{**} defined by (16) and (18) in section 4.2 for the case of a convex, constant returns to scale technology (with capital fixed) are also listed in Table 3 below.

Finally, we use the data in Tables 1 and 2 to construct:

- a chained Fisher (1922) ideal index of net outputs, Yt for year t;
- a chained Fisher ideal index of primary inputs Xt for year t and
- a measure of *index number productivity* in year t equal to t Yt/Xt.

---

[24] We did not compute the quasiconcavity efficiencies since these tend to be close to 1 and are not very informative.

[25] All prices were normalized to equal 1 in the year 1960.

[26] We have three (net) outputs instead of two outputs but the reader need only modify the tests in the obvious ways.

Table 1. Quantity Data on Net Outputs and Primary Inputs for Canada, 1980–2004

Year	y_1	y_2	y_3	x_1	x_2
1980	88.22	23.23	25.38	42.36	36.83
1981	91.73	23.62	26.02	44.11	38.24
1982	85.45	23.20	21.80	42.68	40.07
1983	89.07	24.63	24.01	42.90	40.60
1984	93.38	29.21	28.12	43.97	41.52
1985	98.49	30.63	30.48	45.27	42.82
1986	101.71	31.97	32.68	46.76	44.38
1987	106.53	32.95	34.43	47.92	46.02
1988	112.55	35.95	39.10	49.44	48.04
1989	116.91	36.24	41.39	50.53	50.46
1990	116.22	37.97	42.23	50.88	53.07
1991	114.12	38.66	43.28	49.91	54.92
1992	114.44	41.45	45.31	49.47	56.14
1993	115.95	45.97	48.66	49.68	57.03
1994	119.46	51.83	52.58	50.64	57.94
1995	121.39	56.22	55.60	51.60	59.29
1996	122.85	59.40	58.42	51.87	60.72
1997	130.60	64.35	66.78	52.95	62.06
1998	133.68	70.18	70.19	54.25	64.51
1999	139.19	77.75	75.66	55.87	66.80
2000	145.42	84.61	81.75	57.50	69.42
2001	147.83	81.96	77.62	58.36	72.42
2002	155.53	82.19	78.29	59.70	74.95
2003	162.32	81.51	82.07	60.93	77.73
2004	168.06	85.49	88.78	61.75	80.95

In order to make the resulting index number estimates of Canada's productivity for the years 1980–2004, we normalize the productivities by dividing by Prod^{2002}. This makes the resulting normalized index number estimates of productivity, γ^i, comparable to the profit maximizing estimates of relative efficiency listed in Table 3, since we had $\alpha^*_{2002} = \alpha^{**}_{2002} = 1$ and the year 2002 was the only efficient observation for both α^*_i and α^{**}_i. The normalized index number estimates of productivity are listed in the last column of Table 3.

Looking at Table 3, it can be seen that the various efficiency measures satisfy the following inequalities, which we showed in sections 3 and 4 must be satisfied:

$$\delta^{**}_i \leq \delta^*_i; \tag{25}$$

$$\epsilon^{**}_i \leq \epsilon^*_i; \tag{26}$$

$$\alpha^*_i \leq \epsilon^*_i \leq \delta^*_i; \tag{27}$$

$$\epsilon^{**}_i \leq \delta^{**}_i; \tag{28}$$

$$\alpha^{**}_i \leq \delta^{**}_i. \tag{29}$$

Table 2. Price Data on Net Outputs and Primary Inputs for Canada, 1980–2004

Year	p_1	p_2	p_3	w_1	w_2
1980	3.0783	3.7382	3.3640	4.3250	2.8210
1981	3.4053	4.0361	3.7466	4.6735	3.1366
1982	3.7361	4.1491	3.9089	5.1695	3.2346
1983	3.9537	4.1960	3.9273	5.4053	3.3299
1984	4.1081	4.3480	4.1334	5.6786	3.4856
1985	4.2730	4.4370	4.2510	5.9370	3.5477
1986	4.4630	4.4283	4.3272	6.1151	3.6578
1987	4.6241	4.5167	4.2734	6.5117	3.8049
1988	4.8124	4.5288	4.1715	6.9206	3.9791
1989	5.0277	4.6281	4.1734	7.2986	4.1243
1990	5.2515	4.5938	4.2160	7.6279	4.1099
1991	5.4192	4.4235	4.1456	8.0047	4.0010
1992	5.5112	4.5500	4.3145	8.2749	4.0053
1993	5.6198	4.7522	4.5751	8.4190	4.1214
1994	5.7082	5.0337	4.8661	8.4753	4.3004
1995	5.7797	5.3564	5.0152	8.5948	4.3944
1996	5.8433	5.3863	4.9523	8.7775	4.4662
1997	5.9309	5.3945	4.9883	9.1036	4.6262
1998	5.9969	5.3772	5.1623	9.3415	4.6238
1999	6.0794	5.4361	5.1471	9.5678	4.6415
2000	6.2151	5.7743	5.2620	10.0450	4.7601
2001	6.3336	5.8617	5.4230	10.3032	4.7135
2002	6.4492	5.7705	5.4544	10.4646	4.7970
2003	6.5617	5.6630	5.0758	10.6265	4.8548
2004	6.6784	5.7843	4.9621	10.8718	5.0059

For the Canadian data set, we also find *empirically* that

$$\alpha_i^{**} \le \epsilon_i^{**}. \tag{30}$$

However, we cannot establish the inequality (30) as a *theoretical* certainty. Looking at α_i^* versus α_i^{**}, for the Canadian data, it can be seen that for the most part, $\alpha_i^* \le \alpha_i^{**}$ and sometimes α_i^* is substantially below α_i^{**}; i.e., the relative efficiency of an observation when we assume profit maximizing behavior and a convex technology, α_i^*, is generally less than the corresponding relative efficiency of an observation when we assume profit maximizing behavior subject to a fixed capital constraint and a convex, constant returns to scale technology, α_i^{**}. However, for the years 2003 and 2004, this relationship does not hold.

Perhaps the most interesting thing to note about the results listed in Table 3 is that with the exception of the first two years, the index number

Table 3. Relative Efficiencies for Canada, 1980–2004

Year i	δ_i^*	δ_i^{**}	ϵ_i^*	ϵ_i^{**}	α_i^*	α_i^{**}	γ_i
1980	1.0000	1.0000	1.0000	0.9977	0.8308	0.8847	0.8629
1981	1.0000	1.0000	1.0000	1.0000	0.8480	0.8922	0.8604
1982	1.0000	1.0000	1.0000	1.0000	0.7574	0.8438	0.8422
1983	1.0000	1.0000	1.0000	1.0000	0.7659	0.8659	0.8630
1984	1.0000	1.0000	1.0000	1.0000	0.8163	0.8982	0.8894
1985	1.0000	1.0000	1.0000	1.0000	0.8345	0.9121	0.9015
1986	0.9912	0.9909	0.9893	0.9880	0.8343	0.9072	0.8929
1987	1.0000	1.0000	1.0000	1.0000	0.8465	0.9114	0.9026
1988	1.0000	1.0000	1.0000	1.0000	0.8600	0.9156	0.9095
1989	1.0000	1.0000	1.0000	1.0000	0.8528	0.9042	0.9021
1990	0.9844	0.9810	0.9728	0.9706	0.8345	0.8830	0.8833
1991	0.9824	0.9666	0.9596	0.9437	0.8170	0.8619	0.8655
1992	0.9874	0.9635	0.9601	0.9432	0.8273	0.8665	0.8717
1993	0.9890	0.9525	0.9632	0.9406	0.8457	0.8805	0.8844
1994	0.9924	0.9502	0.9732	0.9497	0.8767	0.9075	0.9088
1995	0.9882	0.9479	0.9704	0.9435	0.8804	0.9113	0.9147
1996	0.9922	0.9449	0.9701	0.9372	0.8857	0.9132	0.9179
1997	1.0000	0.9807	0.9955	0.9526	0.9147	0.9337	0.9355
1998	0.9978	0.9752	0.9892	0.9534	0.9322	0.9436	0.9457
1999	0.9992	0.9982	0.9945	0.9791	0.9580	0.9671	0.9675
2000	1.0000	1.0000	1.0000	1.0000	0.9795	0.9854	0.9838
2001	1.0000	1.0000	1.0000	1.0000	0.9780	0.9806	0.9812
2002	1.0000	1.0000	1.0000	1.0000	1.0000	1.0000	1.0000
2003	1.0000	1.0000	1.0000	1.0000	0.9951	0.9918	0.9926
2004	1.0000	1.0000	1.0000	1.0000	0.9985	0.9910	0.9928

estimates of efficiency, γ_i, are reasonably close to the efficiency estimates, α_i^{**} , which are based on a (variable) profit maximizing model where we assume capital is fixed and assume that there is a convex, constant returns to scale technology. These results are similar to the results obtained by Mendoza (1989; 111), who obtained nonparametric productivity indexes that were quite similar to the corresponding index number measures of productivity[27].

[27] Mendoza (1989; 129–134) also obtained econometric estimates of sectoral technical change for Canada and she compared these estimates with her nonparametric estimates of sectoral technical change. Her results showed that the econometric estimates of efficiency change are simply a highly smoothed version of the corresponding nonparametric estimates. Diewert and Wales (1992; 718) and Fox (1996) showed that econometric estimates of efficiency change were approximately equal to smoothed versions of index number estimates of productivity growth.

7 A Comparison of the Alternative Methods for Measuring Productive Efficiency

We summarize our comparison of alternative methods for measuring the relative efficiency of a number of production units in the same industry in point form.

- Nonparametric or DEA techniques have an overwhelming advantage over index number and econometric methods when *only* quantity data are available. Index number methods cannot be implemented without a complete set of price and quantity data. Econometric methods (i.e., production function methods) are not likely to be successful if only quantity data are available due to limited degrees of freedom[28].
- The relative efficiency of any single observation will tend to decrease as the sample size increases. All three methods have this problem.
- Nonparametric and econometric efficiency scores will tend to increase as we make less restrictive assumptions on the underlying technology; i.e., a quasiconcave technology set is less restrictive than a convex technology set which in turn is less restrictive than a constant returns to scale convex technology set. Index number estimates of efficiency remain unchanged as we change our assumptions on the technology.
- Nonparametric and economic efficiency scores will tend to decrease as we make stronger assumptions about the optimizing behaviour of producers; recall Rule 2 in section 5. It is not clear what will happen to econometric based efficiency scores under the same conditions. Since index number methods are based on the assumption of complete optimizing behaviour we cannot vary our assumptions on optimizing behaviour when using index number methods.
- If we hold the number of observations in our sample constant but disaggregate the data so that the number of inputs or outputs is increased, then nonparametric efficiency scores will tend to increase.[29] However, index number efficiency scores will generally remain unaffected by increasing disaggregation[30] It is not clear what will happen using econometric methods.

[28] Diewert (1992) discusses this point at some length.

[29] As we disaggregate, the objective functions of the various linear programming problems will remain unchanged but the feasible regions for the problems become more constrained or smaller and hence the objective function minimums for the linear programming problems will become larger. Hence, the loss measures will decrease or remain constant and thus efficiency will tend to increase as we disaggregate. This point was first made by Nunamaker (1985). The profit maximization problems (11) and (16) are not affected by disaggregation.

[30] This follows from the approximate consistency in aggregation property of superlative index number formulae like the Fisher and Trnqvist formulae; see Diewert (1978; 889, 895).

- The cost of computing index number estimates of relative efficiency is extremely low; the cost of the nonparametric estimates is low and the cost of computing econometric estimates can be very high if the number of goods exceeds 20 and flexible functional form techniques are used[31].
- When complete price and quantity data are available, the nonparametric estimates based on a constant returns to scale technology and profit maximizing behaviour (subject to one input being fixed) are approximately equal to the corresponding index number estimates. Econometric estimates based on the same assumptions will tend to be similar to the first two sets of estimates (but much smoother in the time series context).
- Nonparametric techniques can be adapted to deal with situations where input prices are available but not output prices. Econometric techniques can also deal with this situation but index number methods cannot be used in this situation[32].
- Nonparametric methods may be severely biased due to measurement errors; i.e., the best or most efficient observation in a DEA study may be best simply because some output was greatly overstated or some important input was greatly understated. Index number methods are also subject to measurement errors but econometric methods may be adapted to deal with gross outliers.

Our overall conclusion is that DEA methods for measuring relative efficiency can be used profitably in a wide variety of situations when other methods are not practical or are impossible to use.

References

Afriat, S.N., "Efficiency Estimation of Production Function", *International Economic Review* **13** (1972), 568–598.

Balk, B.M., *Industrial Price, Quantity and Productivity Indices*, Norwell MA: Kluwer Academic Publishers, 1998.

Charnes, A. and W.W. Cooper, "Preface to Topics in Data Envelopment Analysis", *Annals of Operations Research* **2** (1985), 59–94.

Charnes, A., W.W. Cooper and E. Rhodes, "Measuring the Efficiency of Decision Making Units", *European Journal of Operational Research* **2** (1978), 429–444.

[31] The cost of estimating a fully flexible or semiflexible functional form can be high in terms of the analyst's time in doing the econometric estimation. When curvature conditions are imposed using the normalized quadratic functional form and the number of commodities are large, then in order to ensure convergence of the nonlinear regression using Shazam, it is necessary to gradually increase the rank of the substitution matrix by adding an additional rank one matrix to the already estimated substitution matrix and then rerun the model using the finishing parameter values of the previous model as starting values for the new model and so on. The procedure terminates after an iteration where the log likelihood of the model does not increase significantly.

[32] An exception occurs if there is only one output.

Coelli, T., D.S. Prasada Rao and G. Battese, *An Introduction to Efficiency and Productivity Analysis*, Boston: Kluwer Academic Publishers, 1997.

Debreu, G., "The Coefficient of Resource Utilization", *Econometrica* **19** (1951), 273–292.

Diewert, W.E., "Functional Forms for Profit and Transformation Functions", *Journal of Economic Theory* **6** (1973), 284–316.

Diewert, W.E., "Applications of Duality Theory," pp. 106–171 in M.D. Intriligator and D.A. Kendrick (ed.), *Frontiers of Quantitative Economics*, Vol. II, Amsterdam: North-Holland, 1974.

Diewert, W.E., "Superlative Index Numbers and Consistency in Aggregation", *Econometrica* **46** (1978), 883–900.

Diewert, W.E., "Capital and the Theory of Productivity Measurement", *The American Economic Review* **70** (1980), 260–267.

Diewert, W.E., "The Theory of Total Factor Productivity Measurement in Regulated Industries", pp. 17–44 in *Productivity Measurement in Regulated Industries*, Tom Cowing and R. Stephenson (eds.), New York: Academic Press, 1981.

Diewert, W.E., "The Measurement of Productivity", *Bulletin of Economic Research* **44** (1992), 163–198.

Diewert, W.E. (2005), *Chapter 4: Notes on the Construction of a Data Set for an O.E.C.D. Country*, Lecture notes for Economics 594, Department of Economics, University of British Columbia, Vancouver, Canada, V6T 1Z1. May 2005. http://www.econ.ubc.ca/diewert/594chmpg.htm

Diewert, W.E. and A.O. Nakamura, "Index Number Concepts, Measures and Decompositions of Productivity Growth", *Journal of Productivity Analysis* **19** (2003), 127–159.

Diewert, W.E. and C. Parkan, "Linear Programming Tests of Regularity Conditions for Production Functions," pp. 131–158 in *Quantitative Studies on Production and Prices*, W. Eichhorn, R. Henn, *k*. Neumann and R.W. Shephard (eds.), Vienna: Physica Verlag, 1983.

Diewert, W.E. and T.J. Wales, "Flexible Functional Forms and Global Curvature Conditions", *Econometrica* **55** (1987), 43–68.

Diewert, W.E. and T.J. Wales, "A Normalized Quadratic Semiflexible Functional Form", *Journal of Econometrics* **37** (1988), 327–342.

Diewert, W.E. and T.J. Wales, "Quadratic Spline Models for Producer's Supply and Demand Functions", *International Economic Review* **33** (1992), 705–722.

Färe, R. and C.A.K. Lovell, "Measuring the Technical Efficiency of Production", *Journal of Economic Theory* **19** (1978), 150–162.

Färe, R., S. Grosskopf and C.A.K. Lovell, *The Measurement of Efficiency of Production*, Boston: Kluwer-Nijhoff, 1985.

Farrell, M.J., "The Measurement of Production Efficiency", *Journal of the Royal Statistical Society*, Series A, **120** (1957), 253–278.

Farrell, M.J. and M. Fieldhouse, "Estimating Efficient Production Functions under Increasing Returns to Scale", *Journal of the Royal Statistical Society*, Series A, **125** (1962), 252–267.

Fisher, I., *The Making of Index Numbers*, Houghton-Mifflin, Boston, 1922.

Fox, K.J., "Specification of Functional Form and the Estimation of Technical Progress", *Applied Economics* **28** (1996), 947–956.

Fox, K.J. (ed.), *Efficiency in the Public Sector*, Boston: Kluwer Academic Publishers, 2002.

Hanoch, G. and M. Rothschild, "Testing the Assumptions of Production Theory: A Nonparametric Approach", *Journal of Political Economy* **80** (1972), 256–275.

Hoffman, A.J., "Discussion of Mr. Farrell's Paper", *Journal of the Royal Statistical Society*, Series A, **120** (1957), 284.

Mendoza, M.N.F., *Essays in Production Theory: Efficiency Measurement and Comparative Statistics*, Ph.D. Theses, University of British Columbia, Vancouver, Canada, 1989.

Nunamaker, T.R., "Using Data Envelopment Analysis to Measure the Efficiency of Non-profit Organisations: A Critical Evaluation", *Managerial and Decision Economics* **6** (1985), 58–60.

Samuelson, P.A., *Foundations of Economic Analysis*, Cambridge, MA: harvard University Press, 1947.

Varian, H.R., "The Nonparametric Approach to Production Analysis", *Econometrica* **52** (1984), 579–597.

Finding Common Ground: Efficiency Indices

Rolf Färe[1], Shawna Grosskopf[2], and Valentin Zelenyuk[3]

[1] Oregon State University, Corvallis, OR, USA rolf.fare@oregonstate.edu
[2] Oregon State University, Corvallis, OR, USA shawna.grosskopf@orst.edu
[3] Kyiv Economics Institute (and UPEG/EERC at National University "Kyiv-Mohyla Academy"), Voloska 10, Office 406, 04070, Kiev, Ukraine vzelenyuk@eerc.kiev.ua*

1 Introduction

The last two decades have witnessed a revival in interest in the measurement of productive efficiency pioneered by Farrell (1957) and Debreu (1951). 1978 was a watershed year in this revival with the christening of DEA by Charnes, Cooper and Rhodes (1978) and the critique of Farrell technical efficiency in terms of axiomatic production and index number theory in Färe and Lovell (1978). These papers have inspired many others to apply these methods and to add to the debate on how best to define technical efficiency.

In this paper we try to pull together some of the variants that have arisen over these decades and show when they are equivalent. The specific cases we take up include: 1) the original Debreu-Farrell measure versus the Russell measure—the latter introduced by Färe and Lovell, and 2) the directional distance function and the additive measure. The former was introduced by Luenberger (1992) and the latter by Charnes, Cooper, Golany and Seiford (1985). We also provide a discussion of the associated cost interpretations. The findings are that the common ground is "small" in the sense of the function satisfying it.

2 Basic Production Theory Details

In this section we introduce the basic production theory that we employ in this paper. We will be focusing on the input based efficiency measures here, but the analysis could readily be extended to the output oriented case as well.

To begin, technology may be represented by its input requirement sets

$$L(y) = \{\, x : \ x \text{ can produce } y \}\,, \ y \in \Re^M_+, \tag{1}$$

* We would like to thank W. W. Cooper, D. Primont, R. R. Russell, R. M. Thrall and a referee for their comments. We also thank Pavlo Kostromytskyi and Lisa Duke for the technical support in preparation of the paper.

where $y \in \Re^M_+ = \{y \in \Re^M : y_m \geq 0, m = 1, \ldots, M\}$ denotes outputs and $x \in \Re^N_+$ denotes inputs. We assume that the input requirement sets satisfy the standard axioms, including: $L(0) = \Re^N_+$, and $L(y)$ is a closed convex set with both inputs[4] and outputs[5] freely disposable (for details see Färe and Primont (1995)).

The subsets of $L(y)$ relative toward which we measure efficiency are the isoquants

$$IsoqL(y) = \{x : x \in L(y), \lambda x \notin L(y), \lambda > 1\}, \; y \in \Re^M_+, \tag{2}$$

and the efficient subsets

$$EffL(y) = \{x : x \in L(y), x' \leq x, x' \neq x \Rightarrow x' \notin L(y)\}, \; y \in \Re^M_+. \tag{3}$$

Clearly, $EffL(y) \subseteq IsoqL(y)$ and as one can easily see with a Leontief technology, i.e., $L(y) = \{(x_1, x_2) : \min\{x_1, x_2\} \geq y\}$, the efficient subset may be a proper subset of the isoquant.

Next we introduce two function representations of $L(y)$, namely the Shephard input distance function and the directional input distance function, and discuss some of their properties.

Shephard's (1953) input distance function is defined in terms of the input requirement sets $L(y)$ as

$$D_i(y, x) = \sup_{\lambda}\{\lambda : x/\lambda \in L(y)\}. \tag{4}$$

Among its important properties[6] we note the following

(i) $D_i(y, x) \geq 1$ if and only if $x \in L(y)$, (Representation)
(ii) $D_i(y, \lambda x) = \lambda D_i(y, x)$, $\lambda > 0$, (Homogeneity)
(iii) $D_i(y, x) = 1$ if and only if $x \in IsoqL(y)$, (Indication).

Our first property shows that the distance function is a complete representation of the technology. Property ii) shows that the distance function is homogeneous of degree one in inputs, i.e., the variables which are scaled in (4). The indication condition shows that the distance function identifies the isoquants.

Turning to the directional input distance function introduced by Luenberger (1992)[7], we define it as

$$\vec{\mathbf{D}}_i\,(y, x; g_x) = \sup_{\beta}\{\beta : (x - \beta g_x) \in L(y)\}, \tag{5}$$

where $g_x \in \Re^N_+$ is the directional vector in which inefficiency is measured. Here we choose $g_x = 1^N \in \Re^N_+$. This function $\vec{\mathbf{D}}_i\,(y, x; 1^N)$ has properties

[4] Inputs are freely disposable if $x' \geq x \in L(y) \Rightarrow x' \in L(y)$.
[5] Outputs are freely disposable if $y' \geq y \Rightarrow L(y') \subseteq L(y)$.
[6] For additional properties and proofs, see Färe and Primont (1995).
[7] In consumer theory he calls this the benefit function and in producer theory he uses the term shortage function.

that parallel those of $D_i(y,x)$, and are listed below. For technical reasons the indication property is split into two parts. We note that we require inputs to be strictly positive in part a) of the indication property. The proofs of these properties are found in the appendix.

i) $\vec{\mathbf{D}}_i\,(y,x;\,1^N) \geq 0$ if and only if $x \in L(y)$, (Representation)

ii) $\vec{\mathbf{D}}_i\,(y,x+\alpha 1^N;\,1^N) = \vec{\mathbf{D}}_i\,(y,x;\,1^N) + \alpha$, $\alpha > 0$, (Translation)

iiia) if $\vec{\mathbf{D}}_i\,(y,x;\,1^N) = 0$ and $x_n > 0$, $n = 1,\ldots,N$, then $x \in \mathit{IsoqL}\,(y)$, (Indication)

iiib) $x \in \mathit{IsoqL}\,(y)$ implies $\vec{\mathbf{D}}_i\,(y,x;\,1^N) = 0$, (Indication).

Since we will be relating technical efficiency to costs, we also need to define the cost function, which for input prices $w \in \Re^N_+$ is

$$C(y,w) = \min_x\{wx : x \in L(y)\}. \tag{6}$$

The following dual relationships apply

$$\frac{C(y,x)}{wx} \leq 1/D_i(y,x), \tag{7}$$

and

$$\frac{C(y,x)-wx}{w1^N} \leq -\,\vec{\mathbf{D}}_i\,(y,x;\,1^N). \tag{8}$$

Expression (7) which is the Mahler inequality, states that the ratio of minimum cost to observed cost is less than or equal to the reciprocal of the input distance function. Expression (8) states that the difference between minimum and observed cost, normalized by input prices, is no larger than the negative of the directional input distance function.

These two inequalities may be transformed to strict equalities by introducing allocative inefficiency as a residual.

2.1 The Debreu-Farrell and Russell Equivalence

Our goal in this section is to find conditions on the technology $L(y)$, $y \in \Re^M_+$, such that the Debreu-Farrell (Debreu (1957), Farrell (1957)) measure of technical efficiency coincides with the Russell (Färe and Lovell (1978)) measure. To establish these conditions we redefine the original Russell measure and introduce a multiplicative version. We do this by using the geometric mean as the objective function in its definition rather than an arithmetic mean. Thus our multiplicative Russell measure is defined as

$$\begin{aligned} R_M(y,x) = \min_{\lambda_1\ldots\lambda_N}\Bigg\{\Big(\prod_{n=1}^{N}\lambda_n\Big)^{1/N} &: \\ (\lambda_1 x_1,\ldots,\lambda_N x_N) &\in L(y), \\ 0 < \lambda_n \leq 1, n = 1,\ldots,N &\Bigg\}. \end{aligned} \tag{9}$$

The objective function here is $\left(\prod_{n=1}^{N}\lambda_n\right)^{1/N}$ in contrast to $\sum_{n=1}^{N}\lambda_n/N$ from the original specification in Färe and Lovell (1978). Russell (1985, 1987) criticizes the original measure and a referee points out that this criticism may carry over to the multiplicative measure. For technical reasons we assume here that inputs $x = (x_1, \ldots, x_n)$ are strictly positive, i.e., $x_n > 0$, $n = 1, \ldots, N$.

More specifically in this section we assume that for $y \geq 0$, $y \neq 0$, $L(y)$ is a subset of the interior of $\Re_+^N$.[8]

Note that the Russell measure in (9) has the indication property

$$R_M(y, x) = 1 \quad \text{if and only if } x \in \mathit{EffL}(y). \tag{10}$$

Recall that the Debreu-Farrell measure of technical efficiency is the reciprocal of Shephard's input distance function, i.e.,

$$DF(y, x) = 1/D_i(y, x), \tag{11}$$

thus it is homogeneous of degree -1 in x and it has the same indication property as $D_i(y, x)$.

Now assume that the technology is input homothetic[9], i.e.,

$$D_i(y, x) = D_i(1, x)/H(y), \tag{12}$$

and that the input aggregation function $D_i(1, x)$ is a geometric mean, so that the distance function equals

$$D_i(y, x) = \left(\prod_{n=1}^{N} x_n\right)^{1/N} / H(y). \tag{13}$$

From (4) and the representation property it is clear that the distance function takes the form above if and only if the input requirement sets are of the following form

$$L(y) = H(y) \cdot \left\{\hat{x} : \left(\prod_{n=1}^{N} \hat{x}\right)^{1/N} \geq 1\right\}, \ \hat{x} = \frac{x}{H(y)}. \tag{14}$$

The Russell characterization theorem can now be stated; the proof may be found in the appendix.

Theorem 1: Assume that $L(y)$ is interior to $\Re_+^M$ for $y \geq 0$, $y \neq 0$.

$$R_M(y, x) = DF(y, x) \text{ for all } x \in L(y) \text{ if and only if}$$

$$D_i(y, x) = \left(\prod_{n=1}^{N} x_n\right)^{1/N} / H(y).$$

[8] See Russell (1990) for a related assumption.

[9] For details see Färe and Primont (1995).

Thus for these two efficiency measures to be equivalent, technology must satisfy a fairly specific form of homotheticity—technology is of a restricted Cobb-Douglas form in which the inputs have equal weights. This makes intuitive sense, since technology must be symmetric, but clearly not of the Leontief type. That is, technology must be such that the $IsoqL(y) = EffL(y)$. Of course, it is exactly the Leontief type technology which motivated Färe and Lovell to introduce a measure that would use the efficient subset $EffL(y)$ rather than the isoquant $IsoqL(y)$ as the reference for establishing technical efficiency.

2.2 The Directional Distance Function and the Additive Measure

We now turn to some of the more recently derived versions of technical efficiency; specifically we derive conditions on the technology $L(y)$, $y \in \Re_+^M$ that are necessary and sufficient for the directional distance function to coincide with a "stylized" additive measure of technical efficiency.

The original additive measure introduced by Charnes, Cooper, Golany and Seiford (1985) (hereafter CCGS) simultaneously expanded outputs and contracted inputs. Here we focus on a version that contracts inputs only, but in the additive form of the original measure. Although the original measure was defined relative to a variable returns to scale technology, (see p. 97, CCGS), here we leave the returns to scale issue open and impose only those conditions itemized in Section 2. Finally, we normalize their measure by the number of inputs, N.

We are now ready to define the stylized additive model as

$$A(y,x) = \max_{s_1 \ldots s_N} \left\{ \sum_{n=1}^{N} s_n/N : (x_1 - s_1, \ldots, x_N - s_N) \in L(y) \right\}, \tag{15}$$

where $s_n \geq 0$, $n = 1, \ldots, N$.

This measure reduces each input x_n so that the total reduction $\sum_{n=1}^{N} s_n/N$ is maximized. Intuitively, one can think of this problem as roughly equivalent to minimizing costs when all input prices are equal to one. We will discuss this link in the next section.

The additive measure and the modified Russell measure look quite similar, although the former uses an arithmetic mean as the objective and the modified Russell measure uses a geometric mean. The additive structure of $A(y,x)$ suggests that the directional distance function—which also has an additive structure—may be related to it[10]. To make that link we begin by characterizing the technology for which these two measures would be equivalent. We begin by assuming that technology is translation input homothetic[11], i.e., in

[10] Larry Seiford noted the similarity at a North American Efficiency and Productivity Workhsop.

[11] For details see Chambers and Färe (1998). Chambers and Färe assumed that $F(y)$ depends on the directional vector 1^N. Here we take it as fixed and omit it.

terms of the directional distance function we may write

$$\vec{\mathbf{D}}_i\ (y, x;\ 1^N) = \mathbf{D}_i(0, x;\ 1^N) - F(y). \tag{16}$$

Moreover, we assume that the aggregator function $\vec{\mathbf{D}}_i\ (0, x;\ 1^N)$ is arithmetic mean so that the directional distance function may be written as

$$\vec{\mathbf{D}}_i\ (y, x;\ 1^N) = \frac{1}{N}\sum_{n=1}^{N} x_n - F(y). \tag{17}$$

Note that from the properties of the directional distance function, it follows that it takes the form required above if and only if the underlying input requirement sets are of the form

$$L(y) = \left\{\tilde{x} : \frac{1}{N}\sum_{n=1}^{N} \tilde{x}_n \geq 0\right\} + F(y), \tag{18}$$

where $\tilde{x} = (x_1 - F(y), \ldots, x_N - F(y)$.

We are now ready to state our additive representation theorem (see appendix for proof),

Theorem 2:

$$\begin{aligned}\vec{\mathbf{D}}_i\ (y, x;\ 1^N) &= A(y, x) \text{ for all } x \in \bar{C}(L(y)) = \\ &\{\hat{x} : \hat{x} = x + \delta 1^N, x \in L(y),\ \delta \geq 0\} \\ &\text{if and only if } \vec{\mathbf{D}}_i\ (y, x;\ 1^N) = \frac{1}{N}\sum_{n=1}^{N} x_n - F(y).\end{aligned} \tag{19}$$

Here we see that to obtain equivalence between the additive measure and the directional distance function, technology must be linear and symmetric in inputs, i.e., the isoquants are straight lines with slope = −1.

2.3 Cost Interpretations

The Debreu-Farrell measure has a dual interpretation, namely the cost deflated cost function. Here we show that the multiplicative Russell measure and the additive measure also have dual cost interpretations[12].

Recall that we define the cost function

$$C(y, w) = \min_x \{wx : x \in L(y)\}, \tag{20}$$

[12] It is straightforward to show that the original (additive) Russell measure also has a cost interpretation, despite the claim by Kopp (1981, p. 450) that the Russell measure '. . . cannot be given a meaningful cost interpretation which is factor price invariant.' In this section, we provide such a cost interpretation.

where $w \in \Re^N_+$ are input prices. From the definition it follows that

$$C(y,w) \leq wx, \forall x \in L(y). \tag{21}$$

Now since $DF(y,x)x \in L(y)$ it is also true that

$$C(y,w) \leq w(DF(y,x)x) = wx(DF(y,x)), \tag{22}$$

and

$$C(y,w)/wx \leq DF(y,x). \tag{23}$$

Expression (22) is a direct consequence of (7) and is known as the Mahler inequality expressed in terms of the cost efficiency measure $(C(y,w)/wx)$ and the Debreu-Farrell measure of technical efficiency, $DF(y,x)$. This inequality may be closed by introducing a multiplicative measure of allocative efficiency, $AE(y,x,w)$, so that we have

$$C(y,w)/wx = DF(y,x)AE(y,x,w). \tag{24}$$

To introduce a cost interpretation of the multiplicative Russell measure we note that

$$(\lambda_1^* x_1, \ldots, \lambda_N^* x_N) \in L(y), \tag{25}$$

where λ_n^* $(n = 1, \ldots, N)$ are the optimizers in expression (9). From the assumption that the input requirement sets are subsets of the interior of $\Re^N_+$, it follows that $\lambda_n^* > 0$, $n = 1, \ldots, N$. By (20) and (24) we have

$$C(y,w) \leq (\lambda_1^* w_1 x_1, \ldots, \lambda_N^* w_N x_N), \tag{26}$$

and by multiplication

$$C(y,w)/wx \leq \left(\prod_{n=1}^{N} \lambda_n^*\right)^{1/N} \left[\frac{\lambda_1^* w_1 x_1}{\left(\prod_{n=1}^{N} \lambda_n^*\right)^{1/N} wx} + \cdots + \frac{\lambda_N^* w_N x_N}{\left(\prod_{n=1}^{N} \lambda_n^*\right)^{1/N} wx}\right], \tag{27}$$

or

$$C(y,w)/wx \leq R_M(y,x) \left[\frac{\lambda_1^* w_1 x_1}{\left(\prod_{n=1}^{N} \lambda_n^*\right)^{1/N} wx} + \cdots + \frac{\lambda_N^* w_N x_N}{\left(\prod_{n=1}^{N} \lambda_n^*\right)^{1/N} wx}\right]. \tag{28}$$

Expression (27) differs from the Mahler inequality (22) in that it contains a second term on the right hand side. This term may be called the Debreu-Farrell deviation, in that if $\lambda_1 = \ldots = \lambda_N$, the deviation equals one. That is, if the scaling factors λ_n^* are equal for each n, then (27) coincides with (22). Again, the inequality (27) can be closed by introducing a multiplicative residual, which captures allocative inefficiency.

Turning to the additive measure, we note that

$$(x_1 - s_1^*, \ldots, x_N - s_N^*) \in L(y), \tag{29}$$

where s_n^*, $n = 1, \ldots, N$ are the optimizers in problem (15). Thus from cost minimization we have

$$C(y, w) \leq wx - ws^*, \tag{30}$$

where $s^* = (s_1^*, \ldots, s_N^*)$. From (29) we can derive two dual interpretations: a ratio and a difference version.

The ratio interpretation is

$$C(y, w)/wx \leq 1 - \frac{ws^*}{wx}, \tag{31}$$

which bears some similarity to the Farrell cost efficiency model in (22). Now if $w = (1, \ldots, 1)$, then it follows that the additive model is related to costs as

$$\frac{C(y, 1^N)}{\sum_{n=1}^{N} x_n} \leq 1 - \frac{\sum_{n=1}^{N} s_n^*/N}{\sum_{n=1}^{N} x_n/N} = 1 - \frac{A(y, x)}{\sum_{n=1}^{N} x_n/N}. \tag{32}$$

In this case we see that Debreu-Farrell cost efficiency (the left-hand side) is not larger than one minus a normalized additive measure.

The second cost interpretation is

$$C(y, w) - wx \leq -ws^*, \tag{33}$$

and when $w = (1, \ldots, 1)$ we obtain

$$\frac{C(y, 1^N) - \sum_{n=1}^{N} x_n}{N} \leq -A(y, x). \tag{34}$$

If we compare this result to (8), we see again, the close relationship between the additive measure and the directional distance function.

References

Chambers, R.G., and R. Färe, "Translation Homotheticity," *Economic Theory* **11** (1998), 629–64.

Charnes, A., W.W. Cooper, B. Golany, L. Seiford and J. Stutz, "Foundations of Data Envelopment Analysis for Pareto-Koopmans Efficient Empirical Production Functions," *Journal of Econometrics* **30**(12) (1985), 9–07.

Charnes, A., W.W. Cooper and E. Rhodes, "Measuring the Efficiency of Decision-making Units," *European Journal of Operational Research* **2**(6) (1978), 429–444.

Debreu, G., "The Coefficient of Resource Utilization," *Econometrica* **19** (1951), 273–292.

Färe, R. and C.A.K. Lovell, "Measuring Technical Efficiency of Production," *Journal of Economic Theory* **19** (1978), 150–62.

Färe, R. and D. Primont, *Multi-Output Production and Duality: Theory and Applications*, Kluwer Academic Publishers: Boston, 1995.

Farrell, M., "The Measurement of Productive Efficiency," *Journal of the Royal Statistical Society*, Series A, General, 120, Part 3 253–28, 1957.

Kopp, R., "Measuring the Technical Efficiency of Production: A Comment," *Journal of Economic Theory* **25** (1981), 450–452.

Luenberger, D.G., "New Optimality Principles for Economic Efficiency and Equilibrium," *Journal of Optimization Theory and Applications*, **75** (1992), 22–264.

Russell, R.R., "Measuring of Technical Efficiency," *Journal of Economic Theory* **35** (1985), 1109–26.

Russell, R.R., "On the Axiomatic Approach to the Measurement of Technical Efficiency," in W. Eichhhorn, ed. *Measurement in Economics: Theory and Applications of Economic Indices*, Heidelberg: Physica Verlag, 207–27, 1987.

Russell, R.R., "Continuity of Measures of Technical Efficiency," *Journal of Economic Theory* **51** (1990), 255–267.

Shephard, R. W., *Cost and Production Functions*, Princeton University Press: Princeton, 1953.

Appendix

Proof of (2.5):
i) See Chambers, Chung and Färe (1998, p. 354) for a similar proof.

ii)
$$\begin{aligned}\vec{\mathbf{D}}_i\,(y, x+\alpha 1^N;\, 1^N) &= \sup_\beta \{\beta : (x - \beta 1^N + \alpha 1^N) \in L(y)\} \\ &= \sup_\beta \{\beta : (x - (\beta - \alpha) 1^N) \in L(y)\} \\ &= \alpha + \sup_\beta \left\{\hat{\beta} : (x - \hat{\beta} 1^N) \in L(y)\right\} \quad (\hat{\beta} = \beta - \alpha) \\ &= \vec{\mathbf{D}}_i\,(y, x;\, 1^N) + \alpha.\end{aligned}$$

iiia) We give a contrapositive proof. Let $x \in L(y)$ with $x_n > 0$, $n = 1, \ldots, N$ and $x \notin IsoqL(y)$. Then $D_i(y,x) > 1$, and by strong disposability, there is an open neighborhood $N_\varepsilon(x)$ of x ($\varepsilon = \min\{x_1 - D_i(y,x)x_1, \ldots, x_N - D_i(y,x)x_N\}$) such that $N_\varepsilon(x) \in L(y)$. Thus $\vec{\mathbf{D}}_i\,(y, x;\, 1^N) > 0$ proving iiia).

iiib) Again we give a contrapositive proof. Let $\vec{\mathbf{D}}_i\,(y, x;\, 1^N) > 0$ then $x - \vec{\mathbf{D}}_i\,(y, x;\, 1^N) 1^N \in L(y)$ and since the directional vector is $1^N = (1, \ldots, 1)$, each x_n, $n = 1, \ldots, N$ can be reduced while still in $L(y)$. Thus $D_i(y,x) > 1$ and by the Indication property for $D_i(y,x)$, $x \notin IsoqL(y)$. This completes the proof.

Remark on the proof of iiia): The following figure shows that when the directional vector has all coordinates positive, for example 1^N, then $x_n > 0$, $n = 1, \ldots, N$ is required. In the Figure 1, input vector a has $x_1 = 0$, and $\vec{\mathbf{D}}_i\,(y, x;\, 1^N) = 0$, but a is not on the isoquant.

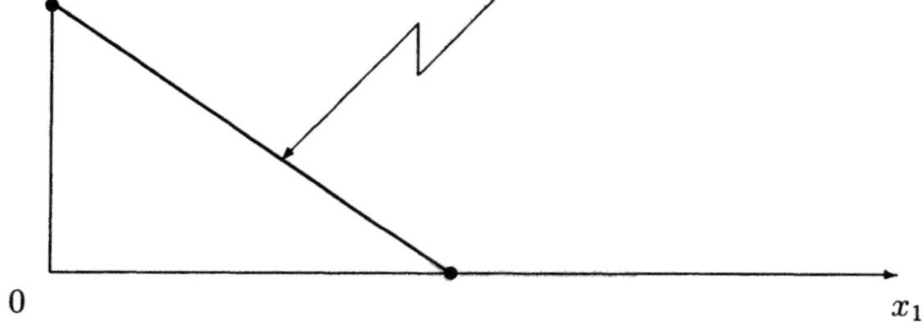

Figure 1. Remark on the proof of iii a).

This problem may be avoided by choosing the directional vector to have ones only for positive x's.

Proof of Theorem 1:

Assume first that the technology is as in (13), then

$$\begin{aligned}
R_M(y,x) &= \min_{\lambda_1\ldots\lambda_N}\left\{\left(\prod_{n=1}^{N}\lambda_n\right)^{1/N} : (\lambda_1 x_1,\ldots,\lambda_N x_N)\in L(y),\right.\\
&\qquad \left. 0<\lambda_n\leq 1, n=1,\ldots,N\right\}\\
&= \min_{\lambda_1\ldots\lambda_N}\left\{\left(\prod_{n=1}^{N}\lambda_n\right)^{1/N} :\right.\\
&\qquad \left. D_i\left(y,\lambda_1 x_1,\ldots,\lambda_N x_N\right)\geq 1, 0<\lambda_n\leq 1, n=1,\ldots,N\right\}\\
&= \min_{\lambda_1\ldots\lambda_N}\left\{\left(\prod_{n=1}^{N}\lambda_n\right)^{1/N} : \left(\prod_{n=1}^{N}\lambda_n x_n\right)^{1/N} /H(y)\geq 1,\right.\\
&\qquad \left. 0<\lambda_n\leq 1, n=1,\ldots,N\right\}\\
&= \min_{\lambda_1\ldots\lambda_N}\left\{\left(\prod_{n=1}^{N}\lambda_n\right)^{1/N} : \left(\prod_{n=1}^{N}\lambda_n\right)^{1/N} \geq H(y)/\left(\prod_{n=1}^{N}x_n\right)^{1/N}\right.\\
&\qquad \left. 0<\lambda_n\leq 1, n=1,\ldots,N\right\}\\
&= H(y)/\left(\prod_{n=1}^{N}x_n\right)^{1/N} = 1/D_i(y,x).
\end{aligned}$$

Since $DF(y,x) = 1/D_i(y,x)$ we have shown that (3) implies $R_M(y,x) = DF(y,x)$.

To prove the converse we first show that

$$R_M(y,\delta_1 x_1,\ldots,\delta_N x_N) = R_M(y,x)/\left(\prod_{n=1}^{N}\delta_n\right)^{1/N}, \qquad 0<\delta_n\leq 1,\ n=1,\ldots,N. \tag{35}$$

To see this,

$$\begin{aligned} R_M(y, \delta_1 x_1, \ldots, \delta_N x_N) &= \min_{\lambda_1 \ldots \lambda_N} \Big\{ \Big(\prod_{n=1}^{N} \lambda_n \Big)^{1/N} \\ &\quad : (\lambda_1 \delta_1 x_1, \ldots, \lambda_N \delta_N x_N) \in L(y), \\ &\quad 0 < \lambda_n \leq 1,\, 0 < \delta_n \leq 1,\, n = 1, \ldots, N \Big\} \\ &= \Big(\prod_{n=1}^{N} \delta_n \Big)^{-1/N} \min_{\lambda_1 \ldots \lambda_N} \Big\{ \Big(\prod_{n=1}^{N} \lambda_n \delta_n \Big)^{1/N} \\ &\quad : (\lambda_1 \delta_1 x_1, \ldots, \lambda_N \delta_N x_N) \in L(y), \\ &\quad 0 < \lambda_n \leq 1,\, 0 < \delta_n \leq 1,\, n = 1, \ldots, N \Big\} \\ &= \Big(\prod_{n=1}^{N} \delta_n \Big)^{-1/N} \min_{\lambda_1 \ldots \lambda_N} \Big\{ \Big(\prod_{n=1}^{N} \hat{\lambda}_n \Big)^{1/N} \\ &\quad : (\hat{\lambda}_1 \delta_1 x_1, \ldots, \hat{\lambda}_N \delta_N x_N) \in L(y), \\ &\quad 0 < \hat{\lambda}_n \leq 1,\, 0 < \delta_n \leq 1,\, n = 1, \ldots, N \Big\} \\ &= R_M(y, x) \Big(\prod_{n=1}^{N} \delta_n \Big)^{-1/N}, \end{aligned}$$

where $\hat{\lambda}_n = \lambda_n \delta_n$, $n = 1, \ldots, N$. Thus (34) holds.

Next, assume that the Debreu-Farrell and the multiplicative Russell measures are equal, then

$$R_M(y, \delta_1 x_1, \ldots, \delta_N, x_N) = R_M(y, x) / \Big(\prod_{n=1}^{N} \delta_N \Big)^{1/N} = DF(y, \delta_1 x_1, \ldots, \delta_N x_N),$$

thus

$$R_M(y, x) = DF(y, \delta_1 x_1, \ldots, \delta_N x_N) \Big(\prod_{n=1}^{N} \delta_N \Big)^{1/N},$$

and

$$DF(y, x) = DF(y, \delta_1 x_1, \ldots, \delta_N x_N) \Big(\prod_{n=1}^{N} \delta_N \Big)^{1/N}.$$

Now we take $\delta_n = 1/x_n$, $n = 1, \ldots, N$ then

$$DF(y, x) = DF(y, 1, \ldots, 1) / \Big(\prod_{n=1}^{N} x_n \Big)^{1/N}.$$

Moreover, since the Debreu-Farrell measure is independent of units of measurement (Russell (1987), p. 215),[10] x_n can be scaled so that $x_n > 0, n =$

[10] This was pointed out to us by R.R. Russell.

$1, \ldots, N$. Thus by taking $H(y) = DF(y, 1, \ldots, 1)$, and using (11) we have proved our claim.

Proof of Theorem 2:

First consider

$$\begin{aligned}
&A(y, x_1 - \delta_1, \ldots, x_N - \delta_N) \\
&= \max_{s_1 \ldots s_N} \left\{ \frac{1}{N} \sum_n s_n : (x_1 - \delta_1 - s_1, \ldots, x_N - \delta_N - s_N) \in L(y) \right\}, \\
&= \max_{s_1 \ldots s_N} \left\{ \frac{1}{N} \sum_n (s_n - \delta_n + \delta_n) : (x_1 - (\delta_1 + s_1), \ldots, x_N - (\delta_N + s_N)) \in L(y) \right\}, \\
&= -\frac{1}{N} \sum_n \delta_n + A(y, x),
\end{aligned}$$

where $s_n \geq 0$, $\delta_n \geq 0$, $n = 1, \ldots, N$.

This is equivalent to

$$A(y, x) = \frac{1}{N} \sum_{n=1}^{N} \delta_n + A(y, x_1 - \delta_1, \ldots, x_N - \delta_N) \tag{36}$$

Take $\delta_n = x_n$ and define $-F(y) = A(y, 0)$, then since equality between the directional distance function and the additive measure holds,

$$\vec{\mathbf{D}}_i\ (y, x;\ 1^N) = A(y, x) = \frac{1}{N} \sum_{n=1}^{N} x_n - F(y). \tag{37}$$

Next, let $x \in \bar{C}(L(y))$, then for some $\hat{x} \in IsoqL\,(y)$, and $\delta \geq 0$,

$$\vec{\mathbf{D}}_i\ (y, x;\ 1^N) = \vec{\mathbf{D}}_i\ (y, \hat{x} + \delta 1^N;\ 1^N) = \vec{\mathbf{D}}_i\ (y, \hat{x};\ 1^N) + \delta, \tag{38}$$

since $\hat{x} \in IsoqL\,(y)$, $\vec{\mathbf{D}}_i\ (y, x;\ 1^N) = \delta$.

Next,

$$\begin{aligned}
A(y, x) \quad &= \max_{s_1 \ldots s_N} \left\{ \tfrac{1}{N} \textstyle\sum_{n=1}^{N} s_n : \sum_{n=1}^{N} (x_n - s_n)/N - F(y) \geq 0 \right\} \\
&= \max_{s_1 \ldots s_N} \left\{ \tfrac{1}{N} \textstyle\sum_{n=1}^{N} s_n : \sum_{n=1}^{N} (\hat{x}_n + \delta - s_n)/N - F(y) \geq 0 \right\} \\
&= \max_{s_1 \ldots s_N} \left\{ \tfrac{1}{N} \textstyle\sum_{n=1}^{N} s_n : \delta + \tfrac{1}{N} \sum_{n=1}^{N} \hat{x}_n - F(y) \geq \tfrac{1}{N} \sum_{n=1}^{N} s_n \right\} \\
&= \delta,
\end{aligned}$$

since $\hat{x} \in IsoqL\,(y)$, thus $\vec{\mathbf{D}}_i\ (y, x;\ 1^N) = A(y, x)$. Q.E.D.

Sources of Manufacturing Productivity Growth: U.S. States 1990–1999

Shawna Grosskopf[1], Kathy Hayes[2], and Lori L. Taylor[3]*

[1] Department of Economics, Oregon State University, Corvallis, OR.
shawna.grosskopf@orst.edu
[2] Dedman College
Southern Methodist University
Dallas, TX 75275. khayes@mail.smu.edu
[3] George Bush School of Government and Public Service
1098 Allen Building, 4220 TAMU
College Station, TX 77843. ltaylor@bushschool.tamu.edu

Summary. In this paper we employ a panel of state level manufacturing data for the U.S. to estimate productivity growth and its sources during the 1990s. Following Kumar and Russell (2002), we augment the usual Malmquist decomposition of productivity growth with a capital deepening component. We find that innovation was the primary determinant of manufacturing productivity growth in all states, but that most states ended the decade further from the production possibilities frontier than they started. Capital deepening contributed to labor productivity growth in all but three states, and explains at least half of the labor productivity growth in a dozen states.

In a second stage, we investigate various policy-related variables and their relationship to productivity growth and its components. We find that a growing technology sector was a strong contributor to labor productivity growth, while a growing public sector was largely a drag. Improvements in labor force quality appear to have had little impact on the pace of technical change or the diffusion of technology, but capital deepening was significantly greater in states with a more highly educated population.

Key words: productivity, capital deepening, Malmquist, state manufacturing

1 Introduction

The literature on the impact of public capital on private productivity has a long history. Recent interest in the question, however, has been sparked by two important papers: Aschauer's provocative analysis suggesting that

* We have benefitted from comments and discussion with Donna Ginther, Steve Brown, Thijs ten Raa, Daniel Henderson and others.

public capital is grossly under provided in the United States (Aschauer 1989) and Munnell's analysis suggesting that state and local public capital is under provided in the United States (Munnell 1990). Munnell's analysis has been particularly influential because she generated a panel data set on public and private capital for the U.S. states that has been used by many subsequent researchers (e.g. Morrison and Schwartz 1994, 1996a,b, Kelejian and Robinson 1997, Holtz-Eakin 1994, Domazlicky and Weber 1998, Boisso, Grosskopf and Hayes 2000). As researchers have refined these seminal analyses, the case for significant under provision of public capital has faded. Holtz-Eakin (1994) and Garcia-Mila, McGuire and Porter (1996) find little evidence that public capital contributes to private sector productivity. Using a cost-function with quasi-fixed factors, Morrison and Schwartz (1994, 1996a,b) find evidence of positive direct productivity impacts of pubic capital but conclude that these direct effects are typically offset by indirect effects on factor accumulation. Brown, Hayes and Taylor (2003) found that not only does growth in public capital tend to discourage the accumulation of private capital and labor, it may also directly discourage output growth. In contrast, Henderson and Kumbhakar (2005) find a positive return to public capital when they use Li-Racine generalized kernal estimation.

A common characteristic of this literature has been that productivity is measured indirectly from an estimated production or cost function. A recent trend has been to use more direct measures of productivity. Domazlicky and Weber (1997, 1998) calculate Malmquist productivity indexes for each of the 48 contiguous states and use them to examine the impact of agglomeration economies and education levels on productivity. They find no relationship between public capital and private productivity. Boisso et al. (2000) also calculate Malmquist productivity indices and then examine the impact of business cycles and various measures of public capital. In contrast to Domazlicky and Weber, Boisso et al. find that the ratio of public capital to private capital has a positive impact on productivity. Boisso et al. also find evidence of spillover effects with respect to highway capital.

In this paper we add to the evidence on direct measures of productivity by augmenting the usual components of Malmquist productivity change to include capital deepening, following Kumar and Russell (2002).[4] We develop new perpetual-inventory estimates of manufacturing capital stocks for states and include those estimates in our analysis. Finally, we investigate the impacts on innovation, diffusion and capital deepening of several policy related instruments including labor quality, high tech share of manufacturing, public capital stocks and the size of state government. We find that capital deepening and technical change are the major sources of labor productivity growth in the period 1990-1999. A growing technology sector was a strong contributor to labor productivity growth, while a growing public sector was largely a drag. Growth in average educational attainment appears to have had little

[4] See also Henderson and Russell (2005) and Weber and Domazlicky (2006).

impact on the pace of technical change or the diffusion of technology, but capital deepening was significantly greater in states with a more highly educated population.

2 Method

We follow Kumar and Russell (2002) who augmented the standard Malmquist productivity index to allow for the identification of productivity changes due to efficiency change, technical change and capital deepening. Before turning to that decomposition, we can relate their decomposition to standard growth accounting approaches as in ten Raa and Mohnen (2002). Let Y denote output, which is a function of capital (K), labor (L) and time (t). To allow for inefficiency define θ as the factor which yields maximum potential output, i.e.,

$$\theta Y = F(L, K, t). \tag{1}$$

If we assume constant returns to scale, then we may normalize output and capital by labor, where $y = Y/L, k = K/L$ thus we may write

$$\theta y = f(k, t). \tag{2}$$

As is usual in the growth accounting literature, we express this in terms of growth rates yielding

$$\hat{y} = \hat{f}_t - \hat{\theta} + \frac{f_k}{f}\hat{k} \tag{3}$$

which states that the growth in output per unit of labor is equal to technical change plus efficiency change plus capital deepening, i.e., the change in the capital labor ratio. This would typically be 'estimated' or deduced from a parametric specification of the production or cost function. Here we replace that function with an estimation of a nonparametric best practice frontier and substitute discrete changes for the derivatives in (3) as discussed below.

Kumar and Russell (2002) arrive at the tripartite decomposition above by generalizing a Malmquist productivity index. The basic building block of these productivity indexes is the Shephard output distance function, which is defined as

$$D(x, y) = \inf\{\theta : y/\theta \in P(x)\}, \tag{4}$$

where $y \in \Re_+^M$ is a vector of outputs, $x \in \Re_+^N$ is a vector of inputs (in our case labor and capital), and $P(x)$ is the output set, i.e., it consists of the set of all outputs producible from a given input vector x. This function has the advantage of readily modeling multi-output technology without requiring data on prices, and identifies deviations from the frontier of technology. It is also easily computed using linear programming methods. For example, we can estimate the distance function for an observation k' in period t as the solution to the following linear programming problem

$$
\begin{aligned}
(D^t(x^t_{k'n}, y^t_{k'm}))^{-1} &= \max \theta \qquad (5)\\
&\text{subject to}\\
\sum_{k=1}^{K} z_k y^t_{km} &\geq \theta y^t_{k'm},\ m = 1, \ldots, M,\\
\sum_{k=1}^{K} z_k x^t_{kn} &\leq x^t_{k'n},\ n = 1, \ldots, N,\\
z_k &\geq 0,\ k = 1, \ldots, K.
\end{aligned}
$$

The $z's$ are intensity variables which serve to construct the technology from the observed data. In our case, the resulting technology would be based on all the states in the sample and would identify the nonparametric best practice frontier of that meta-state technology.

Following Kumar and Russell, we use the distance functions to achieve a tripartite decomposition of labor productivity into technical change, technological catch up and capital deepening. Taking advantage of the fact that the above specified technology satisfies constant returns to scale, we can normalize output and capital by labor, i.e., let $y =$ output/labor, $x =$ capital/labor. Following Kumar and Russell, let c denote the current period and b the previous period, then the tripartite decomposition is defined as follows

$$y^c/y^b = D^c(x^c, y^c)/D^b(x^b, y^b)\left(\frac{D^b(x^c, y^c)}{D^c(x^c, y^c)}\frac{D^b(x^b, y^b)}{D^c(x^b, y^b)}\right)^{1/2} KACCUM \qquad (6)$$

or

$$y^c/y^b = EFF \times TECH \times KACCUM \qquad (7)$$

where EFF is efficiency change (diffusion, or catching up to the frontier), TECH is technical change (innovation or shifts in the frontier) and KACCUM is a residual term capturing the effect of capital deepening (increase in the capital labor ratio). Note that $EFF \times TECH$ yields the traditional Malmquist productivity index proposed by Caves, Christensen and Diewert (1982).

The distance functions are estimated using the programming problem described above with the appropriate substitution of time periods. Thus we will have measures of productivity change for each state for adjacent periods covering the time period 1990–1999.

3 Data and Estimation

We follow a multi-part strategy for evaluating the changes in manufacturing output per worker during the 1990s. In the first stage, we use data on gross state product, employment, and manufacturing capital stocks to generate annual measures of efficiency (the distance functions discussed in the previous section) for U.S. states.

In the second stage of the analysis, we use year-to-year changes in our efficiency measures to decompose changes in manufacturing output per worker into its three components—technical change, efficiency change and capital deepening. We then describe the distributions of these component factors and their relative contributions to productivity growth.

In the final stage of the analysis, we explore possible determinants of our efficiency and productivity measures. Various economists have argued that measured improvements in labor productivity reflect changes in industrial mix, increases in labor force quality, changes in the public capital stock or decreases in the size of the public sector.[5] We use our panel of labor productivity data to examine the impact of each of these factors.

3.1 Data

The Bureau of Economic Analysis (BEA) is the primary source of data for productivity analysis. Annual state-level data on gross state product and employment in manufacturing come directly from the BEA. Following Munnell (1990a,b,c), we estimate net manufacturing capital stocks for each state by apportioning the BEA's national estimates. However, whereas Munnell assumed that manufacturing capital stocks grew at the national rate in most years,[6] we use annual investment data for each state to construct perpetual-inventory estimates of manufacturing capital stocks. These perpetual-inventory estimates are then used to apportion the BEA's national stock estimates for manufacturing capital. See the data appendix for further details.

Data on industrial mix also come from the BEA. Our measure of industrial mix is the high-tech manufacturing sector's share of total manufacturing output. We define high-tech manufacturing as the sum of the industrial machinery (the industry that includes computers), electronics and instruments industries (SIC codes 335,336 and 338).

---

[5] See, for example, Brown, Hayes and Taylor (2003); Cameron (2003); Cook (2004); Domazlicky and Weber (1997, 1998); Kahn and Lim (1998); Grosskopf, Hayes and Taylor (2003), or Taylor and Brown (forthcoming).

[6] Munnell (1990c) decomposes U.S. estimates of private capital into state-level estimates using information from industry censuses to identify each state's share of U.S. capital for that industry in census years. She then assumes that the state shares of private capital are constant for a multi-year period centered on the census year. "Data from the 1972 Census were used to apportion among the states the BEA national stock estimates for 1969 to 1974; 1977 shares were used for the 1975 to 1979 stock estimates; 1982 shares were the basis for the estimates from 1980 to 1984 and 1987 data were used to apportion national asset totals for 1985 and 1986" (Munnell 1990c, pg. 97). Thus, in 1975, 1980 and 1985, growth rates are exaggerated in each industry to "catch up" for the five-year deviations in the state's growth rate from the national average. In all other years, there is no cross-sectional variation in the growth of private manufacturing capital under the Munnell approach.

Data on labor force quality—which we measure as the average educational attainment of the adult population—come from the U.S. Censuses of Population for 1990 and 2000 and the National Center for Education Statistics (NCES). To construct annual estimates of average educational attainment, we first calculate average educational attainment in the two census years.[7] We then use NCES data on degrees conferred (high school diplomas, associates degrees, bachelors' degrees, masters' degrees, first professional degrees and Ph.D. degrees) to generate annual estimates of human capital production in each state. Finally, we use the production data to impute annual changes in average educational attainment for th e state.

Data on public capital stocks come from Brown, Hayes and Taylor (2003). We use their measure of total public capital, divided by the BEA's annual population estimates, as our measure of the public capital per capita.

Finally, we use state and local government noncapital expenditures (net of tuition and health care charges and relative to gross state product) as our measure of government size. The expenditures data come from the annual Censuses and Surveys of Governments.

4 Results

As figure 1 illustrates, there were substantial differences across U.S. states in labor productivity growth in manufacturing during the 1990s. Two states—Louisiana and Delaware—saw declines in output per manufacturing worker, while a handful of states saw labor productivity increase by more than 6 percent per year, on average. New Mexico posted by far the highest gains in labor productivity. At 24 percent per year, New Mexico's increase in output per worker was more than double that of any other state, and nearly six times the national average increase.

Figure 2 illustrates the year-by-year distribution of productivity growth during the 1990s, for the contiguous U.S. states, excluding New Mexico.[8] The markers represent the (output-weighted[9]) average productivity change for each year, while the bars indicate the 5th percentile to 95th percentile ranges.

As the figure demonstrates, productivity growth generally accelerated during the 1990s. For the output-weighted average state, the average rate of productivity growth in the second half of the 1990s (4.7 percent per year) is two

[7] Average educational attainment is a weighted average of the share of the adult population in each educational attainment category (less than high school, high school drop-out, high-school graduate, etcetera) where the weights represent average years of schooling associated with the attainment level.

[8] Given its rate of productivity growth, we consider New Mexico an outlier and exclude it from our analysis.

[9] We follow Zelenyuk (forthcoming) and compute the output weighted harmonic mean to estimate average labor productivity and its components.

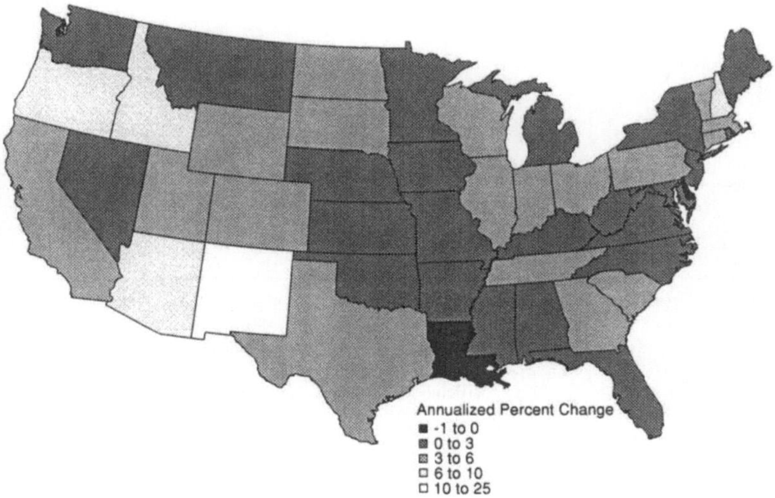

Fig. 1. Changes in the productivity of manufacturing labor 1990–1999

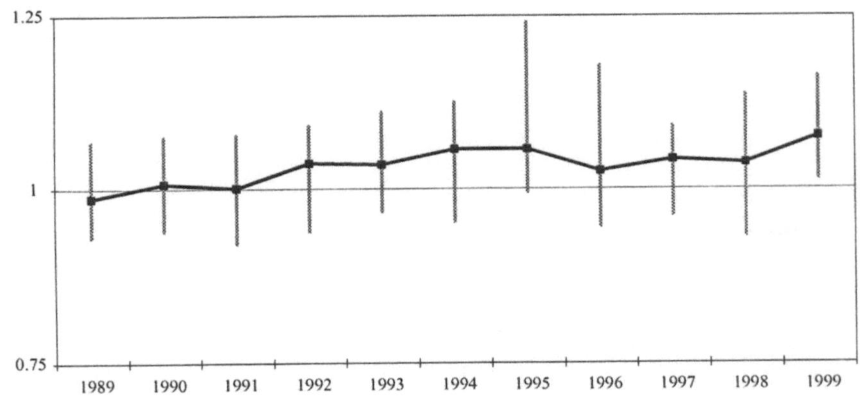

Fig. 2. Labor productivity in manufacturing generally accelerated during the 1990s (year over year changes in output per worker)

percentage points higher than the average rate of productivity growth in the first half of the decade. Thirty-five of the 47 states under analysis experienced more rapid productivity growth after 1994.

Figure 3 illustrates the distributions of technical change, efficiency change and capital deepening. As the figure illustrates, any acceleration in manufacturing productivity during the 1990s is wholly attributable to an acceleration

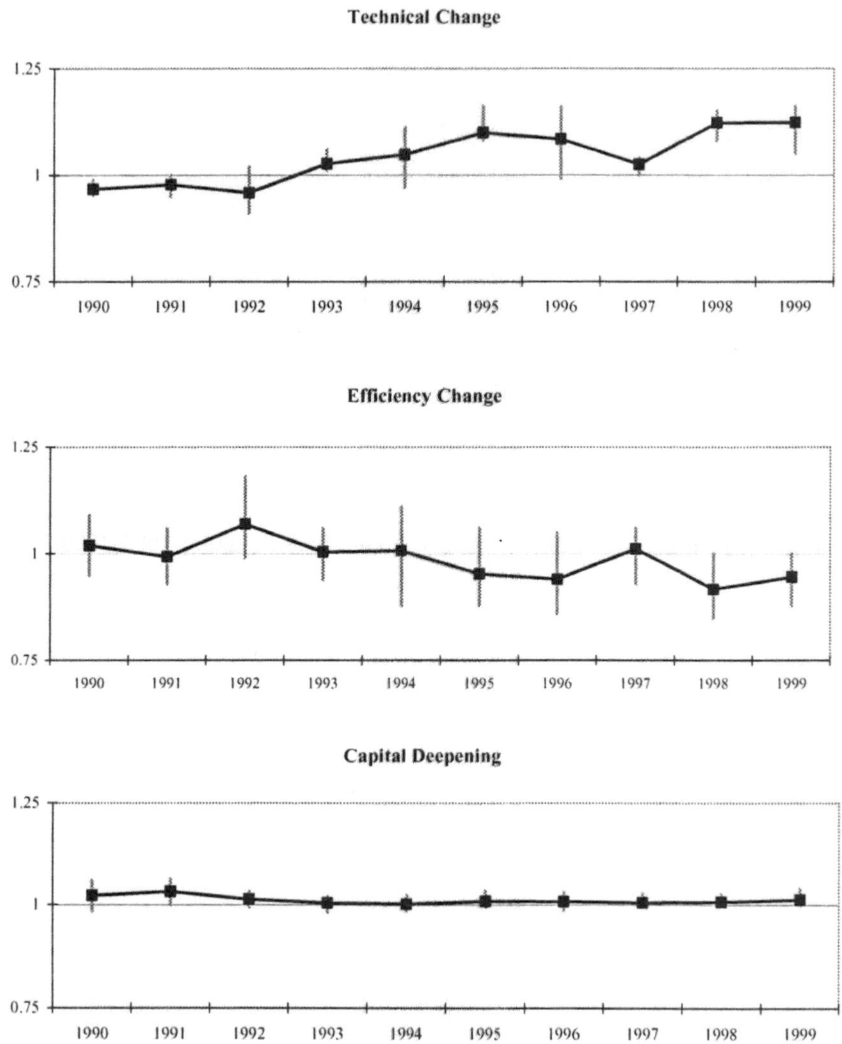

Note: The markers indicate the output-weighted averages for 47 U.S. states. (Alaska, Hawaii and New Mexico are excluded.) The bars indicate the 5th and 95th percentile ranges.

Fig. 3. Sources of Labor Productivity Growth in Manufacturing

in technical change. Capital deepening held steady for most of the decade while efficiency change exhibited a significant downward trend. Average efficiency change was below one during much of the latter half of the 1990s. Apparently the pace of technical change was so rapid that many states had trouble keeping up.

The cumulative impact of a decade of change is striking. (See Table 1.) Technical change was the primary determinant of labor productivity growth

Table 1. Cumulative Changes in State Manf. Productivity: 1990s

State	PROD	EFF	TECH	KACCUM	State	PROD	EFF	TECH	KACCUM
AL	1.249	0.789	1.508	1.051	NC	1.260	0.701	1.542	1.166
AR	1.266	0.761	1.567	1.061	ND	1.414	1.010	1.440	0.972
AZ	2.500	1.348	1.514	1.225	NE	1.268	0.773	1.554	1.056
CA	1.769	0.964	1.516	1.209	NH	2.178	1.077	1.642	1.232
CO	1.416	0.853	1.460	1.138	NJ	1.277	0.730	1.425	1.226
CT	1.666	0.894	1.503	1.240	NV	1.241	0.801	1.448	1.070
DE	0.991	0.616	1.474	1.092	NY	1.291	0.746	1.471	1.177
FL	1.308	0.750	1.540	1.133	OH	1.406	0.876	1.461	1.098
GA	1.412	0.840	1.471	1.142	OK	1.308	0.909	1.413	1.018
IA	1.327	0.879	1.427	1.058	OR	2.418	1.282	1.567	1.204
ID	2.111	1.141	1.438	1.286	PA	1.576	1.004	1.440	1.090
IL	1.423	0.929	1.495	1.024	RI	1.253	0.535	1.720	1.362
IN	1.463	0.929	1.550	1.016	SC	1.439	0.909	1.489	1.064
KS	1.115	0.738	1.429	1.056	SD	1.664	0.858	1.556	1.246
KY	1.247	0.776	1.475	1.090	TN	1.368	0.783	1.484	1.177
LA	0.987	0.800	1.232	1.001	TX	1.501	1.015	1.468	1.008
MA	1.542	0.829	1.515	1.228	UT	1.393	0.829	1.515	1.109
MD	1.302	0.850	1.536	0.997	VA	1.145	0.693	1.486	1.112
ME	1.222	0.773	1.545	1.024	VT	1.407	0.895	1.517	1.036
MI	1.231	0.782	1.562	1.007	WA	1.114	0.679	1.402	1.171
MN	1.213	0.676	1.527	1.175	WI	1.377	0.822	1.528	1.096
MO	1.263	0.687	1.529	1.201	WV	1.148	0.794	1.422	1.018
MS	1.293	0.766	1.540	1.096	WY	1.557	1.068	1.448	1.007
MT	1.045	0.744	1.471	0.955					

PROD is change in labor productivity, EFF is efficiency change, TECH is technical change and KACCUM is change in the capital labor ratio or capital deepening.

in all states, but most states ended the decade further from the production possibilities frontier than they started. Capital deepening contributed to labor productivity growth in all but three states, and explains at least half of the labor productivity growth in a dozen states. In four states—Delaware, Louisiana, Rhode Island and Washington—capital deepening can more than explain growth in output per worker.

4.1 The Usual Suspects

Further analysis can shed additional light on the pattern of productivity gain. In this final stage, we examine the relationship between the rate of productivity change (and its components) and factors frequently used to explain it: changes in industrial mix, increases in labor force quality, increases in the public capital stock or decreases in the size of the public sector.

Our estimation is based on a nine-year panel covering the period 1991-1999 for 47 states.[10] Productivity change and its components are each modeled as a function of the average educational attainment in the state, public capital per capita, the size of the public sector, the share of the manufacturing sector that is high tech manufacturing (all lagged one year) and the changes in each of these factors. Because states that are not on the productivity frontier may have more "room for improvement," the model also includes the state's relative efficiency in the prior year. Fixed effects for time capture national business cycles and other time trends.

Arguably, the initial efficiency level is endogenous. Furthermore, there may be a correlation among the residuals for any given state. Therefore, table 2 presents four variations on a theme. Our first model estimates the relationship between productivity growth and the policy factors using fixed effects for states. The second model incorporates random effects for states. The third model is an instrumental variables regression with state fixed effects. The manufacturing sector's share of gross state product is used as an instrument for the potentially endogenous initial efficiency. Model four incorporates random effects for states into an instrumental variables analysis, using the same instrument as in model three.

As table 2 illustrates, except for the estimated effect of initial efficiency, the estimation is generally insensitive to modeling strategy. Specification tests reject the fixed and random effects models in favor of their IV counterparts.[11]

[10] Alaska, Hawaii and New Mexico are excluded.

[11] A Hausman specification test rejects the random effects model in favor of the IV random effects model, but does not reject the fixed effects model in favor of its IV counterpart. (The probabilities of a greater chi-squared test statistic are 0.0538 and 0.9620, respectively.) However, a Durbin-Wu-Hausman test easily rejects the fixed effects model in favor of the fixed effects IV specification. (The probability of a greater F-statistic is 0.0030.)

Table 2. Influences on Manufacturing Productivity Growth During the 1990s

	State Fixed Eff		State Rand Eff		IV Fixed Eff		IV Rand Eff	
	$\hat{\beta}$	$\hat{\sigma}$	$\hat{\beta}$	$\hat{\sigma}$	$\hat{\beta}$	$\hat{\sigma}$	$\hat{\beta}$	$\hat{\sigma}$
Intercept	2.882	1.296**	1.258	0.120***	3.454	1.338***	2.532	0.709***
Init effic	−0.223	0.053***	−0.047	0.023**	−0.433	0.090***	−0.384	0.095***
High Tech	0.004	0.001***	0.002	0.0002***	0.006	0.001***	0.005	0.001***
Avg H Cap	−0.105	0.101	−0.016	0.009*	−0.116	0.104	−0.082	0.054
Pub Cap	−0.207	0.114*	0.001	0.008	−0.357	0.128***	−0.057	0.056
Govt Size	−0.013	0.006**	−0.003	0.002	−0.016	0.007**	−0.016	0.006***
Change in:								
Hi Tech	0.010	0.001***	0.010	0.001***	0.010	0.001***	0.010	0.001***
Avg H Cap	−1.517	1.776	−0.189	0.283	−3.328	1.919*	−1.341	1.403
Pub Cap	0.272	0.309	0.030	0.220	0.377	0.317	0.581	0.301*
Govt Size	−0.024	0.006***	−0.020	0.005***	−0.024	0.006***	−0.023	0.006***
y92	0.036	0.011***	0.024	0.010**	0.041	0.011***	0.036	0.010***
y93	0.050	0.015***	0.020	0.011*	0.068	0.016***	0.056	0.014***
y94	0.069	0.017***	0.035	0.011***	0.087	0.019***	0.073	0.015***
y95	0.103	0.021***	0.062	0.011***	0.125	0.023***	0.105	0.016***
y96	0.053	0.025**	0.014	0.011	0.070	0.026***	0.046	0.017***
y97	0.050	0.029*	0.015	0.011	0.060	0.030**	0.031	0.018*
y98	0.058	0.034*	0.015	0.011	0.073	0.035**	0.035	0.020*
y99	0.100	0.039***	0.060	0.011***	0.104	0.039***	0.061	0.022***
R-square	0.454		0.368		0.431		0.209	
Num of Obs	423		423		423		423	

Note: Initial efficiency is endogenous in the IV models. The instrument is manufacturing's share of GSP. The asterisks indicate that the coefficient is significantly different from zero at the 1-percent (***), 5-percent (**), or the 10-percent (*) level.

A Hausman test also indicates that the random effects IV model is both efficient and consistent, making it our preferred model.[12]

Our analysis reveals a number of interesting patterns. First, the estimation suggests that initial efficiency has a significant influence on productivity growth. States that start the year far from the production possibilities frontier show more productivity growth than states that start the year on the frontier. The pattern suggests that diffusion or catching up is a significant determinant of regional variations in labor productivity growth.

States with a large or growing high tech share are also much more likely than other states to experience rapid growth in output per worker. Such a pattern is not surprising given other work indicating that the productivity gains in high tech manufacturing are substantially greater than the gains in manufacturing as a whole (e.g. Grosskopf et al. 2002).

On the other hand, states with a large or growing public sector register less productivity growth than other states. One possible interpretation is that a growing public sector crowds out private manufacturing (e.g., as found in Brown et al. 2003). Alternatively, given that budget balance is generally required at the state level, the negative relationship between productivity growth and government growth may simply indicate that taxes discourage private manufacturing activity.

The fixed-effects specifications indicate that public capital is a drag on labor productivity growth, but the fixed effects themselves are highly and positively correlated with public capital per capita.[13] Meanwhile, the random effects specifications indicate that states where public capital stocks per capita are growing experience faster productivity growth than other states. However, the effect is only significant at the 10 percent level and completely disappears when Wyoming data are excluded from the analysis.[14] We can only conclude that the evidence on the impact of public capital deepening is weak and inconclusive.

Intriguingly, there also is no apparent relationship between gains in average educational attainment and labor productivity growth in manufacturing. States where average educational attainment was rising rapidly experienced no greater gains in manufacturing productivity than did other states. In none of the specifications can we reject the hypothesis that both human capital measures are jointly insignificant. In general, the evidence indicates that average educational attainment has no relationship with manufacturing productivity growth. One possible interpretation for this finding is that the educational attainment of the general population is a poor proxy for the educational attainment of manufacturing workers.

---

[12] The chi-squared test statistic is 6.96. The probability of a greater chi-squared is 0.9840.

[13] The Pearson correlation between public capital per capita at the start of the decade and the state fixed effects from the IV model is 0.8875.

[14] Wyoming has significantly more public capital per capita than any other state.

Table 3. The Determinants of Initial Efficiency

State Random Effects

	$\hat{\beta}$	$\hat{\sigma}$
Intercept	−0.6320	0.5709
Manufacturing Share	0.0207	0.0020***
High Tech Share	0.0034	0.0006***
Avg Human Capital	0.0804	0.0448*
Public Capital	0.0524	0.0498
Government Size	−0.0122	0.0045***
y92	0.0124	0.0097
y93	0.0633	0.0107***
y94	0.0583	0.0113***
y95	0.0562	0.0122***
y96	0.0099	0.0135
y97	−0.0279	0.0143*
y98	−0.0258	0.0156*
y99	−0.0874	0.0171***
R-square		0.1366
Number of Observations		423

Note: The asterisks indicate that the coefficient is significantly different from zero at the 1-percent (***), 5-percent (**), or the 10-percent (*) level.

Exploring further, table 3 illustrates the relationship between initial efficiency and the levels of the other explanatory variables. As the table illustrates, states with a relatively large manufacturing sector or a relatively large high tech share tend to be more technically efficient than other states. Manufacturing efficiency also appears to be higher in states where the public sector is smaller or the labor force is more highly educated, all other things being equal. Public capital per capita has no apparent influence on initial efficiency.

Table 4 decomposes the change in output per worker into its three component pieces: technical change, efficiency change and capital deepening.

Table 4. Decomposing Manufacturing Productivity Growth: 1990s

State Random Effects IV Models

	Effic Change		Tech Change		Capital Deep	
	$\hat{\beta}$	$\hat{\sigma}$	$\hat{\beta}$	$\hat{\sigma}$	$\hat{\beta}$	$\hat{\sigma}$
Intercept	2.727	0.732***	0.959	0.186***	0.590	0.161***
Initial Eff	−0.349	0.087***	−0.008	0.101	0.066	0.030**
High Tech Share	0.004	0.001***	0.000	0.000	0.000	0.000
Avg Human Cap	−0.105	0.056*	0.002	0.008	0.032	0.012***
Public Capital	−0.011	0.060	−0.005	0.006	−0.016	0.012
Govt Size	−0.018	0.005***	0.000	0.003	−0.002	0.002
Change in:						
High Tech Share	0.004	0.001***	0.004	0.001***	0.001	0.0003**
Avg Human Cap	−0.040	1.395	0.075	0.251	0.530	0.336
Public Capital	0.253	0.283	0.109	0.283	0.137	0.087
Govt Size	−0.024	0.006***	−0.003	0.004	0.001	0.002
YR92	0.073	0.010***	−0.016	0.008**	−0.018	0.003***
YR93	0.032	0.013**	0.050	0.011***	−0.030	0.004***
YR94	0.039	0.014***	0.061	0.011***	−0.032	0.004***
YR95	−0.002	0.016	0.123	0.011***	−0.024	0.004***
YR96	−0.025	0.017	0.100	0.009***	−0.028	0.004***
YR97	0.013	0.018	0.040	0.009***	−0.027	0.004***
YR98	−0.072	0.021***	0.136	0.009***	−0.028	0.005***
YR99	−0.056	0.023**	0.137	0.013***	−0.018	0.006***
R-square		0.311		0.716		0.195
Number of Obs		423		423		423

Note: All models are instrumental variables with random effects for states. Initial efficiency is treated as endogenous. The instrument is manufacturing's share of GSP. Asterisks indicate that the coefficient is significantly different from zero at the 1-percent (***), 5-percent (**), or the 10-percent (*) level.

All three models are estimated using an instrumental variables, random effects by state specification. In all cases, Hausman tests indicate that the random effects model is both efficient and consistent.[15]

The decomposition reveals additional information about productivity growth. First, as expected, the evidence suggests that starting the period farther from the production possibilities frontier leads to significantly more growth through diffusion. The coefficient on initial efficiency is significantly negative in the efficiency change equation. Somewhat surprisingly, the estimation also reveals that initial efficiency affects capital deepening. States where the manufacturing sector is initially inefficient appear to draw less capital investment (relative to labor growth) than other states. Capital deepening is significantly greater in states that are on or near the production possibilities frontier.

Strikingly, the positive relationship between productivity growth and the high tech sector is found in all three components of productivity growth. An increasing concentration in high tech manufacturing appears to enhance manufacturing productivity not only by inducing technological change, but also by attracting capital investment. Furthermore, states with a large share of manufacturing in high tech industries did a better job of keeping up with technological change (i.e. moving closer to the production possibilities frontier) than did states with a relatively small high tech sector.

On the other hand, changes in government spending appear to affect labor productivity only through their effect on diffusion. States where the public sector is growing are less likely to catch up to the production possibilities frontier (as evidenced by the negative coefficient on the change in government size) but no more likely to grow through innovation or capital deepening.

There is little evidence that labor force quality can explain innovation or the diffusion of technology (efficiency change). The indicators of labor force quality are jointly insignificant in the equations for both components of the standard Malmquist index. However, capital appears drawn to states with a relatively well educated population. States with a high degree of human capital deepening also experience a high degree of physical capital deepening, suggesting that human and physical capital are complements rather than substitutes.

There is no evidence that a lack of public capital affects, innovation, diffusion or capital deepening. Both indicators of public capital are jointly insignificant in all three equations. This finding is generally consistent with Brown, et al. (2003) who found that the growth of public capital tended to discourage the growth of both private capital and private sector labor. Our analysis of labor productivity in manufacturing would not detect influences on factor accumulation that impacted both capital and labor in comparable ways.

---

[15] The probability of a greater chi-squared test statistic is 0.9999, 0.7721 and 0.7868 for efficiency change, technical change and capital deepening, respectively.

5 Conclusions

Careful analysis of recent manufacturing productivity change in the United States provides interesting insights into an important component of economic growth.[16] The analysis reveals that labor productivity in manufacturing accelerated during the 1990s. The pace of technical change picked up sharply, leaving most states further behind the production possibilities frontier. The capital-labor ratio continued to grow, and capital deepening was an important factor in productivity growth for most states.

The growth of the high tech sector was a major contributor to productivity growth in manufacturing during the 1990s. Growth of government, on the other hand, was largely a drag on productivity growth. States with a growing public sector were less likely to catch up to the production possibilities frontier than other states, and there is no evidence that a lack of public capital slowed diffusion, innovation or capital deepening. Growth in average educational attainment appears to have had little impact on the pace technical change or the diffusion of technology, but capital deepening was significantly greater in states with a more highly educated population.

Much remains to be done. A similar analysis for the high tech manufacturing sub-sector is a natural extension, as is that of the services sector both of which experienced even faster productivity growth than manufacturing as a whole (see Anderson and Kliesen (2006)). An extended decomposition to include change in human capital as a component of productivity change following Henderson and Russell (2005) would also be useful. We have not addressed the issue of convergence of labor productivity growth here, but results by Weber and Domazlicky (2006), who also use state data applied to the Kumar and Russell decomposition find that capital deepening and efficiency change have contriuted to β-convergence in labor productivity in manufacturing over the 1977–1996 period. Technical change was divergent, and there was no evidence of σ-convergence over that time period. Since our capital data and time frame differs from theirs, a comparison may prove interesting.

References

Anderson, Richard G. and Kevin L. Kliesen. "The 1990s Acceleration in Labor Productivity: Causes and Measurement" *The Federal Reserve Bannk of St. Louis Review* **88**(3) (2006), 181–202.

Aschauer, David Alan. "Is Public Expenditure Productive?" *Journal of Monetary Economics* **23** (1989), 177–200.

[16] As discussed in Anderson and Kliesen (2006), labor productivity increased even more in the services-producing sectors. They attribute much of the difference to the impact of falling prices of information and communications technology products.

Boisso, D., S. Grosskopf and K. Hayes. "Productivity and Efficiency in the US: Effects of Business Cycles and Public Capital," *Regional Science and Urban Economics* **30** (2000), 663–681.

Brown, Steven P.A., Kathy J. Hayes, and Lori L. Taylor."State and Local Policy, Factor Markets and Regional Growth," *Review of Regional Studies*, **33**(1) (2003), 40–60.

Cameron, Gavin. "Why did UK Productivity Growth Slow Down in the 1970s and Speed up in the 1980s?" *Economica* **70**(277) (2003), 121–41.

Caves, D.W., L.R. Christensen and W.E. Diewert."The Economic Theory of Index Numbers and the Measurement of Input, Output and Productivity." *Econometrica* **50**(6) (1982), 1393–1414.

Charnes, A., W.W. Cooper and E. Rhodes. "Measuring the Efficiency of Decision-making Units." *European Journal of Operational Research* **2**(6) (1978), 429–444.

Cook, David. "Experience and Growth," *Economics Letters* **85**(1) (2004), 53–56.

Domazlicky, B. R, and W. L. Weber. "Productivity Growth and Pollution in State Manufacturing" *Review of Economics and Statistics* **83** (2001), 195–99.

Domazlicky, B. R, and W. L. Weber. "Determinants of total factor Productivity, technological Change and Efficiency Differentials Among States, 1977–86" *Review of Regional Studies* **28**(2) (1998), 19–33.

Domazlicky, B. R, and W. L. Weber. "Total Factor Productivity in the Contiguous United States, 1977–86" *Journal of Regional Science* **37** (1998), 213–33.

Färe, R. *Fundamentals of Production Theory.* Lecture Notes in Economics and Mathematical Systems, Germany: Springer-Verlag, 1988.

Färe, R., S. Grosskopf and C.A.K Lovell. *Production Frontiers*, Cambridge: Cambridge University Press, 1994.

Färe, R., S. Grosskopf, B. Lindgren and P. Roos. "Productivity Developments in Swedish Hospitals: A Malmquist Output Index Approach." Discussion Paper 89–3, Southern Illinois University, 1989.

Färe, R., S. Grosskopf, M. Norris and Z. Zhang. "Productivity Growth, Technical Progress, and Efficiency Change in Industrialized Countries." *American Economic Review*, **84**(1) (1994), 66–83.

Farrell, Michael J. "The Measurement of Productive Efficiency." *Journal of the Royal Statistical Society*, Series A, General, **120**(3) (1957), 253–81.

Garcia-Mila, T., T J. McGuire and R.H. Porter. "The Effect of Public Capital in State-Level Production Functions Reconsidered," *Review of Economics and Statistics* (1996).

Grosskopf, Shawna, Kathy Hayes and Lori L. Taylor. "Productivity, Innovation and Diffusion in the United States: Can Policy put the States on the Technology Frontier?," *mimeo*, 2002.

Henderson, Daniel J. and Subal C. Kumbhakar. "Public and Private Capital Productivity Puzzle: A Nonparametric Approach,' *mimeo*, 2005.

Henderson, Daniel J. and R. R. Russell. "Human Capital and Convergence: A Production-Frontier Approach," *International Economic Review* **46**(4) (2005), 1167–1205.

Holtz-Eakin, Douglas. "Public-Sector Capital and the Productivity Puzzle," *Review of Economics and Statistics* **76** (1994), 12–21.

Kelejian, Harry H. and Dennis P. Robinson. "Infrastructure Productivity Estimation and Its Underlying Econometric Specifications: A Sensitivity Analysis," *Papers in Regional Science* **76** (1997), 115–131.

Jorgenson, D. W. "Information Technology and the U.S. Economy," *American Economic Review* **91**(1) (2001), 1–32.

Kahn, James and Jong-Soo Lim. "Skilled Labor-Augmenting Technical Progress in U.S. Manufacturing," *Quarterly Journal of Economics* **113**(4) (1998), 1281–1308.

Kumar, S. and R. R. Russell. "Technological change, Technological Catch-Up and Capital Deepening: Relative Contributions to Growth and Convergence," *American Economic Review*, **92**(3) (2002), f527–549.

Malmquist, S. "Index Numbers and Indifference Curves." *Trabajos de Estatistica* **4** (1953), 209–242.

Morrison, C.J. and A.E. Schwartz. "State Infrastructure and Productive Performance," *American Economic Review* **86**(5) (1996a), 1095–1111.

Morrison, C.J. and A.E. Schwartz. "Public Infrastructure, Private Input Demand, and Economic Performance in New England Manufacturing," *Journal of Business and Economic Statistics* **14** (1996b), 91–101.

Morrison, C.J. and A.E. Schwartz. "Distinguishing External from Internal Scale Effects: The Case of Public Infrastructure," *Journal of Productivity Analysis*, October (1994), 249–70.

Munnell, A. H. "Why has Productivity declined? Productivity and Public Investment," *New England Economic Review*, Jan-Feb. (1990a), 3–22.

Munnell, A. H. "How does Public Infrastructure Affect Regional Economic Performance?," *New England Economic Review*, Sept.-Oct. (1990b), 3–22.

Munnell, A H. "How Does Public Infrastructure Affect Regional Economic Performance?" in Alicia H. Munnell (ed.) *Is There a Shortfall in Public Capital Investment?*, Federal Reserve Bank of Boston: Boston, 1990c.

Shephard, R.W. *Theory of Cost and Production Functions.* Princeton: Princeton University Press, 1970.

Taylor, Lori L. and Stephen P.A. Brown. "The Private Sector Impact of State and Local Government: Has More Become Bad?," *Contemporary Economic Policy*, forthcoming.

ten Raa, Thijs and Pierre Mohnen. "Neoclassical Growth Accounting and Frontier Analysis: A Synthesis," *Journal of Productivity Analysis* **18**(2) (2002), 111–128.

U.S. Department of Commerce. *Fixed Reproducible Tangible Wealth in the United States, 1925–94* (US Government Printing Office: Washington, DC), 1999.

Weber, William L. and Bruce R. Domazlicky. "Capital Deepening and Manufacturing's Contribution to Regional Economic Convergence," *mimeo*, 2006.

Zelenyuk, Valentin. "Aggregation of Malmquist Productivity Indexes," *European Journal of Operational Research*, forthcoming.

6 Data Appendix

Following Munnell (1990a,b,c), we estimate net manufacturing capital stocks for each state by apportioning the BEA's national estimates. We differ from Munnell in a number of key ways, however. Most obviously, we have extended the data set to cover the period 1977–1999. More importantly, we have based our allocation of the national capital stock estimates on new, perpetual inventory estimates of state level capital stocks.

Munnell(1990c) decomposed U.S. estimates of manufacturing capital into state-level estimates using information from the census of manufacturing to identify each state's share of U.S. capital stocks. She then assumed that the state shares of manufacturing capital were constant for a multi-year period centered on the census year. "Data from the 1972 Census were used to apportion among the states the BEA national stock estimates for 1969 to 1974; 1977 shares were used for the 1975 to 1979 stock estimates; 1982 shares were the basis for the estimates from 1980 to 1984 and 1987 data were used to apportion national asset totals for 1985 and 1986" (Munnell 1990c, pg. 97).

Munnell's approach meant that growth rates in 1975, 1980 and 1985, were exaggerated to "catch up" for the five-year deviations in the state's growth rate from the national average. In all other years, there was no cross-sectional variation in the growth of private manufacturing capital under the Munnell approach.

Because the time series properties of Munnell's capital stock series are problematic, we have adopted a different strategy for apportioning the U.S. capital stocks. We apportioned the U.S. capital stocks in manufacturing using perpetual-inventory estimates of state-level capital stocks that we developed. We have also incorporated improved estimates of national public capital stocks that were not available to Munnell.

BEA now uses a geometric depreciation strategy to generate its capital stock estimates.[17] Following BEA, we calculated our perpetual-inventory estimates of net capital stocks in each state for period t as

$$N_t = \sum_{i=1}^{t} I_i(1 - \delta_T/2)(1 - \delta_t)^{t-1}$$

where $t \geq i, N_t$ is the net capital stock, I_i is investment in year i, and δ_t is the annual geometric rate of depreciation. We assume that the geometric rate of depreciation for each state equals the implicit national rate of depreciation for the manufacturing sector in that year.

Our annual estimates of manufacturing investment by state were based on each state's share of new capital expenditures in the United States. For each year from 1970 forward, we used those shares to apportion real U.S. investment in manufacturing, thereby generating a gross investment series

[17] For more on the construction of the national capital stock series, see U.S. Department of Commerce (1999).

for each state. For the period 1979-81, there are no data on manufacturing investment at the state level, although there are state-level estimates of gross capital stocks for total manufacturing in 1978 and 1981. We used the change in gross stocks between 1978 and 1981 to calculate investment shares for total manufacturing for 1979, 1980 and 1981.

We imputed gross stocks in 1969 by adjusting the estimates of gross capital stocks by industry for each state in 1977 to reflect cumulative real, gross investment over the 1970–77 period. State level estimate of gross capital stocks by industry are only available for 1977 and 1978, and estimates of net capital stocks are not available.

We used our estimates of gross capital stocks in 1969 and gross annual investments from 1970 through 1999 to generate perpetual inventory estimates for each state for the period 1969 through 1999. We then used them to apportion the national estimates of manufacturing capital stocks. Each year, we summed the perpetual-inventory estimates across the states and assigned each state a share of the national manufacturing capital stock according to its share of the sum-of-states estimate.

Nonparametric Estimation of Higher-Order Moments of Technical Efficiency

Daniel J. Henderson

Department of Economics, State University of New York at Binghamton*
djhender@binghamton.edu

Summary. In this paper nonparametric techniques are used to estimate higher-order moments of technical efficiency. The procedures given in this paper allow the moments to be estimated with relative ease, while at the same time not requiring restrictive assumptions on the distribution of inefficiency. The results given by these estimates will allow researchers to gain additional information on the inefficiency of a given firm. As an empirical example, the estimators are applied to a data set examining labor efficiencies of 17 railway companies over a period of 14 years.

Key words: Technical Efficiency, Nonparametric Kernel, Panel Data
JEL Classification: C1, C14, C33

1 Introduction

Technical efficiency refers to a firm's ability to maximize output (minimize inputs) for a given level of inputs (output).[2] Formally, the level of technical efficiency is measured by the distance a particular firm is from the "best practice" frontier. Thus, a firm that sits on the "best practice" frontier is said to be technically efficient. This concept is important to firms because their profits highly depend upon their level of technical efficiency. For example, two firms, that have identical technologies and inputs but different levels of technical efficiency, will have different levels of output. This will create a higher

* The author would like to thank Taradas Bandyopadhyay, Rolf Färe, Shawna Grosskopf, Bill Horrace, Subal Kumbhakar, Chris Parmeter, Subhash Sharma, Aman Ullah and an anonymous referee for helpful comments as well as Léopold Simar for generously providing the data. The GAUSS code used in this paper is available from the author upon request.

[2] The methodology section of this paper will focus on output-oriented technical efficiency (maximization of output) whereas the empiricial example will focus on input-oriented technical efficiency (minimization of inputs). Note that Atkinson and Cornwell (1993) show that these two values are only the same under the assumption of constant returns to scale.

revenue for one firm although both have the same costs, generating a larger profit for the more efficient firm.

For nearly three decades, starting with Aigner, Lovell and Schmidt (1977) and Meeusen and van den Broeck (1977), the stochastic frontier literature has brought forth models to estimate technical efficiency. Many theoretical advances have taken place, but unfortunately researchers appear to be primiarly interested solely in the *mean* of the inefficiency term.

It is well known that higher-order moments can often shed additional and sometimes necessary light on the distribution of a variable. Although most papers in this literature are only intersted in the first moment, there are a few exceptions. Kumbhakar (2002) uses the first three moments of the distribution of inefficiency in order to estimate risk preferences. In another paper, Bera and Sharma (1999) derive the conditional variance of technical efficiency and use it as a measure of production uncertainty. Each of these papers, however, make strong assumptions on the distribution on inefficiency, obviously affecting its outcome.

In this paper nonparametric techniques will be exploited to estimate higher-order moments of technical efficiency. The procedures given in this paper allow the moments to be estimated with relative ease, while at the same time not requiring restrictive assumptions on the distribution of inefficiency. The results given by these estimates will allow researchers to gain additional information on the inefficiency of a given firm. These techniques should be useful, for example, in the risk literature which often examines third moments.

The remainder of this paper is organized as follows. Section 2 describes the methodology whereas the third section gives an empirical example employing the techniques derived in the paper. Finally, Section 4 concludes.

2 Methodology

2.1 Model

This sub-section follows Kneip and Simar (1996) in presenting a nonparametric firm effect model. In their approach a common technological production function is shared by all firms, but differences between the firms are captured by a location effect. The model takes the form

$$y_{it} = m(x_{it}) + \varepsilon_{it}, \tag{1}$$

where $i = 1, 2, ..., N$, $t = 1, 2, ..., T$, $y_{it} \geq 0$ is a scalar output, $x_{it} \geq 0$ is a vector of k inputs and $m(\cdot)$ is an unknown smooth production function. The ε_{it} follow the error component specification ($\varepsilon_{it} = v_{it} + \alpha_i$). The α_i represent producer specific, time invariant individual effects, v_{it} are the random disturbances and are *i.i.d.* $(0, \sigma_v^2)$, and α_i and v_{it} are assumed to be independent of one another and x_{it}. For identifiability, it is assumed that the expected value of the producer effect is zero.

2.2 Estimation of the Unknown Production Function

Often estimation of (1) is performed by replacing $m(x_{it})$ with a parametric production function $(f(x_{it}, \beta))$ and placing distributional assumptions on the error components (e.g., see Kumbhakar and Lovell 2000). These parametric assumptions may not be suitable for all panel data sets. For example, if one assumes a (log) linear specification of the production function and the data generating process is non-linear, then the estimates will most likely be biased.[3] To counter situations such as this, Kneip and Simar (1996) suggest estimating the unknown function nonparametrically. Specifically, they propose using a nonparametric estimator of the Nadaraya (1964) and Watson (1964) type[4] as

$$\widehat{m}(x) = \frac{\sum_i \sum_t y_{it} K\left(\frac{x_{it}-x}{h}\right)}{\sum_i \sum_t K\left(\frac{x_{it}-x}{h}\right)}, \tag{2}$$

where $K\left(\frac{x_{it}-x}{h}\right)$ is a kernel (weight) function[5] and h is the optimal bandwidth (smoothing) parameter. Further, they show that the rate of convergence for m is of the order $O_p\left(NT^{-2/(k+4)} + N^{-1/2}\right)$. By contrast, the standard rate for the fully parametric model is $O_p\left(NT^{-1/2} + N^{-1/2}\right)$. This difference is not large when the number of regressors is small, but the curse of dimensionality quickly becomes prevelant as k increases relative to NT.

Estimation of the bandwidths is typically the most salient factor when performing nonparametric estimation. For example, choosing a very small bandwidth means that there may not be enough points for smoothing and thus one may obtain an undersmoothed estimate (low bias, high variance). On the other hand, when choosing a very large bandwidth, one may include too many points and thus obtain an oversmoothed estimate (high bias, low variance). This trade-off is a well known dilemma in applied nonparametric econometrics and thus researchers often resort to automatic determination procedures to estimate the bandwidths. Although there exist many selection methods, one popular procedure is that of Least-Squares Cross-Validation (LSCV). In short, the procedure chooses the bandwidths which minimize the

---

3 Steps have also been made in the parametric literature to try to account for nonlinearity. For example, the translog production function is widely used in practice and is somewhat flexible. However, there is always some concern whether or not the data generating process is more complex and failure to adequately capture these complex technologies may lead to biases and false conclusions.

4 The asymptotic properties of the Nadaraya-Watson estimator can be found in Pagan and Ullah (1999).

5 Note that generally kernel functions can be any probability function having a finite second moment. In the empirical section below, this paper will follow Kneip and Simar (1996) and employ the Epanechnikov kernel to estimate $\widehat{m}$. Further, it has been shown that the choice of kernel does not seem to matter a great deal (e.g., see Ullah 1988).

LSCV function given by

$$CV(h) = \frac{1}{T}\sum_{i=1}^{N}[y_{it} - \widehat{m}_{-i}(x_{it})]^2, \tag{3}$$

where $\widehat{m}_{-i}(x_{it})$ is computed by leaving out all T observations of the ith firm (leave-one-out-firm estimator).

The rate of convergence of the nonparametric estimator and its reliance on bandwidths causes some to question its relevance. Is it more important to relax distributional and functional form assumptions or should one be concerned with the speed of convergence? While it is true that nonparametric estimators are biased in small samples and suffer from the curse of dimensionality, they are consistent. Alternatively, a misspecified parametric model will be inconsistent and no amount of data can cure that problem.

2.3 Estimation of Technical Efficiency

Once one has obtained a consistent estimate of m, the next step is to obtain firm level estimates of technical efficiency.[6] Having determined a consistent estimator $\widehat{m}$ of m, Kneip and Simar (1996) obtain estimators of α for each i by the method of least squares as

$$\widehat{\alpha}_i = \frac{1}{T}\sum_{i=1}^{T}(y_{it} - \widehat{m}(x_{it})). \tag{4}$$

They also show that the rate of convergence of the producer effect is similar to that of the unknown function, but an additional term is added: $O_p\left(NT^{-2/(k+4)} + N^{-1/2} + T^{-1/2}\right)$.[7]

To obtain non-negative estimates of α_i, the normalization

$$\widehat{u}_i = \max_i \widehat{\alpha}_i - \widehat{\alpha}_i, \tag{5}$$

gives the "shifted" estimates $\widehat{u}_i$. These estimates can be used to estimate producer specific technical inefficiency. Battese and Coelli (1988) argue that

[6] Estimation of the unknown function using nonparametric techniques, although recommended, is not required for the methods described in this subsection. So long as the researcher is able to obtain consistent estimates of the production function, higher-order moments of efficiency can be estimated using the procedures outlined below.

[7] They further show that the rate of convergence can be slightly improved by using an undersmoothed estimate of the unknown function. Specifically, choosing a bandwidth proportional to $NT^{-1/(k+2)}$ instead of $NT^{-1/(k+4)}$ will result in a rate of convergence of the order $O_p\left(NT^{-2/(k+2)} + N^{-1/2} + T^{-1/2}\right)$. Further note that the additional term requires that in practice both N and T must be large.

since the production function is generally defined for the logarithm of the production, firm specific estimates of technical efficiency should be given by

$$\widehat{TE}_i = \exp(-\widehat{u}_i). \tag{6}$$

This setup assures that the values of technical efficiency lie between zero and one. A value of one defines a firm as technically efficient (or a best practice firm) and a value below one deems a firm as inefficient.

Firm level estimates of technical inefficiency can also be obtained by using the mean of the conditional distribution of u given ε. Previously, distributional assumptions on u and v were imposed in order to obtain the conditional distribution.[8] In practice, imposing different distributional assumptions on the error components often leads to different estimates for the efficiencies and more importantly, changes in the rankings of firms. This problem can be avoided with a nonparametric approach which does not require restrictive distributional assumptions. Here nonparametric techniques are exploited to obtain conditional distributions without imposing restrictive parametric assumptions.[9] By first noting that $f(u_i \mid \varepsilon_{i1}, \varepsilon_{i2}, \ldots, \varepsilon_{iT}) = f(u_i \mid \varepsilon_i)$, where $\varepsilon_i \equiv \sum_t \varepsilon_{it}/T$, the sample estimate of the population average of u-values conditional on ε ($\widehat{\gamma}_1(\varepsilon)$) is defined as

$$\widehat{\gamma}_1(\varepsilon) = \widehat{E}(u_i|\varepsilon_i) = \frac{\sum_i \widehat{u}_i K(\frac{\widehat{\varepsilon_i} - \widehat{\varepsilon}}{h})}{\sum_i K(\frac{\widehat{\varepsilon_i} - \widehat{\varepsilon}}{h})}, \tag{7}$$

where the estimate of u_i is taken from (5) and $\widehat{\varepsilon}_i = \sum_t (\widehat{v}_{it} + \widehat{\alpha}_i)/T$. Similarly, firm specific estimates of technical efficiency are then given by

$$\widehat{TE}_i = \widehat{E}(\exp(-\widehat{u}_i)|\widehat{\varepsilon}_i).^{10} \tag{8}$$

2.4 Estimation of Higher-Order Moments

Although these results are intuitive, one can always ask why studies generally only examine the first moment of the conditional distribution. One simple explanation is that given the difficulties in obtaining estimates of higher moments, the importance of higher moments has not been examined sufficiently. An exception is the study by Bera and Sharma (1999). They estimate the first two moments of the conditional distribution using maximum likelihood techniques. Further, they suggest that higher order moments might shed additional light on the behavior of firm-specific efficiency measures.

---

[8] The maximum likelihood approach was first sugested by Jondrow, Lovell, Materov and Schmidt (1982).

[9] To the best knoweledge of this author, this is the first time these techniques have been employed in the efficiency literature.

[10] It should be noted that both (6) and (8) are consistent estimators of technical efficiency as T tends towards infinity.

Here, nonparametric estimates of higher-order moments[11] of technical efficiency will be derived. Similar to above, denoting $\widehat{\gamma}_r(\varepsilon)$[12] as the average of u^r conditional on ε, the estimate of $E(u^r \mid \varepsilon)$ is defined as

$$\widehat{\gamma}_r(\varepsilon) = \widehat{E}(u_i^r|\varepsilon_i) = \frac{\sum_i \widehat{u}_i^r K(\frac{\widehat{\varepsilon_i} - \widehat{\varepsilon}}{h})}{\sum_i K(\frac{\widehat{\varepsilon_i} - \widehat{\varepsilon}}{h})}. \tag{9}$$

Using this result, and the binomial expansion, the nonparametric estimator of the rth conditional moment of u about the mean, for the first four moments, is obtained as

$$\mu_1(u|\varepsilon) = \widehat{\gamma}_1(\varepsilon) \tag{10}$$
$$\mu_2(u|\varepsilon) = \widehat{\gamma}_2(\varepsilon) - \widehat{\gamma}_1^2(\varepsilon) \tag{11}$$
$$\mu_3(u|\varepsilon) = \widehat{\gamma}_3(\varepsilon) - 3\widehat{\gamma}_2(\varepsilon)\widehat{\gamma}_1(\varepsilon) + 2\widehat{\gamma}_1^3(\varepsilon) \tag{12}$$
$$\mu_4(u|\varepsilon) = \widehat{\gamma}_4(\varepsilon) - 4\widehat{\gamma}_3(\varepsilon)\widehat{\gamma}_1(\varepsilon) + 6\widehat{\gamma}_2(\varepsilon)\widehat{\gamma}_1^2(\varepsilon) - 3\widehat{\gamma}_1^4(\varepsilon). \tag{13}$$

Again, the first moment is generally accepted as a relevant indicator for technical inefficiency. Bera and Sharma (1999) define the second moment as production uncertainty due to inefficiency. Here the third and fourth moments are defined as the conditional skewness and kurtosis measures of inefficiency, respectively.[13] Similarly, $E(\exp(-u)^r \mid \varepsilon)$ is defined as

$$\widehat{E}(\exp(-u_i)^r|\varepsilon_i) = \frac{\sum_i \exp(-\widehat{u}_i)^r K\left(\frac{\widehat{\varepsilon_i} - \widehat{\varepsilon}}{h}\right)}{\sum_i K\left(\frac{\widehat{\varepsilon_i} - \widehat{\varepsilon}}{h}\right)} \tag{14}$$

and the first four conditional moments around the mean can be derived as in (10), (11), (12) and (13), respectively.

3 Empirical Example

In this section an empirical example will be used to illustrate the above procedures. Specifically, this example considers the analysis of labor efficiencies of 17 railway companies over a period of 14 years (annual observations). Although the sample size (238 observations) is relatively small, this example will show, from a practical point of view, how the procedures work. Data on the activity of the main international railway companies can be found in the annual reports of the Union Internationale des Chemins de Fer (U.I.C.). The railways retained over the period 1970-1983 can be found in Table 1. One

[11] For a related application of these techniques see Appelbaum and Ullah (1997).

[12] The asymptotic properties of $\widehat{\gamma}_r(\varepsilon)$ for the general case can be found in Singh and Tracy (1970).

[13] For an interpretation of third moments, see Menezes, Geiss and Tressler (1980).

Table 1. Railway Companies

Number	Network	Country	Number	Network	Country
1	BR	Great Britain	10	NS	Netherlands
2	CFF	Switzerland	11	NSB	Norway
3	CFL	Luxemburg	12	ÖBB	Austria
4	CH	Greece	13	RENFE	Spain
5	CP	Portugal	14	SJ	Sweden
6	DB	Germany	15	SNCB	Belgium
7	DSB	Denmark	16	SNCF	France
8	FS	Italy	17	VR	Finland
9	JNR	Japan			

reason for choosing this data set is that it has also been studied in a similar fashion by Hall, Härdle, and Simar (1995), Kneip and Simar (1996), and Park and Simar (1994).

Since this example examines a labor function, the support of m will be bounded from below (the most technically efficient railway company uses the least labor), and thus the firm with the smallest estimated value of α will be deemed the most efficient in the sample. Following Kneip and Simar (1996), the variables used in this example are

y_{it} = labor (total number of employees) / total length of network (in kms)
x_{1it} = total distance covered by trains (in 10^3 kms) / total length of network (in kms)
x_{2it} = ratio of passenger trains in x_{1it} (in %)
x_{3it} = density of network (kms of lines by 100 km^2).

All the variables are in logarithms and have been adjusted for the time trend effect. Note that Kneip and Simar (1996) have placed in the denominator of both y and x_1, the total length of the network, which eliminates the size effect. Further, the variable x_1 represents a rough measure of the output (demand) of the railways, whereas x_2 characterizes some aspects of the demand and x_3 is a physical measure of the density of the network.

Table 2 gives the results for the estimation of m with the optimal bandwidth ($h_{x_k} = 1.86\sigma_{x_k}$, $k = 1, 2, 3$).[14] The first column of numbers in the table are empirical estimates of u_i. These results are identical to those given in Kneip and Simar (1996, pp. 207). For comparison, reported in the second column of numbers are the estimates of ε_i. The remaining columns are

[14] The optimal bandwidth was obtained using the LSCV procedure in equation 3.

Table 2. Estimates for Individual Networks (u_i)

Network	u_i	ε_i	$\mu_1(u\|\varepsilon)$	$\mu_2(u\|\varepsilon)$	$\mu_3(u\|\varepsilon)$	$\mu_4(u\|\varepsilon)$
BR	0.2906	−0.1364	0.3029	0.0047	−0.0002	0.0001
CFF	0.3767	0.0358	0.3495	0.0042	0.0000	0.0001
CFL	0.5275	0.3375	0.4897	0.0031	−0.0002	0.0000
CH	0.3107	−0.0961	0.3133	0.0044	−0.0002	0.0001
CP	0.3288	−0.0598	0.3223	0.0041	−0.0002	0.0001
DB	0.3377	−0.0421	0.3268	0.0040	−0.0002	0.0001
DSB	0.1188	−0.4800	0.1289	0.0035	0.0001	0.0001
FS	0.5243	0.3311	0.4882	0.0032	−0.0002	0.0000
JNR	0.7407	0.7638	0.7373	0.0007	−0.0002	0.0000
NS	0.1337	−0.4502	0.1413	0.0041	0.0003	0.0001
NSB	0.2591	−0.1993	0.2840	0.0055	−0.0002	0.0001
ÖBB	0.4982	0.2788	0.4728	0.0042	−0.0002	0.0000
RENFE	0.3483	−0.0209	0.3323	0.0040	−0.0002	0.0001
SJ	0.0000	−0.7175	0.0333	0.0031	0.0002	0.0000
SNCB	0.3999	−0.0270	0.3307	0.0040	−0.0002	0.0001
SNCF	0.1713	−0.1696	0.2935	0.0051	−0.0002	0.0001
VR	0.3978	0.2078	0.4402	0.0058	−0.0001	0.0001
Median	0.3377	−0.0421	0.3268	0.0041	−0.0002	0.0001

Notes: In the regression function used to estimate each of these values, the dependent variables are in logarithms. Time effects are also controlled for.

estimates of (10)–(13).[15] As expected, $\widehat{u}_i$ and $\widehat{E}(u_i \mid \varepsilon_i)$ are quite similar.[16] The correlation between the two columns is over 98%. Regarding the estimation of the variance, Bera and Sharma (1999) state that $\mu_2(u|\varepsilon)$ should

[15] The Gaussian kernel with the Silverman (1986) adaptive estimate of spread bandwidth was used in the estimation of the higher-order moments. It should also be noted that the results are robust to alternative bandwidth choices.

[16] It should be noted here that the "shifted" estimates are being used instead of the estimates of α_i. However, replacing the shifted estimates with the estimates of the producer effects only results in changes in the means of the distributions, but not the shape of the distributions, the ranking of the firms or the conclusions of the paper.

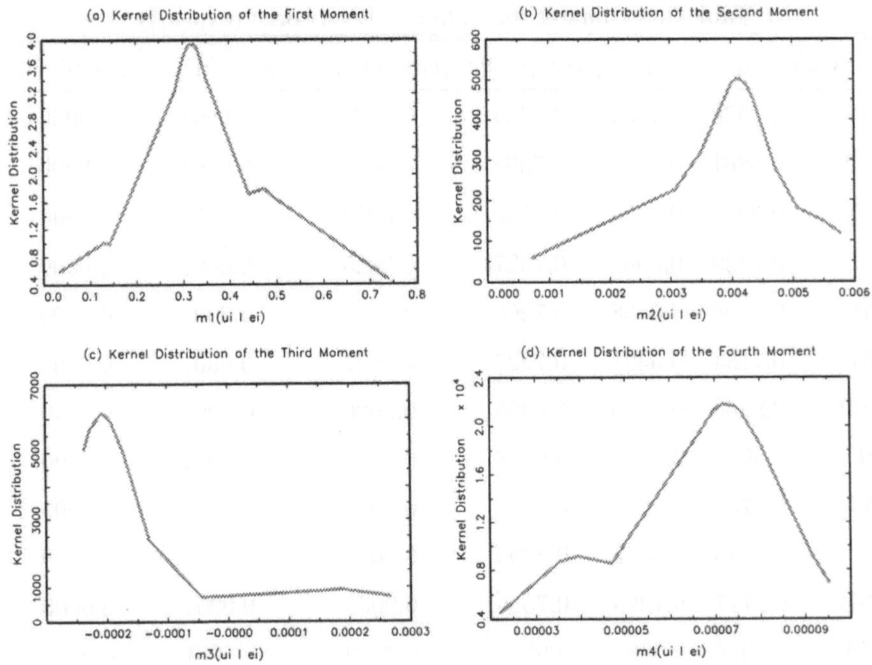

Fig. 1. First Four Moments of E(ui | ei)

be smaller for networks near the frontier. Specifically, they suggest that the most efficient firm will have the least production uncertainty. In this example, SJ is found to be the most efficient firm ($\widehat{u}_i = 0$). Correspondingly, its value for the second moment about the mean (0.0031) is the smallest within the sample. Further, the third moment for SJ is one the largest and the fourth moment is the smallest amongst the networks in the sample.

Kernel density plots of the first four conditional moments about the mean are given in Figure 1.[17] The first thing to notice is the shape of the estimated density in panel (a). It does not appear to be significantly skewed. Typically, in the maximum likelihood approach to efficiency estimation, the distribution of u is often assumed to be highly skewed (e.g., exponential or half-normal).[18] Therefore, it is suggested that assuming one of these distrubitions may be inappropriate for this particular data set. At the same time, panel (c) and Table 2 show that the majority of the conditional third moment values are negative.

[17] The densities were estimated using the Gaussian kernel along with the Silverman (1986) adaptive estimate of spread bandwidth. Again, the results are robust to alternative bandwidth choices.

[18] Note that the shape of the unconditional distribution of u is very similar to that of the conditional distrubtion.

Table 3. Estimates for Individual Networks ($\exp(u_i)$)

Network	u_i	ε_i	$\mu_1(\exp(u)\|\varepsilon)$	$\mu_2(\exp(u)\|\varepsilon)$	$\mu_3(\exp(u)\|\varepsilon)$	$\mu_4(\exp(u)\|\varepsilon)$
BR	0.7478	−0.1364	0.7404	0.0027	0.0001	0.0000
CFF	0.6861	0.0358	0.7065	0.0021	0.0001	0.0000
CFL	0.5901	0.3375	0.6132	0.0013	0.0001	0.0000
CH	0.7329	−0.0961	0.7327	0.0025	0.0001	0.0000
CP	0.7198	−0.0598	0.7260	0.0023	0.0001	0.0000
DB	0.7134	−0.0421	0.7227	0.0022	0.0001	0.0000
DSB	0.8880	−0.4800	0.8806	0.0026	0.0000	0.0000
FS	0.5920	0.3311	0.6148	0.0013	0.0001	0.0000
JNR	0.4768	0.7638	0.4786	0.0002	0.0000	0.0000
NS	0.8749	−0.4502	0.8700	0.0029	−0.0001	0.0000
NSB	0.7717	−0.1993	0.7549	0.0033	0.0001	0.0000
ÖBB	0.6076	0.2788	0.6246	0.0018	0.0001	0.0000
RENFE	0.7059	−0.0209	0.7187	0.0022	0.0001	0.0000
SJ	1.0000	−0.7175	0.9687	0.0027	−0.0002	0.0000
SNCB	0.6704	−0.0270	0.7199	0.0022	0.0001	0.0000
SNCF	0.8425	−0.1696	0.7476	0.0030	0.0001	0.0000
VR	0.6718	0.2078	0.6498	0.0025	0.0001	0.0000
Median	0.7134	−0.0421	0.7227	0.0023	0.0001	0.0000

Notes: See Table 2.

Table 3 and Figure 2 show the corresponding results for the Battese and Coelli (1988) type technical efficiency estimates. The technical efficiency scores are analogous to the estimates of u_i given in Table 2. The estimates of ε_i are, of course, identical to those in Table 2. However, different from the second table, the network closest to the frontier does not have the smallest second moment. However, this is not in contrast to the theory of Bera and Sharma (1988). Although they show in their paper that $\mu_1(u|\varepsilon)$, $\mu_2(u|\varepsilon)$ and $\mu_1(\exp(-u)|\varepsilon)$ decrease montonically with ε_i, $\mu_2(\exp(-u)|\varepsilon)$ does not. Thus, the firm with the highest value of technical efficiency need not have the smallest value of production uncertainty when employing the exponential definition of u. In addition, the distribution of the third moments here is less negative than in Figure 1 and the mode of it appears to be near zero. The corresponding

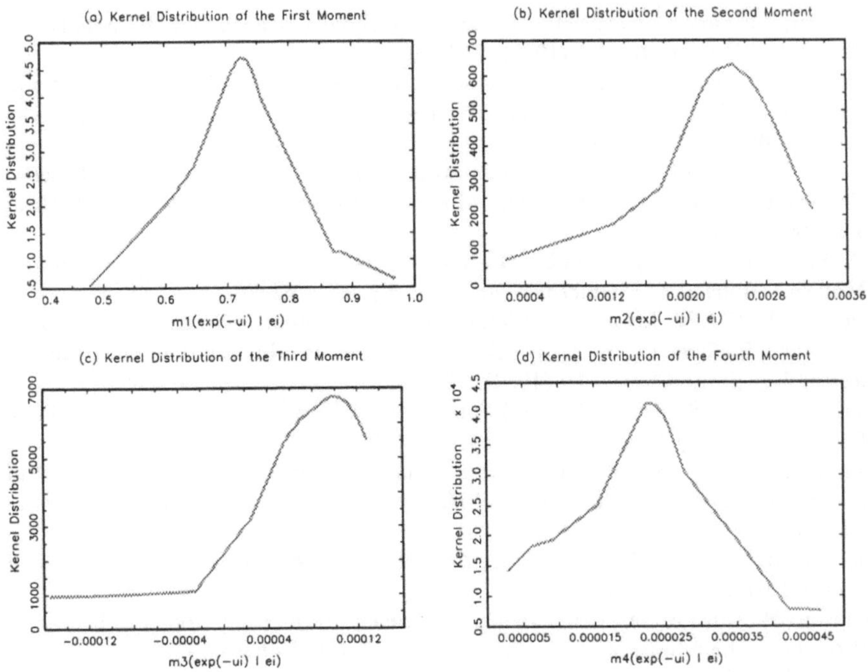

Fig. 2. First Four Moments of E(exp(−ui) | ei)

median, as shown in Table 3, is 0.0001. Finally, as in Figure 1, panel (d) shows positive conditional kurtosis values near zero.

4 Conclusion

In this paper, nonparametric techniques were used to estimate higher-order moments of technical efficiency. These procedures, which are known to give consistent estimates, avoid some of the restrictive distributional assumptions necessary in the maximum likelihood framework. In addition to avoiding parametric specifications, the nonparametric approach shown in this paper is relatively easy to compute for r-th order moment. Finally, these techniques were applied to an empirical panel data set of railway companies.

References

Aigner, D.J., C.A.K. Lovell, and P. Schmidt, "Formulation and Estimation of Stochastic Frontier Production Function Models," *Journal of Econometrics* **6** (1977), 21–37.

Appelbaum, E. and A. Ullah, "Estimation of Moments and Production Decisions Under Uncertainty," *Review of Economics and Statistics*, **79** (1997), 631–37.

Atkinson, S.E., and C. Cornwell, "Measuring Technical Efficiency with Panel Data," *Journal of Econometrics* **6** (1993), 257–61.

Battese, G.E. and T.J. Coelli, "Prediction of Firm Level Technical Efficiencies with a Generalized Frontier Production Function and Panel Data," *Journal of Econometrics*, **38** (1988), 387–99.

Bera, A.K. and S.C. Sharma, "Estimating Production Uncertainty in Stochastic Frontier Production Function Models," *Journal of Productivity Analysis*, **12** (1999), 187–210.

Hall, P., W. Härdle and L. Simar, "Iterated Bootstrap with Application to Frontier Models," *Journal of Productivity Analysis*, **6** (1995), 63–76.

Jondrow, J., C.A.K. Lovell, I.S. Materov and P. Schmidt, "On the Estimation of Technical Inefficiency in the Stochastic Frontier Production Function Model," *Journal of Econometrics*, **19** (1982), 233–38.

Kneip, A. and L. Simar, "A General Framework for Frontier Estimation with Panel Data," *Journal of Productivity Analysis*, **7** (1996), 187–212.

Kumbhakar, S.C., "Specification and Estimation of Production Risk, Risk Preferences and Technical Efficiency," *American Journal of Agricultural Economics*, **84** (2002), 8–22.

Kumbhakar, S.C. and C.A.K. Lovell, *Stochastic Frontier Analysis*, Cambridge University Press, Cambridge, 2000.

Meeusen, W., and J. van den Broeck, "Efficiency Estimation from Cobb-Douglas Production Functions with Composed Error," *International Economic Review*, **18** (1977), 435–44.

Menezes, C., C. Geiss and J. Tressler, "Increasing Downside Risk," *American Economic Review*, **70** (1980), 921–32.

Nadaraya, E.A., "On Estimating Regression," *Theory of Probability Applications*, **9** (1964), 141–2.

Pagan, A. and A. Ullah, *Nonparametric Econometrics*, Cambridge University Press, Cambridge, 1999.

Park, B. and L. Simar, "Efficient Semiparametric Estimation in a Stochastic Frontier Model," *Journal of the American Statistical Association*, **89** (1994), 929–36.

Silverman, B.W., *Density Estimation for Statistics and Data Analysis*, Chapman and Hall, London, 1986.

Singh, R.S. and D.S. Tracy, "Strongly Consistent Estimators of k-th Order Regression Curves and Rates of Convergence," *Zeitschrift für Wahrscheinlichkeitstheorie und Verwandte Gabiet*, **40** (1970), 339–48.

U.I.C., *Statistiques Internationales des Chemins de Fer*, Union Internationale des Chemins de Fer, Paris, 1970–1983.

Ullah, A., "Non-Parametric Estimation of Econometric Functionals," *Canadian Journal of Economics*, **21** (1988), 625–58.

Watson, G.S., "Smoother Regression Analysis," *Sankhya*, **26** (1964), 359–72.

Measuring Inefficiency with Endogenous Innovation

William Schworm

Department of Economics, University of New South Wales, Sydney, Australia.
b.schworm@unsw.edu.au

1 Introduction

Innovation, efficiency and productivity are intertwined concepts that reflect different aspects of production and growth. While these concepts are closely related, distinct literatures have developed around each of these topics. My purpose in this paper is to study these concepts in a model with endogenous innovation causing technical and allocative inefficiency but resulting in productivity growth.

The concept of efficiency and the distinction between technical and allocative efficiency was formally defined by Koopmans (1951). Debreu (1951) and Farrell (1957) proposed a particular measure of technical efficiency. The properties of the Debreu-Farrell and other measures has been studied extensively with important contributions by Russell (1985, 1990), and Färe, Grosskopf and Lovell (1994) and many others. Growth accounting and the measurement of productivity growth are based on the seminal ideas of Solow (1957), Kendrick (1961), Denison (1962), and Jorgenson and Griliches (1967). Barro (1999) has investigated productivity growth in the context of endogenous innovation. Raa and Mohnen (2002) have combined the study of growth accounting with efficiency analysis.

To study innovation, efficiency and growth, I use a simplified version of the lab equipment model of Rivera-Batiz and Romer (1991). This model is explicitly dynamic with investment decisions causing innovation which in turn causes growth. The primary simplification I make in the original model is to assume the intermediate goods are not durable. This eliminates the distinction between transient dynamics and balanced growth and enables a full treatment of the efficiency of a market equilibrium.

This model is applied to three distinct situations: a market economy with a patent system, a market economy without a patent system and an efficient economy in which a social planner dictates production, innovation and consumption decisions. As pointed out by Arrow (1962), a patent system encourages innovation but causes technical and allocative inefficiency. The market economy without a patent system is technically efficient but is allocatively inefficient with a zero growth rate. The efficient economy has sufficient control to obtain an optimal level of innovation without technical or allocative inefficiency.

The equilibrium of the model in each of these scenarios can be described in terms of stationary preferences, a budget constraint and a production possibilities frontier for current consumption and the growth rate. This allows the use of standard measures of technical and allocative inefficiency to evaluate equilibria for the patent and no-patent economies.

The measures of technical and allocative inefficiency can be combined to obtain a measure of overall inefficiency. This measure is consistent with utility evaluations of alternative consumption-growth paths. Therefore, this measure can be used to determine whether the patent system or the non-patent system will be preferred by consumers.

The plan of the paper is as follows. The model is briefly summarized in Section 2. In Section 3, a stationary representation of the preferences, budget constraint and production possibilities is derived. Efficient growth is described in Section 4 while the market equilibrium for the no-patent and patent economy is described in Section 5 and Section 6, respectively. In Section 7 and Section 8, the inefficiencies of the patent and no-patent economies are described. Section 9 compares the inefficiency of the market economy with and without patents. Section 10 concludes.

2 The Model

In this section, I describe a simplified version of the lab equipment model of Rivera-Batiz and Romer (1991). By assuming there are no durable goods in the model, I obtain a simple dynamic model in which to analyze the measurement of technical and economic inefficiency.

2.1 Ideas

The model distinguishes between new ideas and the machines that embody these new ideas. New ideas can be considered as blue prints that enable the production of a new type of machine. Machines cannot be produced until their design has been discovered. Different types of machines are represented as points in $\mathbf{R}$ and lower numbered machines are discovered first. Therefore, the known blue prints at any moment can be represented by $A \in \mathbf{R}$ with all blue prints below A having been discovered and those above waiting discovery.

An economy with knowledge A has a collection of machines denoted by $\mathbf{x}(\mathbf{i})$ for $i \in [0, A]$. The total production of machines, denoted X, is

$$X = \int_0^A \mathbf{x}(i)\, di \tag{1}$$

while the machine aggregate, denoted χ, is

$$\chi = \int_0^A \mathbf{x}(i)^\alpha \, di \tag{2}$$

where $0 < \alpha < 1$ and $\mathbf{x} : [0, A] \mapsto R^n_+$.

2.2 Technology

The economy has three sectors involved with production: the producers of output Y, the producers of machines x, and the producers of new ideas $\dot{A}$.

The production of output Y depends on labour L and an aggregate measure of machines χ as described by the following production function:

$$Y = L^{1-\alpha}\chi. \tag{3}$$

There are competitive conditions with free entry in the Y sector.

Output Y can be converted linearly into consumption goods, machines, and ideas. Units are chosen so that one unit of the consumption good requires one unit of output, Y. The production of a machine of any known type requires $\gamma > 0$ units of Y. The production of a new idea requires $\eta > 0$ units of Y. Therefore, the technology of the economy is described by (1), (2), (3), and

$$Y = C + \eta\dot{A} + \gamma X. \tag{4}$$

Since the machine aggregate is symmetric in types of machines and the cost of producing each machine is the same, the efficient production of machines requires all machines to be produced in the same quantity. Although the market equilibrium in this model is not efficient, the machine aggregate is produced efficiently. Therefore, $x = \mathbf{x}(\mathbf{i})$ for all $i \in [0, A]$ so that $X = Ax$ and $\chi = Ax^\alpha$. The production function can be expressed as

$$Y = AL^{1-\alpha}x^\alpha, \tag{5}$$

and the production possibilities as

$$Y = C + \eta\dot{A} + \gamma Ax. \tag{6}$$

2.3 Preferences

Consumers are identical so that aggregate consumption decisions can be described by the decisions of a representative consumer with a utility function

$$\int_0^\infty e^{\rho t} u(C(t)) \, dt \tag{7}$$

where

$$u(C) = \frac{C^{1-\sigma}}{1-\sigma} \tag{8}$$

for $\sigma \geq 0$.

The representative consumer inelastically supplies L units of labour and owns the initial wealth of the economy.

2.4 Patents

I consider two polar cases of patent rights. The first case has a patent system that assigns full rights to a successful innovator while the second case has no patent system and no protection for a successful innovator. With a patent system, an inventor who develops a new design obtains a permanent patent. This enables the inventor to sell or lease the design to a single producer. Therefore, the producer of each type of machine $i \in [0, A]$ is a monopolist but faces competition by the producers of close substitutes.

Without the patent system, the innovator cannot restrict firms from producing the discovered machine. In this case, there will be free entry into the production of any discovered machine and competitive pricing.

Regardless of the patent system, there is free-entry in the innovation sector. Innovation is not stochastic so any innovators can discover a new design by using η units of output.

2.5 Parameter Restrictions

There are two restrictions imposed on the parameters. The market equilibrium and efficient values for profit and wages are nonnegative if $0 < \alpha < 1/2$. A positive growth rate is feasible if $L^{1-\alpha}x^{\alpha} > \gamma x + \rho\eta$ for at least some values of $x > 0$.

3 A Static Representation

In the model presented, the equilibrium paths are balanced growth paths with no transient dynamics. I show that this permits a "static" representation of the equilibrium in terms of features of the economy that will remain constant over time. The representation has a standard description in terms of the preferences, production possibilities and the budget constraint. This connection to static concepts permits the application of traditional efficiency measurement.

3.1 Preferences

If consumption grows at a constant rate $g > 0$, then utility can be expressed as a function of (C, g). Let $C_t = e^{gt}C$ and express the utility for any (C, g) as

$$\begin{aligned} U(C,g) &= \int_0^\infty e^{-\rho t} e^{(1-\sigma)gt} \tfrac{C^{1-\sigma}}{1-\sigma}\, dt \\ &= \tfrac{C^{1-\sigma}}{1-\sigma} \int_0^\infty e^{-(\rho-(1-\sigma)g)t}\, dt \\ &= \left(\tfrac{C^{1-\sigma}}{1-\sigma}\right)\left(\tfrac{1}{\rho-(1-\sigma)g}\right). \end{aligned} \quad (9)$$

For this utility function, each indifference curve through (C, g) intersects the C-axis at a point $(C^0, 0)$ with $C^0 = \mathbf{C}(C, g)$ defined by

$$\mathbf{U}(\mathrm{C}, \mathrm{g}) = \mathbf{U}(\mathrm{C}^0, 0). \quad (10)$$

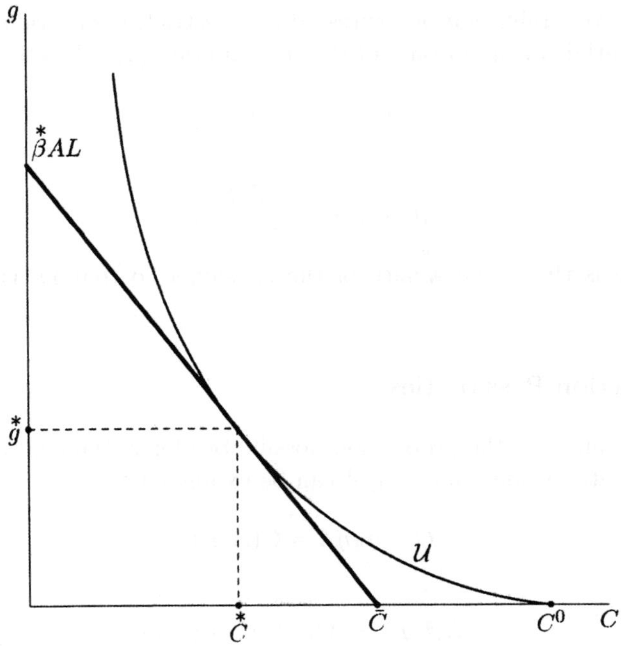

Fig. 1.

This suggests a convenient cardinalization of the utility function with the requirement that $\mathbf{U}(\mathrm{C},0) = \mathrm{C}$ so that

$$\mathbf{U}(\mathrm{C},\mathrm{g}) = \mathbf{U}(\mathrm{C}^0,0) = \mathrm{C}^0 \tag{11}$$

where

$$C^0 = \left(\frac{\rho}{\rho-(1-\sigma)g}\right)^{\frac{1}{1-\sigma}} C. \tag{12}$$

An example of C^0 is shown in Figure 1.

3.2 Budget Constraint

The equilibrium growth paths for the economies studied in this paper will have a constant interest rate r and constant growth rates (g_C, g_W) for consumption and wages, respectively. Therefore, the budget constraint for the consumer can be expressed as

$$\begin{aligned} v_0 A_0 &= \int_0^\infty e^{-rt}(C_t - W_t L)\,dt \\ &= \int_0^\infty e^{-rt}(Ce^{g_C t} - WLe^{g_W t})\,dt \\ &= C\int_0^\infty e^{-(r-g_C)t}\,dt - WL\int_0^\infty e^{-(r-g_W)t}\,dt \\ &= \frac{C}{r-g_C} - \frac{WL}{r-g_W}. \end{aligned} \tag{13}$$

The budget constraint can be expressed as a restriction on available bundles (C, g_C) of initial consumption and the consumption growth rate:

$$C + \mu g_C = r\mu \tag{14}$$

where

$$\mu = v_0 A_0 + \frac{WL}{r - g_W}. \tag{15}$$

Note that μ is the initial wealth of the consumer so that $r\mu$ is permanent income.

3.3 Production Possibilities

By using (5) and (6), the production possibilities for initial consumption and the growth rate for ideas $g_A = \dot{A}/A$ can be expressed as

$$C + g_A \eta A = G(A, L) \tag{16}$$

where

$$G(A, L) = AL^{1-\alpha}x^{\alpha} - \gamma x A \tag{17}$$

for a given level of intermediate goods x. The production of intermediate goods will depend on the patent system and will be discussed further in later sections.

3.4 Balanced Growth

Since there are no transient dynamics in the model, the equilibrium requires an immediate jump to the balanced growth equilibrium at $t = 0$. In order for C to grow at a constant rate, A must grow at the same rate. To maintain balanced growth, the growth rates for (A, C, W) must grow at the same rate. Therefore, $g_A = g_C = g_W$.

4 Efficient Growth

The efficient equilibrium is characterized by a social planner who maximizes the utility of consumers subject to technological constraints.

Net production for the efficient economy is defined by

$$\overset{\star}{G}(A, L) = \max_x \left(AL^{1-\alpha}x^{\alpha} - \gamma A x\right) \tag{18}$$

where the efficient choice of machines is

$$\overset{\star}{x} = \left(\frac{\alpha}{\gamma}\right)^{\frac{1}{1-\alpha}} L. \tag{19}$$

The equilibrium price of machines is $\overset{\star}{p} = \gamma$ so that profit is zero. The net production function can be expressed as

$$\overset{\star}{G}(A, L) = \overset{\star}{\beta} AL \tag{20}$$

where

$$\overset{\star}{\beta} = (1-\alpha)\left(\frac{\alpha}{\gamma}\right)^{\frac{\alpha}{1-\alpha}}. \tag{21}$$

The social planning problem is to choose (C, g) to maximize utility as described in (9) subject to the budget constraint described in (14) and (15). Efficient pricing requires that $v_0 = \eta$ so that the budget constraint can be expressed as

$$C + \eta g A = \overset{\star}{\beta} AL. \tag{22}$$

This implies

$$\begin{aligned} \overset{\star}{g} &= \tfrac{\overset{\star}{\beta}L - \rho\eta}{\sigma\eta} \\ \overset{\star}{C} &= \tfrac{A}{\sigma}(\rho\eta - (1-\sigma)\overset{\star}{\beta}L). \end{aligned} \tag{23}$$

The social planning problem and its solution is shown in Figure 1. The production possibilities frontier is the straight line labeled $\overset{\star}{\beta} AL$. The maximal indifference curve for the consumers and social planner is at the tangency $(\overset{\star}{C}, \overset{\star}{g})$. The utility of $(\overset{\star}{C}, \overset{\star}{g})$ is denoted by C^0.

The social return to new ideas is

$$\overset{\star}{r} = \frac{\overset{\star}{\beta}L}{\eta} \tag{24}$$

while the wage is

$$\overset{\star}{W} = \overset{\star}{\beta} A \tag{25}$$

so that

$$\overset{\star}{r}\eta A + \overset{\star}{W} L = 2\overset{\star}{\beta} AL. \tag{26}$$

Paying both innovators and workers the social value of their marginal product is not feasible since it requires twice the total output of the economy. Of course, this is a consequence of the increasing returns to labour and knowledge.

5 Market Equilibrium with No Patent System

The market equilibrium with no patent system is easily described from the results in the previous section. The net production is the same as in the efficient economy so that the production possibilities are described by (22) and displayed in Figure 1 by the line labeled $\overset{\star}{\beta} AL$.

Without a patent system, there is no market incentive for innovation so that no resources are devoted to the development of new ideas and the equilibrium growth rate is zero. All resources are devoted to current consumption

$$\overline{C} = \overset{\star}{\beta} AL \tag{27}$$

which depends on the economy's initial stock of knowledge. The equilibrium is shown in Figure 1 by the point $\overline{C}$.

6 Market Equilibrium with a Patent System

In this section, we study the market equilibrium in the basic model with a patent system.

The competitive producers of Y maximize profit given the price p for all machines $i \in [0, A]$ and the wage W:

$$\max_x \{AL^{1-\alpha}x^\alpha - pxA\} - WL. \tag{28}$$

Profit maximization and free entry imply the following relations for factor prices:

$$\begin{aligned} pxA &= \alpha Y \\ WL &= (1-\alpha)Y. \end{aligned} \tag{29}$$

The revenue a monopolist may obtain by producing a type of machine is

$$px = \alpha L^{1-\alpha} x^\alpha \tag{30}$$

so the machine producer's optimization problem is

$$\max_x \{px - \gamma x\} = \max_x \left\{\alpha L^{1-\alpha}x^\alpha - \gamma x\right\}. \tag{31}$$

This can be solved for

$$\begin{aligned} \hat{x} &= (\tfrac{\alpha^2}{\gamma})^{\frac{1}{1-\alpha}} L, \\ \hat{p} &= \tfrac{\gamma}{\alpha}, \\ \hat{\pi} &= \alpha(1-\alpha)(\tfrac{\alpha^2}{\gamma})^{\frac{\alpha}{1-\alpha}} L. \end{aligned} \tag{32}$$

Since L is constant, the equilibrium values of $(\hat{x}, \hat{p}, \hat{\pi})$ are constant over time.

Given the production of machines, we can determine net production as

$$G(A, L) = \hat{\beta} AL \tag{33}$$

where

$$\hat{\beta} = (1 - \alpha^2)(\frac{\alpha^2}{\gamma})^{\frac{\alpha}{1-\alpha}} \tag{34}$$

is a constant.

The net production possibilities determines the feasible combinations of consumption and the growth of new ideas:

$$C + \eta g A = \hat{\beta} A L. \tag{35}$$

The value of a new idea at time t, denoted v_t, is the present value of the future profits of producing the machine:

$$v_t = \int_t^{\infty} e^{-R(t,s)} \hat{\pi} \, ds = \hat{\pi} \int_t^{\infty} e^{-R(t,s)} \, ds \tag{36}$$

where

$$R(t,s) = \int_t^s -r(\tau) \, d\tau \tag{37}$$

is the discount rate for $s \geq t$.

Since there is free entry into the innovation sector and η units of output are needed to produce an idea,

$$v_t = \eta \tag{38}$$

or

$$\eta = \hat{\pi} \int_t^{\infty} e^{-R(t,s)} \, ds. \tag{39}$$

Since $\hat{\pi}$ is constant, the interest rate is constant and determined by

$$r = \frac{\hat{\pi}}{\eta}. \tag{40}$$

Since net output must be divided between profits and wage payments,

$$\hat{W} L + \hat{\pi} A = \hat{\beta} A L \tag{41}$$

where

$$\begin{aligned} \hat{\pi} &= (\tfrac{\alpha}{1-\alpha}) \hat{\beta} L \\ \hat{W} &= (1 - \tfrac{\alpha}{1-\alpha}) \hat{\beta} A. \end{aligned} \tag{42}$$

The interest rate is determined in the production sector as

$$\hat{r} = \frac{\alpha}{1-\alpha} \frac{\hat{\beta} L}{\eta} \tag{43}$$

by using (40) and (42).

Using (38), the budget constraint in (14) and (15) can be written as

$$C + \mu g = r\mu \tag{44}$$

where

$$\mu = \eta A + \frac{WL}{r - gw}. \tag{45}$$

The consumer with preferences described in (9) facing this budget constraint will choose

$$\begin{aligned} \hat{g} &= \tfrac{r-\rho}{\sigma} \\ \hat{C} &= (\rho - (1-\sigma)r)\tfrac{\mu}{\sigma} \end{aligned} \tag{46}$$

where $\mu = v_0 A_0 + \frac{\hat{W}L}{r-g}$.

Using the equilibrium factor prices in (40) and (42) implies

$$\begin{aligned} \hat{g} &= \tfrac{1}{\sigma\eta}(\tfrac{\alpha}{1-\alpha})\hat{\beta}L - \rho\eta) \\ \hat{C} &= \tfrac{A}{\sigma}\{\sigma - \tfrac{\alpha}{1-\alpha})\hat{\beta}L + \rho\eta\}. \end{aligned} \tag{47}$$

The market equilibrium is shown in Figure 2 by the point $(\hat{C}, \hat{g})$. The consumer's budget constraint is the dashed line while the production possibilities frontier is the straight line labeled $\hat{\beta}AL$. The consumers choose consumption and the growth rate to maximize utility at $(\hat{C}, \hat{g})$. For this to be an equilibrium, it must be on the production possibilities curve.

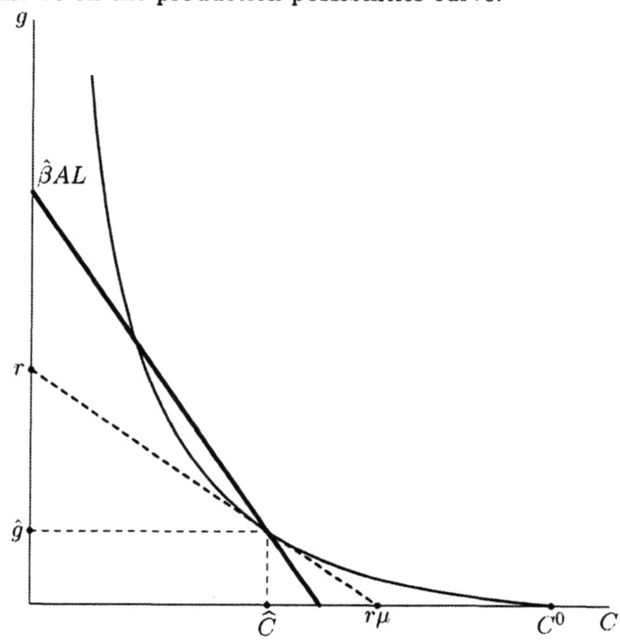

Fig. 2.

7 Inefficiency in the Economy with Patents

The economy with a patent system is both technically and allocatively inefficient. In this section, I present a method of measuring the technical inefficiency, allocative inefficiency and total inefficiency in an economy with a patent system.

7.1 Technical Inefficiency

The monopoly pricing and restricted production of machines implies an inefficient allocation of output between intermediate goods and consumption goods. This restricts the production possibilities in the economy as displayed in Figure 3. The lines labeled $\overset{\star}{\beta}AL$ and $\hat{\beta}AL$ are the production possibilities frontier for the efficient economy and the market economy with patents, respectively. Since $\hat{\beta} < \overset{\star}{\beta}$, the net production possibilities for the market economy are a subset of the production possibilities for an efficient economy.

The Debreu-Farrell measure of technical efficiency is the proportional reduction of the input L that could be achieved if production is technically efficient and the output vector (C, g) remains the same. Formally, the measure of technical efficiency is the minimal value of λ such that

$$\hat{C} + \eta\hat{g}A = \overset{\star}{\beta}\lambda AL \tag{48}$$

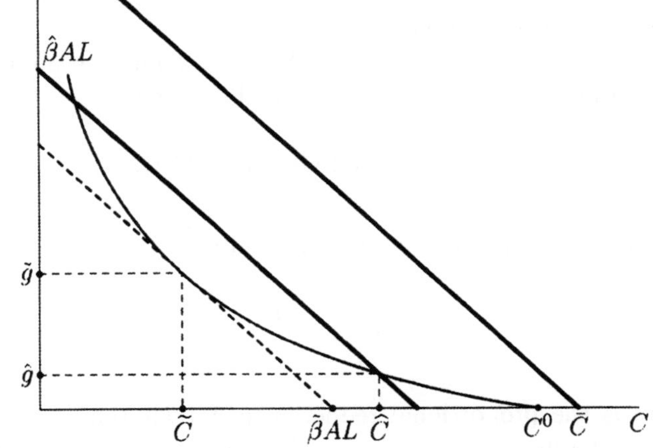

Fig. 3.

which can be written as

$$\hat{\beta}L = \overset{\star}{\beta}\lambda L. \tag{49}$$

To transform the Debreu-Farrell measure of technical efficiency into a measure of technical inefficiency, define $I_T = 1 - \lambda$ so that a technically efficient economy has $I_T = 0$ and increases in inefficiency increase I_T. Then,

$$I_T = 1 - \frac{\hat{\beta}}{\overset{\star}{\beta}}. \tag{50}$$

7.2 Measuring Economic Inefficiency

The economy with a patent system is economically inefficient as well as technically inefficient. The growth rate in the patent economy is determined by the decisions of households who save by buying shares of intermediate goods producers. These decisions are based on the market rate of interest which is less than the social return to innovation.

The patent system enables machine producers to earn a monopoly profit which can be captured by the innovator. However, profit is insufficient to support innovation at an efficient level. In the market economy, the social value of an idea is $\hat{\beta}L$ and for the innovator to capture this benefit, the machine producer would need to earn a profit of $\hat{\beta}L$. But the maximal profit for machine producers is shown in (42) to be less than this. Therefore, the patent system does not enable the innovator to capture the full benefit of a new idea.

The economic inefficiency is displayed in Figure 3. As demonstrated in the previous section, the consumer's indifference curve is not tangent to the production possibilities curve. The representative consumer may be made better off by changing $(\hat{C}, \hat{g})$ to any point on the production possibilities curve that is above the indicated indifference curve.

To obtain a measure of economic inefficiency, define the minimal cost of obtaining the utility level of the market equilibrium by

$$\tilde{\beta}AL = \min_{(C,g)}\{C + \eta g \mid \mathbf{U}(\mathrm{C}, \mathrm{g}) \geq \mathbf{U}(\hat{\mathrm{C}}, \hat{\mathrm{g}})\}. \tag{51}$$

The measure of economic inefficiency is defined as

$$I_E = 1 - \frac{\tilde{\beta}}{\hat{\beta}}. \tag{52}$$

This measure is the proportional reduction of labour that can achieve the same utility as the market equilibrium $(\hat{C}, \hat{g})$ by improving the allocation of net output to consumption and growth.

7.3 Overall Inefficiency

A simple measure of total inefficiency λ can be defined by

$$I = 1 - \frac{\tilde{\beta}}{\overset{\star}{\beta}}. \tag{53}$$

Since $1-I_E$ and $(1-I_T)$ can be interpreted as economic and technical efficiency measures, respectively, the measure of total inefficiency can be decomposed as follows:

$$I = 1 - (1 - I_T)(1 - I_E). \tag{54}$$

8 Inefficiency of the Economy without Patents

As shown above, the market economy without a patent system is technically efficient so that $I_T = 1$. As shown in Figure 4, however, this economy is economically inefficient. The equilibrium for the no-patent economy is indicated by $\overline{C}$ and the utility of this equilibrium is $\overline{C}$. The indifference curve for this level of utility is shown in the figure.

As before, define the minimal cost of obtaining the utility level of the market equilibrium by

$$\tilde{\beta}AL = \min_{(C,g)} \{C + \eta g \mid \mathbf{U}(\mathrm{C}, \mathrm{g}) \geq \overline{\mathrm{C}}\}. \tag{55}$$

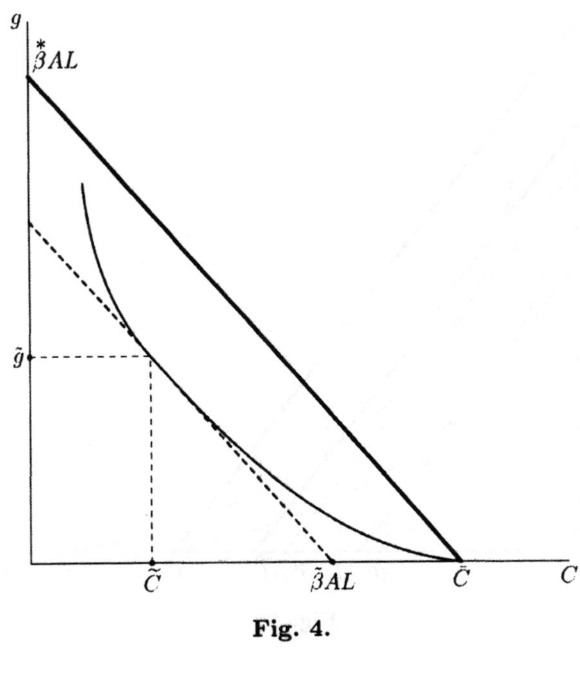

Fig. 4.

The measure of economic inefficiency is

$$I_E = 1 - \frac{\tilde{\beta}}{\overset{\star}{\beta}}. \tag{56}$$

The measure of total inefficiency I is equal to the measure of economic inefficiency

$$I = I_E \tag{57}$$

since there is no technical inefficiency for the market economy with no patents.

9 Comparing Institutions

The total inefficiency of the two economies with and without patents provides a meaningful comparison of the institutions. The utility of the equilibrium in each economy can be represented by $\mathbf{U}(\hat{\mathrm{C}}, \hat{\mathrm{g}})$ and $\overline{C}$, respectively. Denote the inefficiency in the patent economy by I^1 and the inefficiency in the no-patent economy by I^0. Then,

$$\mathbf{U}(\hat{\mathrm{C}}, \hat{\mathrm{g}}) \geq \overline{\mathrm{C}} \Longleftrightarrow \mathrm{I}_1 \leq \mathrm{I}_0. \tag{58}$$

The relationship is displayed in Figure 5 in the situation with $\mathbf{U}(\hat{\mathrm{C}}, \hat{\mathrm{g}}) > \overline{\mathrm{C}}$ so that the patent equilibrium has a higher utility than the no-patent system.

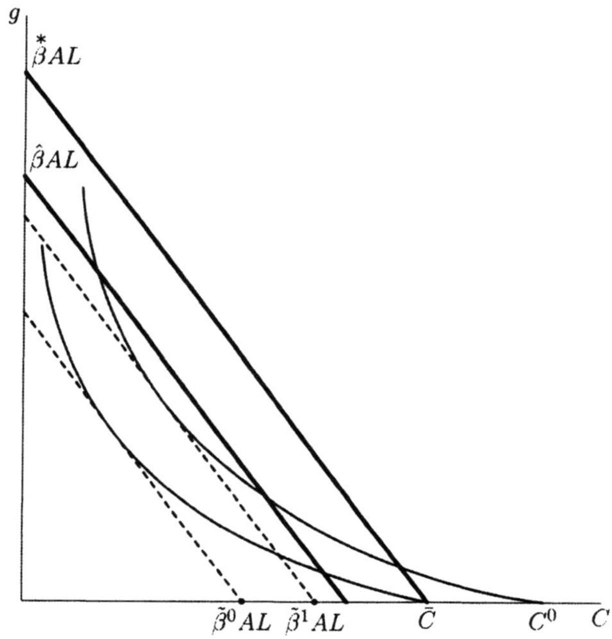

Fig. 5.

The indifference curve through the patent equilibrium must lie above the indifference curve for the no-patent equilibrium as shown in the figure. Therefore, the tangencies will have the indicated relationship and $\tilde{\beta}^0 \leq \tilde{\beta}^1$. Therefore, $I^1 \leq I^0$.

A situation in which the no-patent equilibrium has a higher utility than the patent equilibrium is shown in Figure 3. Although not all the curves are displayed, it is clear that $I^1 \geq I^0$.

10 Conclusion

The specific results obtained in this paper are a consequence of the tight structure imposed on the model. First, we have used a Cobb-Douglas production function for the economy. This simplifies the pricing problem for the monopolistic machine producers and permits the identification of production parameters with factor shares. Second, we assume machines are non-durable and there are no durable assets in the economy. This simplifies the dynamics and permits a welfare analysis in a relatively simple context. Third, we assume that consumption goods, machines and ideas are produced with the same factor proportions. This enables us to represent the economy with a one sector model. It is important but substantially more difficult to relax each of these assumptions.

The model analyzed in this paper assumes innovation expands product variety with no obsolescence of old products as in Romer (1990) and Rivera-Batiz and Romer (1991). Models developed by Grossman and Helpman (1991) and Aghion and Howitt (1992) treat innovation as improving the quality of products so that new products may make old products obsolete. The techniques developed in this paper could be usefully applied to these models.

Vives (2005) has investigated the innovation decisions by firms in much more general circumstances than used in this paper. It would be useful but difficult to eliminate many of the restrictive functional forms exploited in this paper.

Many existing growth models with endogenous innovation have transient dynamics as well as balanced growth paths and this is an important generalization. However, this would eliminate the simple stationary representation of the equilibria and seriously complicate the inefficiency measurement.

References

Aghion, Philippe, and Peter Howitt, "A Model of Growth Through Creative Destruction", *Econometrics*, **60**(2) (1992), 323–351.

Arrow, Kenneth J., "Economic Welfare and the Allocation of Resources for Invention", in *The Rate and Direction of Inventive Activity: Economic and Social Factors*, National Bureau of Economic Research, 609–625, 1962.

Barro, Robert J., "Notes on Growth Accounting", *Journal of Economic Growth*, **4**(2) (1999), 119–137.

Debreu, Gerard, "The Coefficient of Resource Utilization", *Econometrics*, **19** (1951), 273–292.

Denison, Edward F., *The Sources of Economic Growth in the United States and the Alternatives Before Us*, Washington, D.C., Committee for Economic Development, 1962.

Färe, Rolf, Shawna Grosskopf, and C.A. Knox Lovell, *Production Frontiers*, Cambridge University Press, 1994.

Farrell, M.J., "The Measurement of Production Efficiency", *Journal of the Royal Statistical Society, Series A*, **120** (1957), 253–261.

Grossman, Gene M., and Elhanan Helpman, "Quality Ladders and the Theory of Growth", *Review of Economic Studies*, **58**(1) (1991), 43–61.

Jorgenson, Dale W., and Zvi Griliches, "The Explanation of Productivity Change", *Review of Economic Studies*, **34** (1967), 249–280.

Kendrick, John W., *Productivity Trends in the United States*, Princeton University Press, 1961.

Koopmans, Tjalling C., "Analysis of Production as an Efficient Combination of Activities", in *Activity Analysis of Production and Allocation*, edited by Tjalling C. Koopmans, Wiley Publishers, 1951.

Raa, Thijs ten and Pierre Mohnen, "Neoclassical Growth Accounting and Frontier Analysis: A Synthesis", *Journal of Productivity Analysis*, **18** (2002), 111–128.

Rivera-Batiz, Luis A., and Paul M. Romer, "Economic Integration and Endogenous Growth", *Quarterly Journal of Economics*, **106**(2) (1991), 531–555.

Romer, Paul M., "Endogenous Technical Change", *Journal of Political Economy*, **98**(5) (1990), S71–S102.

Russell, R. Robert, "Measures of Technical Efficiency", *Journal of Economic Theory*, **35** (1985), 109–126.

Russell, R. Robert, "Continuity of Measures of Technical Efficiency", *Journal of Economic Theory*, **51**(2) (1990), 255–267.

Solow, Robert M., "Technical Change and the Aggregate Production Function", *Review of Economic Studies*, **39** (1957), 312–320.

Vives, Xavier, "Innovation and Competitive Pressure", unpublished manuscript, 2005.

Don't Aggregate Efficiency But Disaggregate Inefficiency

Thijs ten Raa

Tilburg University, Box 90153,5000 LE Tilburg, the Netherlands `tenRaa@UvT.nl`

1 Introduction

Recently Bob Russell published an impossibility result with Chuck Blackorby. The gentlemen argue that it is impossible to aggregate efficiency indices. Since some of us make a descent living decomposing the efficiency of an economy into sectoral contributions the question is if we are crooks. This paper attempts to give an answer to this question.
Blackorby and Russell (1999) state:

> Perhaps more disturbing is the fact that the principal indexes proposed by Debreu (1951) and Farrell (1957), by Färe and Lovell (1978) and by Zieschang (1983) cannot satisfy these [aggregation] conditions for any technologies, even linear ones.

The subsequent relaxation of these aggregation conditions by Blackorby and Russell (1999) offers little comfort:

> In particular, the [relaxed] aggregation condition provides a rationalization of the Debreu/Farrell efficiency measure, albeit for a very restrictive (linear) class of technologies.

A first step in the process of recovery from bad news is to take stock of the issues. I shall clarify a number of things. First, what are efficiency measures? The Debreu/Farrell name, however much in the air as a reference for a general measure of efficiency, is misleading. The Debreu and Farrell measures would better be delineated vis-à-vis each other. Second, can we disaggregate these measures?

Predecessors disaggregating inefficiency, albeit implicitly, are Färe and Grosskopf (2004, pp. 110–14) who determine aggregate industry output (and the corresponding distance function) allowing for reallocations of inputs between firms and—the source they credit for this approach—Johansen (1972). This paper can be considered to generalize the approach and offer a dual analysis.

The upshot of this paper is a redirection of the measurement of efficiency: top-down instead of bottom-up. I hope the reader will feel better again.

2 Efficiency Measures: Debreu and Farrell or Diewert?

Consider an economy comprising l commodities, m consumers, with preference relationships $\succeq_i$ and observed consumption vectors $\mathbf{x}_i^0 \in \Re^l$ $(i = 1, \ldots, m)$, and n production units with sets of possible (net) input vectors $Y_j \subset \Re^l$ containing the observed input vector $\mathbf{y}_j^0$ $(j = 1, \ldots, n)$. A combination of consumption vectors and an input vector is *feasible* if the total sum does not exceed the vector of *utilizable physical resources*, $\mathbf{z}^0$, which is the datum of the economy. This constraint is binding for the observed inputs:

$$\sum \mathbf{x}_i^0 + \sum \mathbf{y}_j^0 = \mathbf{z}^0 \tag{1}$$

The *better set* of net consumption vectors is defined by

$$\mathbf{B} = \sum \mathbf{x}_i : \mathbf{x}_i \succeq_i \mathbf{x}_i^0, i = 1, \ldots, m + \sum Y_j \tag{2}$$

Debreu (1951) defines the coefficient of resource allocation by

$$\rho = Max\ \mathbf{p}(\mathbf{z}) \cdot \mathbf{z} / \mathbf{p}(\mathbf{z}) \cdot \mathbf{z}^0 \text{ subject to } \mathbf{z} \in \mathbf{B}^{min} \tag{3}$$

Coefficient ρ measures the distance from the set of minimally required physical resources, $\mathbf{z} \in \mathbf{B}^{min}$ to the utilizable physical resources, $\mathbf{z}^0$, in the metric of the supporting prices (which indicate welfare indeed). Debreu (1951, p. 284) proves that the distance or the Max in (3) is attained by

$$\mathbf{z} = \rho \mathbf{z}^0 \in \mathbf{B}^{min} \tag{4}$$

In modern terminology, this result means that ρ is the *input-distance function*, determined by the program

$$Min\ \rho \text{ subject to } \sum \mathbf{x}_i + \sum \mathbf{y}_j \leq \rho \mathbf{z}^0, \mathbf{x}_i \succeq_i \mathbf{x}_i^0, \mathbf{y}_j \in Y_j \tag{5}$$

Farrell (1957) decomposes efficiency in technical efficiency and allocative efficiency. He notes the similarity between his technical efficiency measure and the Debreu coefficient of resource utilization. Indeed, both concepts are defined through proportionate input contractions. Nonetheless, the analogy is sheer formality and confusing at a conceptual level. It suggests that Farrell takes the Debreu coefficient, augments it, and thus constructs a more encompassing overall measure. It is the other way round; the sway of the Debreu coefficient is far greater than that of Farrell's measure. Particularly Farrell's allocative efficiency measure is a partial (dis)equilibrium concept, conditioned on prices. It takes into account the cost reduction attainable by changing the mix of the inputs, given the prices of the latter. The Debreu coefficient, however, is a general (dis)equilibrium concept. It measures the technical and allocative inefficiency in the economy given only its fundamentals: resources, technology, and preferences. Prices are derived and enter the definition of the Debreu coefficient, see (3). Debreu *proves* that the coefficient can be freed from these prices, by formula (4) or nonlinear program (5). Prices remain implicit, however. They support the better set in the point of minimally required physical resources and will be revealed in this paper. The Debreu coefficient measures technical and allocative inefficiency, both in production and consumption, solving the formidable difficulty involved in assessing prices, referred to by Charnes, Cooper, and Rhodes (1978, p. 438). Farrell refrains from this, restricting himself to technical efficiency and price-conditioned allocative efficiency.

The formal analogy between the Debreu coefficient and the Farrell measure of technical efficiency prompted Färe and Lovell (1978) to coin the phrase "Debreu-Farrell measures of efficiency." This is confusing. Debreu's coefficient of resource allocation encompasses both Farrell's technical efficiency and his allocative efficiency measures, plus frees the latter from prices. On top of this, Debreu's coefficient also captures consumers' inefficiencies. The confusion persists. In a very recent review of Farrell's contribution Førsund and Sarafoglou (2002, footnote 4) state

> (Debreu) worked only from the resource cost side, defining his coefficient as the ratio between minimised resource costs of obtaining a given consumption bundle and actual costs, for given prices and a proportional contraction of resources.

Debreu (1951) calculates the resource costs not of a given consumption bundle, but of an (intelligently chosen) Pareto equivalent allocation. (And the prices are not given, but support the allocation.)

Yet, let me bridge the difference. Following Diewert (1983), I limit inefficiency to production by assuming Leontief preferences. Under this assumption Debreu's program (5) can be shown to reduce to

$$Min\ \rho \text{ subject to } \sum_i \mathbf{x}_i^0 + \sum_j \mathbf{y}_j \leq \rho \mathbf{z}^0, \mathbf{y}_j \in Y_j \tag{6}$$

The detail is in ten Raa (2003) who calls the consequent ρ the *Debreu-Diewert efficiency measure.*

3 An Example

Let us consider an economy producing a single consumption good. Denote the inputs by vector **I**. The available stock of inputs is $\mathbf{I}^0$. The production possibilities are given by two production functions, one for each unit: F_1 and F_2. The observed inputs are $\mathbf{I}_1^0$ and $\mathbf{I}_2^0$. Efficiency program (6) reads

$$Min\ \rho \text{ subject to } \sum \mathbf{x}_i^0 \leq F_1(\mathbf{I}_1) + F_2(\mathbf{I}_2) \text{ and } \mathbf{I}_1 + \mathbf{I}_2 \leq \rho \mathbf{I}^0 \tag{7}$$

The solution denotes the Debreu-Diewert efficiency of the economy. Denote the efficient inputs by $\mathbf{I}_1$ and $\mathbf{I}_2$ and contrast them with the observed inputs. The question is: How efficient are the units? It may very well be that both units produce the maximum output given their inputs, but that the distribution of inputs is inefficient. For example, if there is only one input and the units have the same, strictly concave production function, say F, then the efficient distribution of inputs is fifty/fifty. This example, however simple, conveys the message of Blackorby and Russell (1999). The efficiency of the units in the sense of maximizing output given the inputs does not imply that the constellation of the two units is efficient.

Is there no way to cope with this example? My idea is to look at profits, not at market prices, but at shadow prices. Choosing the consumption good as numeraire, the shadow prices of the inputs are their marginal products or the vector of partial derivatives $F'(\rho\mathbf{I}^0/2)$, evaluated at the optimum. These input prices will be intermediate, higher than the marginal product of a big unit, smaller than the marginal product of a small unit (assuming concavity). I shall consider the small unit relatively efficient. The big unit will pick up more inefficiency.

4 Back to the Model

Let the production possibility set be given by $Y_j = \{\mathbf{y}_j : F_j(\mathbf{y}_j) \geq 0\}$ where the differentiable functions F_j are concave. (In the previous example these functions map $(\mathbf{I}, -x)$ into $F_j(\mathbf{I}) - x$: the value of the production function of the previous section at input vector l minus output. Since the functions are concave the differentiability assumption can be dropped and the subsequent analysis would be in terms of subgradients.) Efficiency program (6) reads

$$Min\ \rho \text{ subject to } \sum_i \mathbf{x}_i^0 + \sum_j \mathbf{y}_j \leq \rho \mathbf{z}^0, F_j(\mathbf{y}_j) \geq 0 \tag{8}$$

Unlike the Blackorby and Russell (1999) condition, F_j need not be linear. Consequently, (8) is a nonlinear program. According to Wolfe (1961) the dual program is

$$Max_{\rho,\mathbf{y},\mathbf{p},\boldsymbol{\tau}}\ \rho - \mathbf{p}(\rho\mathbf{z}^0 - \sum \mathbf{y}_j - \sum \mathbf{x}_i^0) - \boldsymbol{\tau}\mathbf{F}(\mathbf{y}) \tag{9}$$
$$\text{subject to } \mathbf{pz}^0 = 1, \mathbf{p} = \boldsymbol{\tau}\mathbf{F}'(\mathbf{y}), \text{ and } \mathbf{p}, \boldsymbol{\tau} \geq 0$$

and by his Theorem 2 (9) has the same solution value as (8). Here $\mathbf{F}$ is the vector with components F_j and $\mathbf{F}'$ is the matrix with the j-th row displaying the partial derivatives of F_j. Notice that the first two terms in (9) cancel by the first dual constraint.

The analysis becomes highly transparent if we assume constant returns to scale, or, in Blackorby and Russell (1999) jargon, linear homogeneity. In this case Blackorby and Russell (1999) argue that the inputs must be perfect substitutes and the outputs must be perfect substitutes. This prohibitive restriction rules out CES functions and even the case of fixed input coefficients, and reduces (9) to a linear program. Under general linear homogeneity, however, (9) remains a nonlinear program, but the third and fifth terms in (9) cancel by the second dual constraint and Euler's theorem. Hence only the fourth term remains and we obtain

$$Max_{\mathbf{y},\mathbf{p},\boldsymbol{\tau}}\ \mathbf{p}\sum \mathbf{x}_i^0 \text{ subject to } \mathbf{p}\mathbf{z}^0 = 1, \mathbf{p} = \boldsymbol{\tau}\mathbf{F}'(\mathbf{y}), \text{ and } \mathbf{p}, \boldsymbol{\tau} \geq 0 \qquad (10)$$

And, by Wolfe's Theorem 2,

$$\rho = \mathbf{p}\sum \mathbf{x}_i^0 \qquad (11)$$

Now value the observed inputs and resources, see equation (1), by the shadow prices. Substituting (10) and (11), and rearranging terms, I obtain

$$1 - \rho = \sum \mathbf{p}\mathbf{y}_j^0 \qquad (12)$$

On the left hand side is inefficiency and on the right hand side are losses at shadow prices. (Remember $\mathbf{y}_j^0$ are net input vectors.) The shadow prices are given by the second dual constraint of (9) or (10), namely $\mathbf{p} = \boldsymbol{\tau}\mathbf{F}'(\mathbf{y})$. These are the marginal products of the efficient units. If a unit is inefficient, that is within its own frontier—$F_j(\mathbf{y}_j) > 0$—then $\tau_j = 0$ by the phenomenon of complementary slackness (which is equivalent to Wolfe's Theorem 2) and it plays no role in price formation.

5 Another Example

Consider an economy with one input (L) and one output (Y). The production possibilities for two units (1 and 2) are $Y \leq L$ and $Y \leq \beta L$, respectively. The observed allocation is $(Y_1^0, L_1^0) = (1/2, 1/2), (Y_2^0, L_2^0) = (1/2\ \beta, 1/2)$. Notice that both units are efficient in the sense of being on their frontiers. Blackorby and Russell (1999) argue that output (input) aggregation of efficiency indices is possible only if the efficiency indices are ratios of linear functions of input and output quantities and the aggregate index is a weighted average. Moreover, these functions must be common to all units. This implies the first of the following statements.

I. *The economy is efficient if and only if* $\beta = 1$.
II. If $\beta < 1$, the efficient allocation is
$(Y_1, L_1) = (1/2 + 1/2\beta, 1/2 + 1/2\beta), (Y_2, L_2) = (0, 0)$. Hence efficiency $\rho = 1/2 + 1/2\ \beta$ and inefficiency $1 - \rho = 1/2 - 1/2\ \beta$.
III. If $\beta > 1$, the efficient allocation is
$(Y_1, L_1) = (0, 0), (Y_2, L_2) = (1/2 + 1/2\ \beta, 1/2\beta^{-1} + 1/2)$. Hence efficiency $\rho = 1/2\ \beta^{-1}$ and inefficiency $1 - \rho = 1/2 - 1/2\beta^{-1}$.

To decompose inefficiency, let us first determine the shadow prices. The first dual constraint, see (9) or (10) normalizes the shadow price of the input to 1. The shadow price of the output is 1 in cases I and II and β^{-1} in case III.

I. Both units make zero losses at shadow prices, hence pick up zero inefficiency. This is in perfect agreement with Blackorby and Russell (1999).
II. At shadow prices the losses of the units are $1/2 - 1/2$ and $1/2 - 1/2\ \beta$, respectively. The inefficiency is imputed entirely to the second unit. Indeed, it should be out of business.
III. At shadow prices the losses of the units are $1/2 - 1/2\ \beta^{-1}$ and $1/2 - 1/2\ \beta\beta^{-1}$, respectively. The inefficiency is imputed entirely to the first unit. Indeed, it should be out of business.

The point of the example is that inefficiency has been decomposed in cases where efficiency cannot be aggregated according to Blackorby and Russell (1999). The result holds for nonlinear technologies, like CES functions, including the limiting case of a Leontief function.

6 Conclusion

To determine the efficiency of a constellation of production units we need the following data.

a. The inputs and outputs of each unit
b. The production possibilities of each unit

Notice that this is no more than what is required by Blackorby and Russell (1999).

I suggest we proceed as follows. The first step is to compute the efficiency of the system of the units. This is done by contracting the total input of the system subject to the condition that total output is preserved, allowing for reallocations of the inputs and outputs between the units. The percentage by which contraction is feasible is the inefficiency in the economy. The second step is to compute the shadow prices of the contraction program. They are the marginal products of the efficient units. The output shadow prices will be low, as they reflect best practice costs. The third step is to value the units (in terms of profits) at shadow prices. Under constant returns to scale the best practice units break even; their values are zero. The other units incur losses though. This paper has shown that the losses sum to the aggregate inefficiency. This completes the decomposition of inefficiency.

The inefficiency of a unit can have two sources. First, the unit may operate within its possibility frontier. Second, the unit may produce the wrong output vector, not the one implied by the optimal allocation of inputs between units. This allocative source of firm inefficiency should not be neglected. If one neglects it, one obtains impossibility results on the aggregation of efficiency indices. If one takes it into account, inefficiency can be disaggregated. The upshot is that efficiency scores may be aggregated when reallocations are allowed. This differs from the negative result obtained by Blackorby and Russell (1999). With Richard Nixon, let me conclude, "I am not a crook."

References

Blackorby, Charles and R. Robert Russell, "Aggregation of Efficiency Indexes", *Journal of Productivity Analysis* **12** (1999), 5–20.

Charnes, A., W.W. Cooper, and E. Rhodes, "Measuring the Efficiency of Decision Making Units", *European Journal of Operational Research* **2** (1978), 419–444.

Debreu, Gerard, "The Coefficient of Resource Utilization", *Econometrica* **19**(3) (1951), 273–292.

Diewert, W. Erwin, "The Measurement of Waste Within the Production Sector of an Open Economy", *Scandinavian Journal of Economics* **85**(2) (1983), 159–179.

Färe, Rolf, and Shawna Grosskopf, New Directions: Efficiency and Productivity, Kluwer, Boston, 2004.

Farrell, M.J., "The Measurement of Productive Efficiency", *Journal of the Royal Statistical Society Series A*, **120**(III) (1957), 253–281.

Førsund, Finn R., and Nikias Sarafoglou, "On the Origins of Data Envelopment Analysis", *Journal of Productivity Analysis* **17** (2002), 23–40.

Johansen, Leif, *Production Functions*, North-Holland, Amsterdam, 1972.

Jorgenson, Dale W., and Zvi Griliches, "The Explanation of Productivity Change", *Review of Economic Studies* **34**(3) (1967), 308–350.

ten Raa, Thijs, Debreu's Coefficient of Resource Utilization, the Solow Residual, and TFP: The Connection by Leontief Preferences, CentER DP 111, 2003.

Wolfe, Philip, "A Duality Theorem for Nonlinear Programming", *Quarterly of Applied Mathematics* **19**(3) (1961), 239–244.

Zieschang, K., "An Extended Farrell Technical Efficiency Measure", *Journal of Economic Theory* **33** (1983), 387–396.

Index

MIX
Papier aus verantwortungsvollen Quellen
Paper from responsible sources
FSC® C105338

If you have any concerns about our products,
you can contact us on
ProductSafety@springernature.com

In case Publisher is established outside the EU,
the EU authorized representative is:
Springer Nature Customer Service Center GmbH
Europaplatz 3, 69115 Heidelberg, Germany

Printed by Libri Plureos GmbH
in Hamburg, Germany